29998

Nathaniel Hawthorne

Revised Edition

Twayne's United States Authors Series

Lewis Leary, Editor

University of North Carolina, Chapel Hill

TUSAS 75

Nathaniel Hawthorne

Revised Edition

By Terence Martin

Indiana University

Twayne Publishers • *Boston*

29998

Nathaniel Hawthorne
Revised Edition

Terence Martin

Copyright © 1983 by G. K. Hall & Company
All Rights Reserved
Published by Twayne Publishers
A Division of G. K. Hall & Company
70 Lincoln Street
Boston, Massachusetts 02111

Book Production by Marne B. Sultz
Book Design by Barbara Anderson

Printed on permanent/durable acid-free
paper and bound in the United States of
America.

Library of Congress Cataloging in
Publication Data

Martin, Terence.
    Nathaniel Hawthorne.

        (Twayne's United States authors series; TUSAS 75)
        Bibliography: p. 196
        Includes index.
        1. Hawthorne, Nathaniel, 1804-1864
        —Criticism and interpretation.
    I. Title. II. Series.
    PS1888.M34 1983   813'.3   82-23419
    ISBN 0-8057-7384-3
    ISBN 0-8057-7427-0 (Paperback)

Contents

About the Author

Preface

Chronology

Chapter One
Life and Career   1

Chapter Two
The Neutral Ground of Fiction   28

Chapter Three
The Tales: Method and Achievement   43

Chapter Four
Six Tales   72
>"The Minister's Black Veil"
>"The May-pole of Merry Mount"
>"Young Goodman Brown"
>"Rappaccini's Daughter"
>"Ethan Brand"
>"My Kinsman, Major Molineux"

Chapter Five
The Scarlet Letter   105

Chapter Six
The House of the Seven Gables   128

Chapter Seven
The Blithedale Romance   147

Chapter Eight
The Marble Faun   163

Chapter Nine
Furthering a Significant Legacy   181

Notes and References   189
Selected Bibliography   196
Index   217

About the Author

Terence Martin is Professor of English at Indiana University. He has spent two years abroad as Visiting Professor of American Literature at the University of Dijon in France and has lectured in Germany, Poland, and India, as well as at numerous universities in this country. For the year 1963–64 he was awarded a fellowship by the American Council of Learned Societies to explore the relation of pragmatism and American fiction. He has published widely on American writers from Washington Irving and James Fenimore Cooper to Willa Cather and Ken Kesey in such journals as *New England Quarterly, American Literature, Kenyon Review*, and *Nineteenth-Century Fiction.* His study *The Instructed Vision: Scottish Common Sense Philosophy and the Origins of American Fiction* was published in 1962, and he brought out an edition of *The Scarlet Letter* in 1967. Professor Martin has recently completed a four-year term on the Editorial Board of *American Literature.* Currently, he is serving on the Advisory Council of the Nineteenth-Century American Literature Division of the Modern Language Association. He teaches both graduate and undergraduate courses on Hawthorne and other American writers at Indiana University.

Preface

Since his death in 1864 Hawthorne has held a sure place as one of our most significant writers. He was the only American author to have a volume devoted to him in the nineteenth-century English Men of Letters Series (Henry James's *Hawthorne* in 1879). No appraisal of American literature has ignored his achievement. So enduring has been his reputation, so consistently has his work been read, that there has been no need to rediscover his fiction or to proclaim a Hawthorne revival. The writer who once referred to himself as "the obscurest man of letters in America" has weathered literary fashions in a way that would have surprised him perhaps more than anyone else.

The last decade has been a particularly interesting one for students of Hawthorne's tales and romances. The major event has been the progress and virtual completion of the Centenary Edition of his work which makes Hawthorne available to us in reliable and authoritative texts and thus serves as the basis for sound scholarship. The discovery of Hawthorne's "Lost Notebook," surely the happy surprise of the decade, has also added to our understanding of an aspiring and often frustrated writer—even as it has tempted hopeful scholars to rummage through antique cabinets in search of similar treasures. And the publication of significant biographical and critical studies has brought us to see more clearly than ever before the complex relation between Hawthorne's life and art.

My purpose in the revised edition of this book is to bring the reader to a responsible understanding of Hawthorne's achievement in fiction. To that end I have brought the results of important recent scholarship to bear on my discussion and have sharpened the focus of ideas that remain basic to my sense of Hawthorne as a writer. My chapter organization remains fundamentally the same. Initially (in chapter 1), I have sought to define the contours, issues, and recurrent imaginative patterns that shaped Hawthorne's career, then (in chapters 2 and 3) to explore the method of creation by means of which his fiction came into being. The problem of how to tell a story led Hawthorne to put great emphasis on what I term the *conditions* of fiction. He required—and is frequently explicit about his need for—

an imaginative latitude which would free him from the constraints of the everyday world and give him access to "the kingdom of possibilities." The strategy or method he used to attain such latitude became a formative part of the way in which he conceived fiction. The *how* and the *what* of Hawthorne's work are not, of course, finally separable. But by attending to how he created his tales and romances, we come to see more clearly what—in the fullest sense—he achieved.

Because Hawthorne's best work in short fiction enacts concisely the deepest concerns of his imagination, I have focused in chapter 4 on six representative tales that amply repay individual analysis. Chapters 5 through 8 are devoted to Hawthorne's major romances: assuming a knowledge of his method of imaginative creation, these chapters assess the accomplishments, difficulties, and inevitable limitations of Hawthorne's art at its expansive best. My final chapter suggests the manner in which Hawthorne articulated and passed on the humanistic legacy of Western literature. What he has to tell us about the human condition is not new; he would be the last to think so. But the quality of his telling keeps it persistently from being old. And in coming to know his fiction well, we begin to see its essential relevance to significant writing in our own century.

As my discussion will make clear, I am indebted to those who have written on Hawthorne before me. Intelligent and sensitive criticism awaits anyone who would study Hawthorne. The spirit of that criticism has encouraged me to develop my own perceptions and approaches to the subject, hopefully in ways that will contribute to the ongoing dialogue concerning Hawthorne's work. For quick and efficient research when I needed it most, I wish to thank Barbara B. Martin. For a grant in aid of research I am grateful to the Indiana University Graduate School.

Terence Martin

Indiana University

Chronology

1804   Nathaniel Hawthorne born on July 4 in Salem, Massachusetts.

1808   Hawthorne's father dies in Surinam, Dutch Guiana.

1809   Hawthorne family moves to the Manning house in Salem.

1813–1815   Injury to foot curtails Hawthorne's youthful physical activity.

1818   Family moves to Raymond, Maine.

1819   Attends Samuel Archer's school in Salem.

1820   Tutored by Benjamin L. Oliver in preparation for college. Family returns to Salem.

1821–1825   Attends Bowdoin College, Brunswick, Maine.

1828   *Fanshawe: A Tale* published anonymously at Hawthorne's expense.

1830–1837   Publishes numerous tales and sketches (all anonymous or pseudonymous) in periodicals.

1836   March to August, edits the *American Magazine of Useful and Entertaining Knowledge.*

1837   *Peter Parley's Universal History,* one of Samuel Goodrich's *Peter Parley* series for children.

1837   *Twice-Told Tales.*

1838   Engagement to Sophia Peabody.

1839–1840   Measurer of salt and coal at the Boston Custom House.

1841   *Grandfather's Chair,* historical stories of New England for children and youthful readers, written while working at the Boston Custom House.

1841   April to November, lives at Brook Farm Community, West Roxbury, Massachusetts.

1842   Marries Sophia Peabody in Boston, July 9.

1842   Second (and expanded) edition of *Twice-Told Tales*.

1842–1845   Lives at the Old Manse, Concord, Massachusetts.

1844   Daughter Una born.

1845   Edits Horatio Bridge's *Journal of an African Cruiser*.

1846   Son Julian born.

1846   *Mosses from an Old Manse*.

1846–1849   Surveyor in the Salem Custom House.

1850   *The Scarlet Letter*.

1850–1851   Lives in Lenox, Massachusetts.

1851   Daughter Rose born.

1851   *The House of the Seven Gables, The Snow-Image and Other Twice-Told Tales*, and *True Stories from History and Biography*.

1851–1852   Lives at West Newton, Massachusetts.

1852   *The Blithedale Romance, A Wonder-Book for Girls and Boys*, and the *Life of Franklin Pierce* (a campaign biography).

1852–1853   Lives at the Wayside, Concord, Massachusetts.

1853   *Tanglewood Tales for Girls and Boys*.

1853–1857   Serves as United States consul at Liverpool. Appointed by President Franklin Pierce.

1854   Revised edition of *Mosses from an Old Manse*.

1857–1859   Lives in Rome and Florence.

1859   Returns to England. Finishes *The Marble Faun*, begun in Florence in 1858.

1860   *The Marble Faun*. Returns to the Wayside in Concord.

1863   *Our Old Home* (dedicated to Franklin Pierce).

1864   Dies May 19 at Plymouth, New Hampshire, and is buried May 23 at Sleepy Hollow Cemetery, Concord.

Chapter One

Life and Career

When Hawthorne finished *The Scarlet Letter* on February 3, 1850, he had been a writer for almost twenty-five years. The new book, he wrote to his friend Horatio Bridge, promised to succeed: not only did James T. Fields speak of it "in tremendous terms of approbation," but a reading of the conclusion had broken Sophia Hawthorne's heart "and sent her to bed with a grievous headache"—"which I look upon," said Hawthorne, "as a triumphant success." Judging from the effect of the story on his publisher and on his wife, Hawthorne thought he might "calculate on what bowlers call a ten-strike." Characteristically, however, he refused to make such a calculation. "Some portions of the book are powerfully written," he acknowledged; "but my writings do not, nor ever will, appeal to the broadest class of sympathies, and therefore will not obtain a very wide popularity. Some like them very much, others care nothing for them, and see nothing in them."

A lifelong tendency to depreciate his work underlies Hawthorne's refusal to calculate on "a ten-strike" for *The Scarlet Letter.* When in May, 1850, for example, he saw "Peter Goldthwaite's Treasure" and "The Shaker Bridal" published as original stories in the London *Metropolitan*, he condemned the English for their piracy but pitied them for being "poor enough to perk themselves in such false feathers as these"; the two stories seemed to him "painfully cold and dull." From England in 1854 he wrote to Fields that some of the "blasted allegories" in *Mosses from an Old Manse* struck him as alien and obscure; six years later he agreed with his favorite critic, E. P. Whipple, that characters in these tales are "introduced, not as thinking, but as the illustration of thought"—even as he brushed aside Whipple's praise of his achievement in fiction.[1] Years of striving had brought Hawthorne to see clearly the special qualities of his work, its strengths and limitations. And he tended to judge the work of early years relentlessly, with remarkable objectivity. His twice-told tales, he wrote (prefatorily in the 1851 edition),

have the pale tint of flowers that blossomed in too retired a shade,—the coolness of a meditative habit, which diffuses itself through the feeling and observation of every sketch. Instead of passion there is sentiment; and, even in what purport to be pictures of actual life, we have allegory, not always so warmly dressed in its habiliments of flesh and blood as to be taken into the reader's mind without a shiver. Whether from lack of power or an unconquerable reserve, the Author's touches have often an effect of tameness; the merriest man can hardly contrive to laugh at his broadest humor; the tenderest woman, one would suppose, will hardly shed warm tears at his deepest pathos. The book, if you would see anything in it, requires to be read in the clear, brown, twilight atmosphere in which it was written; if opened in the sunshine, it is apt to look exceedingly like a volume of blank pages.[2]

Hawthorne is thorough enough as a self-critic not to rest content with such a judgment of the tales but to make a point of their place and meaning in his career. They are not, he admits readily, profound; more remarkably, they "seldom, if ever, show any design on the writer's part to make them so. They have none of the abstruseness of idea, or obscurity of expression, which mark the written communications of a solitary mind with itself." The tales are not, that is, "the talk of a secluded man with his own mind and heart (had it been so, they could hardly have failed to be more deeply and permanently valuable)" but they are the "very imperfectly successful" attempts of such a man "to open an intercourse with the world." They never need "translation." Their style is "the style of a man of society."

With the publication of *The Scarlet Letter* Hawthorne had begun the most public decade of his life. He had made the tale his own form in a final way, and he would now move to achievement in the Romance. From the vantage point of 1851 he views the tales and sketches in *Twice-Told Tales* as "the memorials of very tranquil and not unhappy years." Years of trial, years of effort, had become in retrospect years of progress and tranquility: for Hawthorne had succeeded fully in establishing his identity as an author; though he doubted the size of his audience, he could know all the more surely that he was talking not to himself but to others—and that he had been doing so all along.

The Poet and the Bookkeeper

Hawthorne grew up with access to books. Temperament and circumstances (an injury to his foot at the age of nine reduced his physical activity for almost two years) helped to form a youthful habit of reading in the classics of English literature. Among his early favorites were Spenser's *Faerie Queene*—supposedly the first book he ever purchased with his own money—Bunyan's *Pilgrim's Progress*, Thomson's *Castle of Indolence*, and the plays of Shakespeare. The influence of Bunyan was daily in evidence; in the Manning household, where Mrs. Hawthorne and her children lived after the death of her husband in 1808, two cats were named Apollyon and Beelzebub. And Hawthorne later named his first child Una, after Spenser's heroine.

When Hawthorne was twelve, his family moved to Raymond, Maine, on Lake Sebago, and into a house belonging to Robert Manning. For three years Nathaniel enjoyed the outdoor life of the region. Later he was to say that he first picked up his "accursed habits of solitude" amid the freedom of these years. But he regretted his mother's decision to send him back to Salem for schooling. "I wish I was in Raymond, and I should be happy," he wrote to his younger sister Louisa, in September, 1819; but study, his own reading, and a part-time job as bookkeeper for his Uncle Robert's stagecoach line involved much of his time in the ensuing months. In the same letter to Louisa he mentioned having read *Waverly, The Mysteries of Udolpho, The Adventures of Ferdinand Count Fathom, Roderick Random*, and the "first volume" of the *Arabian Nights*. The following year he mentioned his reading again to Louisa:

I have bought the Lord of the Isles and intend either to send or to bring it to you. I like it as well as any of Scott's other Poems. I have read Hogg's Tales, Caleb Williams, St. Leon & Mandeville. I admire Godwin's Novels, and intend to read them all. I shall read The Abbott by the Author of Waverly as soon as I can hire it. I have read all Scott's Novels except that. I wish that I had not that I might have the pleasure of reading them again. Next to them I like Caleb Williams.

When in that year Louisa came to Salem for tutoring, she and her brother attended dancing school, founded the Pin Society (with themselves as the two members), and brought out several issues of the *Spectator*, a hand-printed paper which featured poetry by Louisa and assorted essays and humorous editorials by Nathaniel.

Hawthorne's work as a bookkeeper for his Uncle William brought him a salary of a dollar a week. Though he welcomed the dollar, he was sorry that his work kept him from literary pursuits. "No Man," he lamented to his sister Elizabeth in 1820, "can be a Poet & a Book-keeper at the same time." Exaggerated and self-dramatic, the statement has its obvious comic quality. But it also testifies to an attitude that was to be pervasive in the course of Hawthorne's career. The man of imagination and the man of business (to take his terms "Poet" and "Book-keeper" in their widest significance) consistently seemed to Hawthorne two distinct if not always antipathetic individuals. In his lifetime, terms of service in government offices seemed temporarily to anesthetize his creative imaginaton. Yet such business was necessary if he was to support his family; as a writer he secured only seasons of financial security. During his years as a consul in England (1853–57), he could fill his English journal with delightful and perceptive observations, but he could not be his own kind of poet or artist while he was engaged in consular business. Frustration was evident: if he had enough money, he wrote William D. Ticknor from England, he would "kick the office to the devil, and come home again"—for he missed both his Wayside home and his pen.

In his fiction, the distinction between the outer man, the man of affairs, and the inner man, the man of imagination and creativity, supplies dramatic tension in a number of Hawthorne's works. The "scholar-idealist," in Randall Stewart's phrase, is of course a recurrent figure in Hawthorne's tales and romances—and he may be, in some manifestations, a poet. But the relation between the poet and his antitype—the bookkeeper—derives from a configuration of characters. The youthful scholar Fanshawe and the more socially oriented Edward Walcott in *Fanshawe*, for example, find echoes in the characters of Septimius Felton and Robert Hagburn in the late and incomplete "Septimius" manuscripts. Peter Goldthwaite, man of fancy, and John Brown, practical man of business, embody the thematic forces at work in "Peter Goldthwaite's Treasure." In "The

Artist of the Beautiful," Owen Warland is juxtaposed with Peter Hovenden, Robert Danforth, Annie, and the child. And in "The Snow-Image," Mr. Lindsey's disbelief in a childish miracle stands in opposition to Mrs. Lindsey's faith in and consequent acceptance of the miraculous.

Hawthorne's early distinction between the poet and the book-keeper—or, rather, the quality of that distinction as he sustained it—yields what may be the central ambivalence in the career of a man whose art, at its best, thrived on ambivalence. For as the distinction is articulated in fiction, Hawthorne demonstrates various and tentative attitudes toward both types of men. Fanshawe, for example, who uses intense study as a means of self-destruction, is portrayed sympathetically by Hawthorne. Yet the obvious doom written deeply into his character spells a limitation in Fanshawe's being. Momentarily inspired into a love of life by Ellen Langton, he ultimately relinquishes hope of winning her hand in order to resume his courtship of death. The pattern of withdrawal and return which pervades Hawthorne's fiction finds an inverse beginning in *Fanshawe*: withdrawn when we first meet him, Fanshawe effects only a momentary relation to society, then withdraws finally to solitude, study, and death. But in a story of this kind, someone must marry the beautiful Ellen Langton. And so Edward Walcott, bookkeeper as student, does the honors. Because Edward exists in a way that Fanshawe does not, Hawthorne can present him as a likable young man. Edward Walcott embraces as a matter of course the things which make up ordinary life; if he lacks Fanshavian brilliance, he offers no antagonism to it.

In *Fanshawe*, the poet meets opposition only from himself. In "The Artist of the Beautiful," however, the scorn, ignorance, and shallow sensibility of the world victimize the artist, who must work, if he is to work, out of a determined mesalliance to society. As an artist Owen Warland succeeds; he succeeds even more significantly by being able to transcend the destruction of his creation; but he is forced into, even as he willingly adopts, a position of asociality or even antisociality if he is to create at all. The poet and the bookkeeper have never been farther apart; and the implications are disturbing for both.

As presented in "Peter Goldthwaite's Treasure," the man of business saves the man of fancy from utter ruin. Hawthorne's conception in this tale is significant: at one time in the past Peter Goldthwaite and John Brown have been in partnership; after the partnership dissolves, Peter goes through years of foolish hopes and financial disasters, finally tearing down his house in a vain effort to find legendary wealth. John Brown, meanwhile, prospers unspectacularly. No doubt John Brown is dull, unexciting, and basically unimaginative. But he rescues Peter Goldthwaite, arrests a career of sterility and self-destruction, and promises to protect the man of deluded imagination from his own fantasies. When John Brown plays the role of Mr. Lindsey in "The Snow-Image," however, he is blind to all but common sense; unable to withstand his bleak, unknowing, factual stare, the marvelous melts away before his eyes without his realizing what has happened. In Mr. Lindsey's world, the bookkeeper would be unaware of the poet's existence.

"Septimius Felton" offers a final presentation of the characters who have evolved from Hawthorne's conception of the poet and the bookkeeper. The action of the narrative takes place during the Revolutionary War. The poet, Septimius Felton, is now searching for the elixir of life; he feels that human existence, thrust on man gratuitously, is a kind of cosmic joke that can be set right for him only by the success of his experiments (though he recognizes the further "absurdity" that he might die "just at the moment when he should have found out the secret of everlasting life"). But Hawthorne satirizes this artist who seeks to create the uncreatable: Septimius wastes his life in a search for life—in his way he is as foolish as Peter Goldthwaite, although Hawthorne in portraying Septimius neither qualifies the idea of irresponsibility nor rescues the artist from the cancer of obsession. Ultimately, Septimius dismisses the Revolution from his consciousness, so absorbed is he by his personal quest for existential independence: "he knew nothing, thought nothing, cared nothing about his country, or his country's battles." The concerns of the inner world have reduced the affairs of the outer world to meaningless incident.

But for Robert Hagburn, bookkeeper as soldier, the outer world becomes the arena of life and achievement. Robert fights hard for his country and is decorated for valor; he wins honor, glory—and consequently a kind of immortality inconceivable to Septimius. One must always be astonished at the rapid change in Robert Hagburn from country bumpkin to gentleman officer, scar slanting dashingly down from his temple in one version of the story, arm resting gracefully in a sling in another; but there is no doubt that his life grows richer and larger in scope while that of Septimius grows mean and small in relation to the self-inflicted poverty of his imagination.[3] Robert also, as one might expect, wins the girl (though Hawthorne provides a second girl, Sybil Dacy, for Septimius, their strange romance ends predictably with her death). And Robert, in a highly articulate speech, formulates the notion of "dying well" as the only thing that can give meaning to life. Robert Hagburn is the public hero, Septimius Felton the fool even of a private world. The poet and the bookkeeper have taken their final, surprising, and still tentative forms in Hawthorne's fiction. The poet has become the embryo existentialist hero, for whom Hawthorne has mounting disdain; the bookkeeper, in a time of national crisis, becomes not only the hero in and of history, but a figure who is "fit to be the founder of a race," one who anticipates later, more romantic, and differently conceived protagonists in American fiction.

When Hawthorne complained that no man could be a poet and a bookkeeper at the same time, he had four years of college ahead of him. Though he had some misgivings about his Uncle Robert's underwriting the cost of his education, he had become "quite reconciled" to the idea of attending college. "Yet four years of the best part of my life is a great deal to throw away," he could not help thinking prior to his entrance at Bowdoin in the fall of 1821. He was undecided about a profession—or so he wrote to his mother. To be a minister seemed dull and out of the question. Lawyers frequently starved to death, but physicians lived off the infirmities of their fellow men. "Oh that I was rich enough to live without a profession!" But what, he asked, coming to the point of his letter and to the idea forming in his mind, "do you think of my becoming an author, and relying for support upon my pen? Indeed, I think the illegibility of my handwriting is very author-like. How proud you would feel to see my works praised by the reviewers, as equal to the proudest productions of the scribbling sons of John Bull. But authors are always poor devils, and therefore Satan may take them."

One must appreciate the sportive manner of these remarks without being disarmed by it. The joke is serious: the idea of becoming an author appeals strongly to Hawthorne. It is wise, I think, always to be prepared to take Hawthorne seriously; only in that way can one estimate the quality of his humor. In "The Custom-House," for example, he imagines his great-grandsires denigrating his work as an author:

No aim, that I have ever cherished, would they recognize as laudable; no success of mine—if my life, beyond its domestic scope, had ever been brightened by success—would they deem otherwise than worthless, if not positively disgraceful. "What is he?" murmurs one gray shadow of my forefathers to the other. "A writer of story-books! What kind of a business in life—what mode of glorifying God, or being serviceable to mankind in his day and generation,—may that be? Why, the degenerate fellow might as well have been a fiddler!"

The tone of the imaginary dialogue is jocular; Hawthorne is having his little game with his "stern and black-browed" Puritan ancestors. But the tone should not distract us from seeing that *what* Hawthorne says here is thoroughly true. He knew his ancestors as well as any man could know them in 1850; he knew as a matter of course that they would deplore his writing of fiction. What is equally important, however, is that he knew himself: with reflexive irony he adds that let them scorn him as they will, "strong straits of their nature have intertwined themselves with mine"—which means, of course, that scorn them as he will, a Puritan legacy is his. Though the Puritans repudiate Hawthorne the writer they cannot repudiate Hawthorne the descendant, who claims or admits kinship with them, and through them—or through that part of him which was forever theirs—casts doubt on the value of his life's work. "The bane of your life has been self-distrust," wrote Horatio Bridge to Hawthorne in 1836; and, although he meant that Hawthorne distrusted the quality of his work, he might correctly have added that the primary difficulty derived from a fundamental doubt about the efficacy of fiction. Having decided to be a writer, Hawthorne found it extremely difficult to sustain a belief in the value of his fiction. It is well to remember, of course, that a deep mistrust of the imagination was a part of Hawthorne's contemporary environment. One did not have to be descended from the Puritans to criticize fiction for being untrue to life. Hawthorne seems never to have been caught in the shallows of such didactic criticism. But living in his time and place, and being Hawthorne, he was unable to project a sustained image of the artist in vital contact with society. The result was a sense of doubt that is a part of his career as a writer.

Bowdoin College was both new and small when Hawthorne began his studies in the fall of 1821. The college had opened in 1802 with an entering class of eight, and the enrollment in 1821 was only one hundred and fourteen. As much as anything else, the simple fact that no member of his family had attended college before suggests how special the young Hawthorne seemed to his relatives. At Bowdoin, he met some of the men who came to be his close friends in later years. Bridge, Jonathan Cilley, and Longfellow were members of his class; Franklin Pierce, the future president, was in the class ahead.[4] Hawthorne joined a literary society, and he belonged also to the more convivial Pot-8-o Club. He played cards, paid his fines for breaking the rules, went for long walks, refused to take part in declamation exercises, demonstrated ability in Latin and English composition, and graduated eighteenth in a class of thirty-eight in September, 1825.

Clearly, Hawthorne did not make a full commitment to academic success. During his years at Bowdoin he was often distracted from formal study by his desire to be a writer. He may have been working on *Fanshawe* and on the collection of tales entitled "Seven Tales of My Native Land" at this time—conflicting evidence from his sister Elizabeth leaves us unsure. Following his graduation, he returned to his mother's house. The family had moved back to Salem in the summer of 1822, and thus to Salem Hawthorne went to live and write.

The Years of Anonymity

The years 1825 to 1837 have traditionally been termed the years of solitude in Hawthorne's life. Early biographers at times stressed the degree of his solitude to the point of making him seem a morbid recluse. Later students of Hawthorne's life have made such an image seem exaggerated by taking a closer look at biographical details. The habit of making seasonal trips, for example, took Hawthorne into society. In the fall of 1828 he very much enjoyed a trip to New Haven with his Uncle Samuel Manning. In August, 1831, again with his Uncle Samuel, he visited New Hampshire and saw the Shaker Village at Canterbury. Impressed and amused by Shaker customs, he described the village in a letter to his sister

Louisa; "if it were not for their ridiculous ceremonies," he added, "a man might do worse than join them." Twenty years later, however, in August, 1851, he described the Shaker settlement at Hancock in his notebook in terms of disgust and disdain. He had visited the settlement while on a picnic with Herman Melville, Evert Augustus Duyckinck, and his own son Julian. The principal dwelling house, he wrote, contained

no bathing or washing facilities in the chambers; but in the entry there was a sink and wash-bowl, where all their attempts at purification were to be performed. The fact shows that all their miserable pretense of cleanliness and neatness is the thinnest superficiality; and that the Shakers are and must needs be a filthy sect. And then their utter and systematic lack of privacy; the close function of man with man, and supervision of one man over another—it is hateful and disgusting to think of; and the sooner the sect is extinct the better—a consummation which, I am happy to hear, is thought to be not a great many years distant.

The Shakers, he concluded, "are certainly the most singular and bedevilled set of people that ever existed in a civilized land."

A thorough review of Hawthorne's activities in this period does not dispel the idea that he lived and worked, for the most part, alone. Life in the Hawthorne home made seclusion eminently possible. Elizabeth Peabody, Sophia's sister, reports Hawthorne's saying that both his sister Elizabeth and his mother "take their meals in their rooms, and my mother has eaten alone ever since my father's death." According to this account, the "witty and original" Elizabeth Hawthorne stayed much in her room; Hawthorne is reported to have said that he had "scarcely seen her in three months." And Madame Hawthorne's chamber (she was styled Madame Hawthorne following her husband's death) was virtually the sovereign territory of a semi-recluse, seldom invaded unless by little Una and Julian in the years leading up to her death.

The chronic inability of the Hawthorne family to communicate on matters of personal import enhanced Nathaniel's reserve. Perhaps the most notable instance of such embarrassed and embarrassing reticence came later—when at the age of thirty-seven Hawthorne could not bring himself to tell his mother and his sisters of his engagement to Sophia. Within his family, he admitted, there seemed "to be a tacit law that our deepest heart-concernments are not to be spoken of." As one would expect, Sophia conveyed the necessary information about the engagement. As one might not expect, no member of the Hawthorne family attended the wedding. Yet, as Hawthorne's notebook entry on the day before his mother's death (in 1849) attests, powerful emotion lay beneath a taciturn surface. "I love my mother," Hawthorne wrote; "but there has been, ever since my boyhood, a sort of coldness of intercourse between us, such as is apt to come between persons of strong feelings, if they are not managed rightly." Although he knew that he would deeply regret her death, he "did not expect to be much moved" as he went to visit his mother's bedside. Kneeling next to the bed, he heard her murmur, indistinctly, "an injunction to take care of my sisters"; and then, "I found the tears slowly gathering in my eyes. I tried to keep them down; but it would not be—I kept filling up, till, for a few moments, I shook with sobs. For a long time, I knelt there, holding her hand; and surely it is the darkest hour I ever lived."

Made up of strongly attached yet reticent people each of whom maintained a well-developed sense of solitude, the Hawthorne household thus gave Nathaniel the privacy he required when he returned from Bowdoin. And because he devoted himself to his writing, he required a good bit. Supported financially by his mother and by his Manning uncles, Hawthorne worked steadily at his craft. More than anything else, the years 1825 to 1837 seem to have served his career as a writer in a unique and perhaps necessary way. For as he said later in a letter to Franklin Pierce, "It needs long thought with me, in order to produce anything good...."

In his preface to the 1851 edition of *Twice-Told Tales*, Hawthorne claimed the "distinction" of having been, "for a good many years, the obscurest man of letters in America." As a writer he was understandably obscure. For all of his work before the publication of *Twice-Told Tales* in 1837 appeared anonymously or pseudonymously. Most often, a tale or sketch was unsigned. At times, authorship was indicated by a conventional tag referring to a previously published story—"by the author of 'The Gentle Boy,'" for example, or "by the author of 'The Gray Champion.'" Again, Hawthorne might appear as Ashley A. Royce, the Reverend A. A. Royce, or Oberon. Hawthorne thus stood apart from the public image of the poet that he was slowly creating. Not only that, but in addition he was appearing under such different forms that any such image would be diffused even in a society accustomed to the convention of anonymity and perhaps more practiced than we might be in recognizing authorship by means of style and mode of presentation.

Two factors contributed much to his identity being hidden from the public during these years. First of all, what he saw as the failure of his earliest work discouraged him from announcing himself to the public. When the publisher seemed to procrastinate, Hawthorne recalled his first collection of tales ("Seven Tales of My Native Land") and, according to Bridge, "burned the manuscript, in a mood half savage, half despairing." Two of the tales, Hawthorne said, "chanced to be in kinder custody at the time," and hence escaped the fire. One of these was "Alice Doane's Appeal," which Hawthorne revised and published in the *Token* in 1835. The identity of the other tale is unknown.

In 1828 *Fanshawe* was published anonymously at Hawthorne's expense, and, had he had his way, it too would have been burned shortly afterward. Extremely dissatisfied with *Fanshawe*, he endeavored to suppress it in every way he could. "He called in and destroyed all the copies he could reach," reports Bridge; "at his request I burned my copy, and we never alluded to *Fanshawe* afterwards." In later years James T. Fields recalled that, when he asked about *Fanshawe*, Hawthorne "spoke of it with great disgust." Not even in 1851, after the success of *The Scarlet Letter* had made his fame secure, would Hawthorne relent: "You make inquiry about some supposed former publication of mine," he wrote to Fields: "I cannot be sworn to make correct answers as to all the literary or other follies of my nonage; and I earnestly recommend you not to brush away the dust that may have gathered over them." Such statements reveal unequivocally Hawthorne's attitude toward *Fanshawe*. But the depth of his inner repudiation of the book is best tested by negative evidence. Throughout the years of their courtship and marriage, despite his profound love for Sophia, Hawthorne never told her that he had written *Fanshawe*. After his death when confronted with a copy, she innocently denied his authorship.

Editorial problems and policies likewise contributed to Hawthorne's anonymity. In 1829 he had written to publisher Samuel G. Goodrich, who was also editor of the annual *Token*, about a second collection of his work to be called "Provincial Tales." Goodrich read the tales, as he said, "with great pleasure." He liked "The Gentle Boy" and what he called "My Uncle Molineaux" particularly well. But although he promised to use his "influence to induce a publisher to take hold of the work," Goodrich seems to have preferred to publish the tales individually in the *Token*. In May, 1831, after Hawthorne had apparently given up the idea of having the collection published in book form, Goodrich wrote that he had made "very liberal use" of the permission Hawthorne had given him to publish the tales in the *Token*. "I have already inserted four of them; namely, 'The Wives of the Dead,' 'Roger Malvin's Burial,' 'Major Molineaux,' and 'The Gentle Boy.'" Then comes the significant admission: "As they are anonymous, no objection arises from having so many pages by one author, particularly as they are as good, if not better, than anything else I get." Accordingly, these four tales appeared in the *Token* for 1832.

Together with Park Benjamin, who became editor of the *New-England Magazine* in 1835, Goodrich was undoubtedly pleased not to reveal how much of his fiction he was obtaining from one author. Benjamin incurred Hawthorne's displeasure by dismantling the framework of a third group of tales, "The Story-Teller," so that the tales could appear separately in his magazine.[5] Throughout the early 1830s two, three, or four of Hawthorne's tales appeared in each issue of the *Token*; the 1837 issue contained nine of his pieces. And in 1835, the *New-England Magazine* had published eight of his tales and sketches. The editors knew they had a good thing in Hawthorne. "I shall want three or four sketches from you for the next volume, if you can finish them," wrote Goodrich in the fall of 1836. Hawthorne was publishing a great deal, with relatively little remuneration. To augment his income he edited the *American Magazine of Useful and Entertaining Knowledge* for Goodrich from March to August, 1836. And despite a growing dissatisfaction with Goodrich, Hawthorne assembled—with assistance from his sister Elizabeth—*Peter Parley's Universal History* for him in 1836. The popular history made a good deal of money for the publisher, but little for the author.

Thus the circumstances of periodical publication, following on the heels of Hawthorne's early disappointment with his work, helped to sustain his posture of anonymity. In 1836, harried by the scrambling work (and the lack of money) connected with his editing of the

American Magazine of Useful and Entertaining Knowledge and having seen three projected collections of tales exploited for magazine publication since 1829, Hawthorne was understandably in low spirits about his writing. One letter to Bridge contained "a kind of desperate coolness" that struck Hawthorne's friend as dangerous. Bridge had repeatedly urged Hawthorne to come before the public in his own name. "I've been thinking of how singularly you stand among the writers of the day," he wrote in 1836, "known by name to very few, and yet your writings admired more than any others with which they are ushered forth.... Your articles in the last 'Token' alone are enough to give you a respectable name, if you were known as their author." And Bridge, who had always given Hawthorne encouragement, now suited action to words: unknown to Hawthorne, he arranged for the publication of a volume of tales and supplied $250 to guarantee the publishers against loss. Thus, *Twice-Told Tales* was contracted for publication. The volume, containing eighteen of the thirty-six tales and sketches previously published in periodicals, appeared in March, 1837.

Only later did Hawthorne discover Bridge's role in the publication of *Twice-Told Tales*. Remembering that and Bridge's unwavering faith in his ability since their days at Bowdoin, he expressed his gratitude in the dedicatory letter which prefaced *The Snow-Image and Other Twice-Told Tales* in 1851: "If anybody is responsible for my being at this day an author," he wrote publicly to Bridge, "it is yourself." In 1854, with Bridge in need of money and Hawthorne for the first time in his life relatively affluent as United States consul at Liverpool, his generosity took a private form when he loaned Bridge $3,000, with or without collateral, as he said, for two years or "till the day of doom."

Response to *Twice-Told Tales* was favorable, if not widespread. Hawthorne sent a complimentary copy to his former Bowdoin classmate Longfellow, hoping, as he admitted later, that Longfellow might perform a "kind office" for the book. And Longfellow's review, published in the *North American Review* in July, 1837, praised Hawthorne warmly—the review, indeed, was more a gush of friendship than a critical evaluation. The modest title of the volume, promising only the tedium of a twice-told tale, may have (as Bridge thought) kept some people from buying it; but it sold well enough to enable the publisher to refund Bridge's guarantee of $250. After twelve years of writing in what he called his "dismal chamber," Hawthorne had established a literary reputation that went beyond the confines of editorial offices. He now stood before the public as an artist.

A Quest for Achievement

As he looked back on the twelve years following his graduation from Bowdoin, Hawthorne tended to give them a certain dramatic function in the evolution of his career. After the publication of *The Scarlet Letter* he saw them as twilight years of obscurity; in the midst of self-discoveries in love, he portrayed them romantically as years during which he had lived an uncertain half-life. In his preface to *The Snow-Image*, for example, he wonders if there was "ever such a weary delay in obtaining the slightest recognition from the public, as in my case. I sat down by the wayside of life, like a man under enchantment, and a shrubbery sprang up around me, and the bushes grew to be saplings, and the saplings became trees, until no exit appeared possible, through the entangling depths of my obscurity." And in one of the best known of his letters to Sophia (written from his old chamber in 1840), he formulates the notion of having been imprisoned for many years until he met her:

Here I have written many tales—many that have been burned to ashes—many that doubtless deserved the same fate. This deserves to be called a haunted chamber; for thousands upon thousands of visions have appeared to me in it; and some few of them have become visible to the world. If ever I should have a biographer, he ought to make great mention of this chamber in my memoirs, because so much of my lonely youth was wasted here, and here my mind and character were formed; and here I have been glad and hopeful, and here I have been despondent; and here I sat a long, long time, waiting patiently for the world to know me, and sometimes wondering why it did not know me sooner, or whether it would ever know me at all—at least, till I were in my grave. And sometimes (for I had no wife then to keep my heart warm) it seemed as if I were already in the grave, with only life enough to be chilled and benumbed. But oftener I was happy—at least, as happy as I then knew how to be, or was aware of the possibility of being. By and by, the world found me out in my lonely chamber, and called me forth—not, indeed, with a loud roar of acclamation, but rather with a still, small voice; and forth I went, but found nothing in the world that I thought preferable to my old solitude, till at length a certain Dove was revealed to me, in

the shadow of a seclusion as deep as my own had been. And I drew nearer
and nearer to the Dove, and opened my bosom to her, and she flitted into
it, and closed her wings there—and there she nestles now and forever,
keeping my heart warm, and renewing my life with her own. So now I
begin to understand why I was imprisoned so many years in this lonely
chamber, and why I could never break through the viewless bolts and bars;
for if I had sooner made my escape into the world, I should have grown
hard and rough, and been covered with earthly dust, and my heart would
have become callous by rude encounters with the multitude; so that I
should have been all unfit to shelter a heavenly Dove in my arms. But
living in solitude till the fulness of time was come, I still kept the dew
of my youth and the freshness of my heart, and had these to offer to my
Dove.

   While this account of his solitary years is not wholly inaccurate,
it is obviously shaped to be part of a statement of love. Like all
(articulate) lovers, Hawthorne seizes upon his love as the great
reality of his life; all that has come before is dreamlike, unreal—at
best, a necessary prologue to living. He fashions a rhetoric to accommodate the central fact of meeting and loving Sophia. And
the language of such a letter creates a reality of its own which
reinforces the manner in which Hawthorne wishes to view his
early career. He could stand outside that reality, it is true, and mock
his earlier life, saying (to Sophia) that visitors to his chamber in
future years would point out with rapture his bed, his washstand,
his looking-glass, his pine table and flag-bottomed chair, his chest
of drawers, his shoebrush. But his final sense of his early career was
shaped in the context of love and public success.
   Hawthorne met Sophia in the fall of 1838. His letters during
four years of courtship and, when occasion demanded, after their
marriage reveal an idyllic relationship such as can only come into
being when one siezes upon love as a way of seeing oneself and the
world anew. Their love, they felt, was unique: "Nothing like our
story was ever written, or ever will be," he wrote to Sophia in 1840.
Only by means of their love had Hawthorne come to know himself.
"You only," he wrote, "have taught me that I have a heart,—you
only have thrown a light, deep downward and upward into my soul.
You only have revealed me to myself; for without your aid my best
knowledge of myself would have been merely to know my own
shadow. . . . Do you not comprehend what you have done for me?"

Sophia is "Belovedest," "Dearest Heart," "Dearest Unutterably," and—frequently after 1844—"Sweetest Phoebe." She is a "sinless Eve," who gives him reality and makes "all things real" for him. Sophia binds him to the world; he yields always to her "superior wisdom." And, importantly, Sophia believes that "home . . . is the great arena" for woman, where she "can wield a power which no king or conqueror can cope with."

As we have seen, Hawthorne had admitted that with his mother and sisters his "deepest heart-concernments" could not be mentioned: "I cannot gush out in their presence," he continued in a letter to Sophia; "I cannot take my heart in my hand and show it to them." It is small wonder that he gushed out to Sophia, the person to whom he could finally show his heart. At times his outpourings are highly exaggerated, and they may strike a reader for whom they were never meant as silly. But it balances our sense of the serious and solitary Hawthorne to realize that he could be giddy with happiness and as syrupy as anyone writing love letters, that he would solemnly tell Sophia he never read her letters without first washing his hands. To a man who once fancied that to be a Paul Pry, observing human affairs without becoming embroiled in them, was a desirable form of existence, who came to imagine peerlessly the capacity of the human being for isolation and the fearful consequences of losing touch with human kind—to such a man, Sophia represented, simply and fully, life. He loved her not simply as if she had saved him from disaster but as if she were constantly saving him from disaster. And Sophia, semi-invalid for years, treating her chronic headaches with laudanum and unable to venture out when there was an east wind, clung to Hawthorne with a need that complemented his. Yet, we recall, Hawthorne never mentioned to Sophia that he had written *Fanshawe*.

In January, 1839, Hawthorne was appointed measurer of salt and coal in the Boston Custom House at an annual salary of $1,500. His earlier interest in securing the post of historian on a South Sea Exploring Expedition had resulted in disappointment despite the efforts of friends on his behalf. Now, with Sophia his intended wife, he felt the need of the security offered by a regular salary. For two years he stayed in the Boston Custom House, working hard, writing to Sophia of his "coal-begrimed visage and salt-befrosted locks." But early in 1841 he invested $1,000 in George Ripley's famous utopian community of Brook Farm and went to live there. Several weeks after his arrival he wrote enthusiastically to his sister Louisa that he was "transformed into a complete farmer." He had loaded manure carts, planted potatoes and peas, milked cows, and "gained strength wonderfully,—grown quite a giant, in fact." He praised the natural beauty of the place and seemed pleased with the brotherhood: "The whole fraternity eat together; and such a delectable way of life has never been seen on earth since the day of the early Christians." He signed the letter, "Nath. Hawthorne, *Ploughman.*"

But Hawthorne had not gone to Brook Farm out of Transcendentalist or Socialist convictions. The avid reformer of any kind was an object of his suspicion. He had wondered if Brook Farm might afford a satisfactory and economical home for Sophia and himself when they were married. When he came to believe that it would not—toward the end of 1841—he left the community. Romantic enchantment had given way to sweaty disenchantment.

After their marriage in 1842 Hawthorne and Sophia lived at the Old Manse in Concord, the house in which Emerson had written *Nature* in 1836. The three years at the Old Manse were perhaps the happiest of Hawthorne's life. The Old Manse journal kept jointly by Hawthorne and Sophia reveals a shared world of delights and simple joys. But the difficulty of earning a living was a nagging problem that could not be wished away. Hawthorne's letters to Bridge during this period reveal both a careful attention to expenditures and the idea that the poet might once again have to become the bookkeeper to support his family. "I did not come to see you," he wrote in March, 1843, "because I was very short of cash, having been disappointed in money that I expected from three of four sources. My difficulties of this sort sometimes make me sigh for the regular monthly payments of the custom-house." The irony of his situation, he wrote two months later, was that "nobody's scribblings seem to be more acceptable to the public than mine; and yet I shall find it a tough scratch to gain a respectable support by my pen. Perhaps matters may mend; at all events, I am not eager to ensconce myself in an office, though a good one would certainly be desirable." But the tone of such letters does not convey the full reality of the situation: so pressing did financial matters become that for several months late in 1844 Sophia moved to her family home in Boston and Hawthorne to his in Salem. Five years later, with his family now including two children (Una and Julian), Hawthorne's financial condition was again precarious following his dismissal from the Salem Custom House. Among those who came to his aid was George Hilliard, who took up a collection among Hawthorne's friends and presented the money to an embarrassed, but needy, Hawthorne as a gift. Only after he became consul at Liverpool was Hawthorne in a position to return Hilliard's "gift," with interest.

In the three years following his marriage Hawthorne published almost two dozen tales and sketches. He had long been, as he later said, "burrowing into our common nature for the purpose of psychological romance." And now his "burrowing" took on the new form that one finds in such pieces as "A Virtuoso's Collection," "The Hall of Fantasy," "The Celestial Rail-road," "A Select Party," "Earth's Holocaust," and "The Christmas Banquet." These are not tales in the ordinary sense. In each of them Hawthorne assembles groups of people or things who move through time or space and thereby illustrate some fundamental truth, or aberration, of human nature.

"The Procession of Life," in which he seeks to organize large groups of human beings according to principles that have a greater reality than the principles of social organization, affords a term with which to describe these tales as a group. They are, in one way or another, processionals. They reflect a growing social awareness on Hawthorne's part, or, rather, the manner in which Hawthorne's imagination confronted the fact of his social awareness. The best of these tales, "The Celestial Rail-road," is a masterful allegorical satire based on Bunyan's *Pilgrim's Progress*. In it Hawthorne pokes fun at the optimistic, pastel religiosity of his day and replaces Bunyan's giants Pope and Pagan with a new monster of German birth, Giant Transcendentalist. Though they embody Hawthorne's fundamental themes, the processionals do not represent literary achievement of high merit. In the light of his best work, they should probably be considered a misstep. Nonetheless, with their expansive movement and their focus on the collective rather than on the individual, they do show us an interesting stage in Hawthorne's concern with the form of the tale. They suggest that he was not averse to experimentation to adapt that form to his particular needs.

Hawthorne's processionals were included in *Mosses from an Old Manse,* which appeared in 1846. The collection of tales was well received; it contributed to a reputation that had been growing since the publication of *Twice-Told Tales.* But there were those who pre-

ferred Hawthorne's first book. Poe, for example, who had praised
Hawthorne's genius and originality in a review of *Twice-Told Tales*,
objected to the allegory and the lack of originality in *Mosses*. And
Melville, reading *Twice-Told Tales* after having lavished praise on
Mosses, felt that the quality of the "earlier vintage" surpassed that
of the later. Hawthorne himself, in the preface to *Mosses*, announced
that unless he could "do better" he would publish no more collections
of tales. *Mosses*, however, contains some of Hawthorne's excellent
work—"The Old Manse," for example; "Rappaccini's Daughter";
"The Birth-Mark"; and, perhaps most notably, "Young Goodman
Brown" (first published in 1835), which Hawthorne had passed over
for both the first and second editions of *Twice-Told Tales*. His new
collection was not entirely made up of the "blasted allegories" which
he later deprecated.

The substance of many of Hawthorne's tales (more so in *Twice-
Told Tales* than in *Mosses*) came from his reading in the documents
of colonial history. Cotton Mather's *The Wonders of the Invisible
World*, his *Magnalia Christi*, and Increase Mather's *Remarkable Provi-
dences* offered up to Hawthorne the public essence of Puritanism.
Books such as Felt's *Annals of Salem*, John Winthrop's *Journal*, and
the *Diary* of Samuel Sewell supplied him with information and with
a personal sense of what it meant to be a Puritan.

But if the matter of Hawthorne's work frequently derives from
sources in American colonial history, the manner owes much to the
great writers of English literature—to Spenser and Bunyan, to Shakespeare and Milton, to Scott, and to the lesser Gothic romancers. The
question here is not one of "influence" in any narrow sense; Hawthorne assimilated the mode and moral quality of his favorite writers,
digested it and made it his own, so that it came to be a pervasive
aspect of his work. Spenser and Bunyan, with their allegorical vitality,
were of special and enduring importance to a writer whose art required a means of access to the moral world. The Gothic romance
bequeathed devices and machinery which haunted Hawthorne's fiction
from *Fanshawe* to *The Marble Faun*. Other writers, such as Swift,
Dante, Madame de Staël, and Tieck, had an importance for the genesis
of individual tales. But the allegorical and the Gothic traditions of
English literature exercised a persistent effect on Hawthorne's creative
imagination. When he brought these traditions to bear on the
material of Puritanism, the result was allegory transmuted, Gothic-

ism refined. At its best, the result could be "Young Goodman Brown." In April, 1846, Hawthorne secured an appointment as Surveyor of the Salem Custom House at an annual salary of $1,200. The prospects of an "office" had materialized, happily for Hawthorne's financial position. But the cost of being the bookkeeper once again was virtually to relinquish the role of the poet. Though his job was undemanding, Hawthorne wrote little during his three years in the Custom House. Dismissed in January, 1849, he was somewhat frustrated and bitter; the machinations of small-time politics, he felt, had victimized him. But, encouraged by Sophia, he turned to his writing and by early February, 1850, completed *The Scarlet Letter.* A career that had taken shape during long years of anonymity, that had struggled through intermittent and necessary terms of business life, had resulted in the writing of an American classic.

The Public Decade—and the Final Years

The early 1850s were for Hawthorne a time of intense literary activity. *The Scarlet Letter* was followed by *The House of the Seven Gables* (1851) and by *The Blithedale Romance* (1852). And Hawthorne was finding the energy for other writing as well. *True Stories from History and Biography* (1851), *A Wonder-Book for Girls and Boys* and the *Life of Franklin Pierce* (both 1852), and *Tanglewood Tales for Girls and Boys* (1853) evidence his versatility and his efforts to write for varied markets. Moreover, in an effort to gain maximum financial advantage from the increasing importance of his name, he followed the advice of James T. Fields and agreed to the publication of *The Snow-Image and Other Twice-Told Tales* (1851), to a new edition of *Twice-Told Tales* (1851), and to a new edition of *Mosses from an Old Manse* (1854). At no other period of his life did Hawthorne set himself so prodigally before the public.

Winter months seem to have been the best for writing. On February 4, 1850, with *The Scarlet Letter* just completed, Hawthorne declined an invitation from Bridge partly for financial reasons "and partly because I can ill spare the time, as winter is the season when my brain-work is chiefly accomplished." *The House of the Seven Gables* would not be finished by November, 1850, he wrote to Fields, "for I am never good for anything in the literary way till after the first autumnal frost. . . ."[6] He was ready to enjoy the summer, he told

Fields in 1851, "and to read foolish novels, if I can get any, and smoke cigars, and think of nothing at all; which is equivalent to thinking of all manner of things." Between December, 1851, and April, 1852, he completed *The Blithedale Romance.* When Hawthorne did get to work as a writer, he worked to good purpose.

Hawthorne preferred *The House of the Seven Gables* to *The Scarlet Letter*, which seemed to him "positively a h——l f——d story, into which I found it almost impossible to throw any cheering light." Of the two romances, *Seven Gables* struck him as "more characteristic" of his mind, "more proper and natural" for him to write, "more sure of retaining the ground it acquires." Yet he told Bridge that in his next romance he meant to put in "an extra touch of the devil"; "I doubt whether the public will stand two quiet books in succession without my losing ground." *Blithedale*, as we know, came next; and although he doubted that Bridge would like it, Hawthorne admitted that "it has met with a good success, and has brought me—besides its American circulation—a thousand dollars from England." At present, he added, "I rather think your friend stands foremost there as an American fiction-monger." Public success spelled at least temporary financial security.

The combination of financial and literary success bred an increasing desire to work: again to Bridge (after the publication of *Seven Gables*), Hawthorne wrote that "as long as people will buy, I shall keep at work, and I find that my facility for labor increases with the demand for it." With *Blithedale* completed, he announced his intention of beginning a "new" romance—"more genial than the last"—in "a day or two." But the period of burgeoning literary activity was over. The "new" romance never appeared. It was not until 1860 that Hawthorne published another romance—*The Marble Faun*, his last completed work of fiction.

During his residence at the Old Manse in the 1840s, Hawthorne had come to know the Concord literati—without partaking of their Transcendental efforts. Never, he wrote in "The Old Manse," was "a poor little country village infested with such a variety of queer, strangely-dressed, oddly-behaved mortals, most of whom took upon themselves to be important agents of the world's destiny, yet were simply bores of a very intense water." These seekers and thinkers surrounded Emerson, whose magnetism Hawthorne readily acknowledged. Indeed, he said, there had been times in his life when he would have sought from Emerson "the master word that should solve me the riddle of the universe"; being happy, however, he had no question to put at the present time. Thus he admired Emerson "as a poet of deep beauty and austere tenderness, but sought nothing from him as a philosopher." More to his liking was Thoreau, "a healthy and wholesome man to know." At times, Thoreau's addiction to principle might make Hawthorne judge him a difficult companion; but his intimacy with nature and his qualities as a literary man commanded Hawthorne's enduring respect.[7]

With Melville, whom he came to know well during his residence at Lenox in 1850 and 1851, Hawthorne established a significant friendship, attenuated finally by their vast differences in temperament. Emerson and other Concord neighbors had felt the pressure of Hawthorne's silence; "Hawthorne rides well his horse of the night," Emerson had once remarked. But Melville, fourteen years younger than Hawthorne and filled with admiration for him, simply ignored Hawthorne's reserve in the blinding light of his own exuberance. They talked—"about time and eternity," as Hawthorne said of one evening, about "things of this world and the next, and books, and publishers, and all possible and impossible matters." They corresponded—and even granting Melville's extravagant rhetoric, Hawthorne must have struck a common chord of perception, and struck it generously, for Melville to erupt in thanksgiving for his "joy-giving and exultation-breeding letter" about *Moby-Dick*, just off the press. "I was lord of a little vale in the solitary Crimea," wrote Melville, "but you have given me the crown of India. . . . A sense of unspeakable security is in me this moment, on account of your having understood the book." A pattern of insistence in this friendship was set by Melville's beguiling need for resonant understanding. As James R. Mellow says, Melville had found an ideal friend in Hawthorne— "father, brother, inspired mentor, intelligent audience."[8] Melville assumed the complementary roles—son, brother, irrepressible student, uninhibited performer—with a natural joy. In a postscript to one letter he added with manic self-awareness that Hawthorne need not bother to write or visit or talk: "I will do all the writing and visiting and talking myself."

Melville's review of *Mosses from an Old Manse* had early testified to his respect for Hawthorne's work (and to his hopes for American literature). His personal regard for Hawthorne led him to write in 1851 that he would leave the world "with more satisfaction for having come to know you. . . . The divine magnet is on you, and my magnet responds." And his most encompassing tribute remains the dedication of *Moby-Dick*: "In Token of my admiration for his genius, *This book is inscribed to* NATHANIEL HAWTHORNE." In England five years later, Hawthorne, on his part, showed a profound understanding of Melville's restlessness: the two had talked again of belief and immortality—subjects, said Hawthorne, about which Melville "had persisted ever since I knew him, and probably long before." Melville, he felt, "can neither believe, nor be comfortable in his unbelief; and he is too honest and courageous not to try to do one or the other. If he were a religious man, he would be one of the most truly religious and reverential; he has a very high and noble nature, and is better worth immortality than most of us." According to Arlin Turner, Hawthorne may not have recognized "the urgency" of Melville's need for "sympathy and guidance" in 1850. After getting a good start on *The House of the Seven Gables*, he did hold "his importunate young friend at arm's length" until even the proofreading was completed. Any student of American literature must, I think, lament the fact that Hawthorne's emotional makeup led him to shy away from the vulnerable expressions of wonder and rejoicing one finds in Melville's letters and reported conversations. As Turner concludes, "there is evidence throughout the remaining forty years of Melville's life that he thought he had been rebuffed by Hawthorne, and that he felt a genuine regret for his loss."[9]

If in the early 1850s Hawthorne presented himself to the public, in the middle years of that decade the public presented itself to him. From the time he secured his appointment from President Franklin Pierce and assumed the lucrative position of United States Consul at Liverpool, Hawthorne received a steady stream of callers: merchant seamen with grievances; American citizens seeking legal, financial, or perhaps emotional assistance; exiles in search of help. Virtually overwhelmed at first by what he called the "rascally set of sailors, . . . dirty, desperate, . . . pirate-like," who filled the entry to his office, he responded with a greater involvement in the affairs of others than he had formerly had occasion to show. His generosity to Delia Bacon, an American whose idea that Francis Bacon and others wrote the plays we attribute to Shakespeare generally made people avoid her, is worthy of note. Not only did he listen to her obsession sympathetically; he spent over $1,000 to have her book on the subject published ("the last of my benevolent follies," he wrote to Ticknor), and, at Miss Bacon's request, even provided a preface that was as delicate as it was evasive. The years 1853–57 brought Hawthorne into direct contact with distress and inhumanity. They also introduced him to England and to an idea of homecoming which, until the end of his life, he would seek to articulate in fiction.

The obvious financial advantage of the consular post, plus a desire to see England, made Hawthorne want very much to go abroad at this time. And see England he did, with a shrewd and critical intelligence, as his journal entries show. A record of his observations, he hoped, would prove useful for an English romance he was planning to write. But that romance was never to be completed. A series of essays on England, first published in the *Atlantic Monthly* and then collected under the title *Our Old Home* in 1863, came instead from these sketches and observations in his journal—a charming but disappointing harvest from the rich soil of his recorded English experiences. Appropriately, Hawthorne dedicated *Our Old Home* to Franklin Pierce, the man who had made his English years possible.

But this dedication was a studied act of gratitude. For Pierce, out of his desire to hold the Union together, had consistently advocated a cautious, moderate policy regarding slavery. To many he seemed far less a patriot than a temporizer. His popularity, never of magnitude in the North, had waned appreciably. By insisting that *Our Old Home* be dedicated to Pierce, Hawthorne thus made a point of his good will toward a man exceedingly out of fashion. Emerson, indeed, was so irritated by Hawthorne's public thanks to Pierce that he ripped the dedicatory pages from his copy of the book.

Hawthorne resigned from the consulate in August, 1857, and early in 1858 he left for Italy. There during the last years of the decade he met artists and poets as a peer, visited cathedrals and museums as an amateur critic of art, and perceived the mighty dimensions of the past as an American. Still the man of letters of established reputation, he was gathering force for a romance which would embody some significant aspect of his years abroad. Italy challenged Hawthorne as no other experience in his life had done. As we shall see in considering *The Marble Faun*, it came to represent to him the antithesis of home. All too often, he could view the rich legacy of the Italian past only through the distracting lens of the Italian present. He could not ignore, for example, the dirt of Roman byways and even less the ever-present beggars whose importuning numbers exceeded the capacity of one man's charity. His daughter Una's illness in November, 1858, cost him anxious days and weeks in an environment in which he was and felt himself to be essentially a stranger. Hawthorne's Italian experience was rich in implication for him; but it was also complex. Out of it, however, did come the idea for a new romance engendered by his contemplation of the Faun of Praxiteles. In 1859, with no emotional misgivings, he left Italy for England, where he would write *The Marble Faun.*

In 1860 Hawthorne returned to the United States and to his former home at the Wayside. William Dean Howells visited him in 1862 and was struck by his "sombre and brooding" look—just the look "such a poet should have" had. After a walk, some conversation, and tea, Hawthorne pointed to a bookcase "where there were a few books toppling about on the half-filled shelves, and said, coldly, 'This is my library.' " Men, not books, Howells decided, were the objects of Hawthorne's study. As Howells was leaving, Hawthorne volunteered to give him a note of introduction to Emerson; it read simply, "I find this young man worthy." With the spirit of a pilgrim Howells enjoyed his visit with Hawthorne, but he admitted that "there was a great deal of silence in it all, and at times, in spite of his shadowy kindness, I felt my spirits sink." Hawthorne's capacity for silence was undiminished. Yet graciousness and lack of ostentation seemed to Howells the most impressive things about him.

Hawthorne visited Washington in 1862 and, together with a delegation from Massachusetts, called on President Lincoln. Though it has since become the most famous passage in the essay, his description of Lincoln was omitted (with his consent) from an article, "Chiefly About War Matters," which he contributed to the *Atlantic* in July, 1862. Homely, "yet by no means repulsive or disagreeable," Lincoln seemed to Hawthorne "the pattern American"; his coarse features were "redeemed, illuminated, softened, and brightened" by the kind and sagacious look in his eyes. Yet Hawthorne could stand apart and make his judgment: although the President was clearly "honest at heart, and thoroughly so," yet in some way he seemed "sly,—at least, endowed with a sort of tact and wisdom that are akin to craft, and would impel him, I think, to take an antagonist in the flank, rather than to make a bull-run at him right in front." Hawthorne's oblique praise of Lincoln resolves itself into personal assessment; the reticent man of New England is attempting to measure the raw man of the West. "On the whole," Hawthorne concluded, he liked Lincoln and was as glad to have him for President as he would be to have anyone else. During the final years of his life Hawthorne began work (several times) on a romance dealing with an American claimant to an English estate and on another dramatizing the idea of immortality, neither of which he was able to complete.[10] The fragments he left (six in all, some extensive, some brief) reveal a series of attempts to make old strategies of creation viable once again; frustration and disappointment were the results of his inability to do so. The years of the Civil War marked the end of Hawthorne's career. For Whitman they were the "years of parturition"; for Hawthorne they were years of a final imaginative decline. In a context of war, with the psychic energies of the nation indentured to concerns of victory and defeat, his attempts to bring his kind of fictional reality into coherent form met with failure. He could not breathe vitality into the idea of an American claiming a lost estate in England or into the idea of an elixir of life when the life of the nation itself was at stake. The fact of the Civil War, of course, does not fully account for the deterioration of Hawthorne's creative abilities. Failing health also contributed to his difficulties. And perhaps he would have been unable to complete a romance under even the most favorable of circumstances. As later analysis of his work will show, however, the overpowering reality of the war must have constituted a staggering problem to one who created fiction in the mode that Hawthorne did.

On the day after Hawthorne's funeral, in May, 1864, Emerson wrote in his journal: "I thought him a greater man than any of his works betray. . . ." The statement reveals (uniquely) a sense of Hawthorne's stature as a human being. But an artist will be judged finally by the quality of his art. And in the best of his tales, in his romances—and especially in *The Scarlet Letter* (a "ten-strike"' after all)—Hawthorne created an art of unchallenged significance. Not only did he succeed in opening "an intercourse with the world" of his own time; in his work the poet transcended, even as he has survived, the bookkeeper to achieve an enduring fame.

Chapter Two

The Neutral Ground of Fiction

A Strategy of Creation

"The Present, the Immediate, the Actual, has proved too potent for me," wrote Hawthorne to Franklin Pierce in the preface to *Our Old Home* in 1863. "It takes away not only my scanty faculty, but even my desire for imaginative composition, and leaves me sadly content to scatter a thousand peaceful fantasies upon the hurricane that is sweeping us all along with it, possibly, into a Limbo where our nation and its polity may be as literally the fragments of a shattered dream as my unwritten Romance."

For Hawthorne, wearily at work on "The Dolliver Romance," these were new words to an old tune. The American Civil War was certainly an overwhelming reality to him. His absence from the United States during the years 1853 to 1860 had caused the war to loom before him with paralyzing suddenness. Out of an increasing depression he came to see it as "the most inevitable event that ever happened." But from the beginning of his career Hawthorne had contended with "the Present, the Immediate, the Actual." He had always felt that "the hard, hot, practical life of America" constricted his imagination. To write fiction he consistently sought to lessen the pressure of the actual, to dilate reality for the purposes of his imagination. The incomplete "Septimius" manuscripts are understood most clearly as displacements of one war for another, the backdrop of the American Revolution substituting for the insistent reality of the Civil War. The fragility of such a displacement is suggested in "Septimius Norton" when on the eve of the Revolution Robert Hagburn observes that "we are in for a civil war," and in "Septimius Felton" when Robert provides an unwitting gloss on Hawthorne's artistic difficulties by telling Septimius that "this is not a generation for study, and the making of books. . . ."

Out of a need to shield his imagination from the recalcitrant glare of the American present, Hawthorne evolved certain fundamental strategies of creation which did much to define the nature of his achievement as a writer. The prefaces to his major romances contain what is, in effect, a theory of fiction based on the supposition that art requires a domain of its own if it is to flourish. Thus, he explains in the preface to *The House of the Seven Gables*, the latitude of fashion and material afforded by the romance is congenial to his imagination. His concern in *The Blithedale Romance* is "to establish a theatre, a little removed from the highway of ordinary travel, where the creatures of his brain may play their phantasmagorical antics, without exposing them to too close a comparison with the actual events of real lives." Older countries, Hawthorne realizes, have granted a traditional privilege to the romancer so that "his work is not put exactly side by side with nature." Among Americans, however, "there is as yet no such Faery Land, so like the real world, that, in a suitable remoteness, one cannot well tell the difference, but with an atmosphere of strange enchantment, beheld through which the inhabitants have a propriety of their own. This atmosphere is what the American romancer needs." The difficulty of creating fiction under such circumstances, Hawthorne admits, "has always pressed very heavily" upon him. In writing *Blithedale*, he has "ventured to make free" with his memory of Brook Farm as being "essentially a day-dream, and yet a fact," as something which offers "an available foothold between fiction and reality."

The same theory of fiction evokes Hawthorne's statement concerning the romance and America in the preface to *The Marble Faun*. As the setting for that romance, he explains, Italy afforded him "a sort of poetic or fairy precinct, where actualities would not be so terribly insisted upon, as they are, and must needs be, in America. No author, without a trial, can conceive of the difficulty of writing a Romance about a country where there is no shadow, no antiquity, no mystery, no picturesque and gloomy wrong, nor anything but a common-place prosperity, in broad and simple daylight, as is happily the case with my dear native land." He hopes that it will be very long before America furnishes appropriate themes for romance: for "Romance and poetry . . . need Ruin to make them grow." In 1837 Hawthorne had singled out the lack of materials as a particular burden for a writer like himself who had seen relatively little of life. By 1860 he had seen a great deal more of life, and the lack of suitable materials revealed itself as a lack of perspective. Significantly, Hawthorne rejoices in the very problem he defines so persuasively. As an American of his time, he approves of all that makes American society so different and consequently so difficult for the man of imagination. As an artist, however, he announces once again that he has had to seek out a fairy precinct, a region removed from the actual, in which to locate the world of his fiction.

In "The Custom-House," which stands as the portal to *The Scarlet Letter*, Hawthorne formulates a metaphor basic to his thinking about fiction. Moonlight tempered by the dim light of a hearth fire, he writes, contributes to a creative mood; a nearby mirror portrays everything "one remove further from the actual, and nearer to the imaginative"; finally, one arrives at a "neutral territory, somewhere between the real world and fairy-land, where the Actual and the Imaginary may meet, and each imbue itself with the nature of the other." As Leo B. Levy has pointed out, Hawthorne's original notebook account of sitting by the fireside in a moonlit room one evening does not include the teams "Actual," "Imaginary," and "neutral territory" so crucial to his discussion in "The Custom-House."[1] As additions, these terms suggest Hawthorne's desire to convert a provocative description of atmosphere into a functioning explanation of the creative process. Admittedly, Hawthorne's neutral territory has only a metaphorical existence; but as a metaphor with an ontological burden it held a great attraction for him. He structured his thinking about reality in the terms of this metaphor. He assumed, for the purposes of his art, a basic division of reality into the actual, on the one hand, and the imaginary, on the other. History, daylight, wakefulness, and fact frequently become alternative terms for the actual; darkness, dream, and mystery constitute alternatives for the imaginary.

Between these two kinds of reality lies the neutral ground, where the actual and the imaginary interpenetrate. When Hawthorne says that during the whole of his Custom House experience moonlight, sunshine, and the glow of firelight were "just alike" in his eyes, he is speaking in emphatic metaphorical language of his inability to make the necessary distinctions for invoking the strategy of the neutral ground. The Salem Custom House, slow as its traffic may have been, epitomizes in his sketch the world of actuality, a world uncongenial to his imagination. Although the scarlet letter, as Hawthorne tells us, was in the Custom House, *The Scarlet Letter* was not and could not have been.

In the first half of the nineteenth century, as R. W. B. Lewis reminded us some years ago, Americans tended to define their society in terms of hope, promise, and innocence.[2] Europe was mired in "folly, corruption, and tyranny," wrote Noah Webster, virtually as part of a chorus; America, on the other hand, was fresh, unspoiled, a land happily delivered from the past. "No people," a writer in the *North American Review* announced in 1818, have ever had such advantages: "We are free from any of those institutions transmitted to us from past ages, by which other nations are enthralled, and held back, and allied to the ignorance and vice of their progenitors." The American mind is not "crippled and deformed by prejudices" but is free from "moral infection," free also from institutions that "oppress and bear down the truth." In short, the writer concludes, "we are favoured beyond all example; almost beyond any previous imagination of what might possibly be attained."[3]

Such statements are representative of a national disposition. When Hawthorne in 1860 saw "no shadow" in America, but only a "broad and simple daylight," he was—it is important to remember—reflecting an attitude that had prevailed throughout his culture for more than a half century. The basic antithesis of his terms is instructive: broad daylight dispels shadow just as wakefulness dispels dream; a world of fact crowds out fiction. From England came a view of the New World structured in analogous terms. To explain the difficulties of the American novelist, for example, a writer in the *Edinburgh Review* in 1829 observed that "no ghost, we will venture to say, was ever seen in North America." For ghosts "do not walk in broad day; and the night of ignorance and superstition which favours their appearance, was long past" before the United States came into being.[4] A society that insists on seeing itself in terms of daylight, wakefulness, and fact perforce depreciates shadow, dream, and ghostly apparitions. And Hawthorne, as a writer who was part of such a society, felt a need to attenuate in some way the necessary glare of the American present, to remove his fiction—if he was to have fiction—from the tyranny of what he called the "actual." The metaphor of a neutral ground served to describe conditions by means of which his work could come into being.

In various forms, Hawthorne's concept of a neutral ground pervades both his fiction and his description of its genesis. *Blithedale*, as we have noted, offers "an available foothold between fiction and reality"; it is "essentially a day-dream and yet a fact." Italy serves as a poetic or fairy precinct in *The Marble Faun*. Rappaccini's garden becomes a dreamlike enclosure governed by magic that baffles perception. And Hawthorne is not alone in formulating such strategies. Washington Irving's observation in "Westminster Abbey" that the exploits of the Crusader formed "the connecting link between fact and fiction; between the history and the fairy tale" evinces a concern for something, someone, in this case a figure blurred by time, to *embody* a middle ground. Edgar Allan Poe in his "Marginalia" locates certain "*fancies*" which exist only "at those mere points of time where the confines of the waking world blend with those of the world of dreams." Poe is attracted to this "border-ground," this "point of blending between wakefulness and sleep," just as Hawthorne finds a fascination in the "conscious sleep" of the "haunted mind." In the historical romance, both Walter Scott and James Fenimore Cooper employed the idea of a neutral or middle ground. Scott's border country and Cooper's frontier—the latter defined by the ever-moving figure of Leatherstocking—stand typically between the wild and the civilized as the matrix of their fiction. These two writers give geographical location to what is for Hawthorne primarily a state of mind, for Irving a perspective on nostalgia, and for Poe an opportunity to play at terror.

Without some kind of strategy for visualizing a middle ground, the work of writers who cast history and fiction, daydream and fact, into antithetical modes could take bizarre form. Jeremy Belknap's *The Foresters* (1792), an epistolary account of the American Revolution, is humorously albeit fatally impaled by allegory. Isaac Mitchell's *The Asylum; or, Alonzo and Melissa* (1811) attempts to introduce an aura of mystery by setting a Gothic castle and a moat in Connecticut. Perhaps the most instructive example of all is Samuel Woodworth's *The Champions of Freedom; or, the Mysterious Chief* (1816), a narrative dealing with the War of 1812. When, in an elaborate preface, a friend of the author objects to "absurd" incidents in the manuscript, Woodworth replies that "the absurdity of the *incidents* must not be imputed to me . . . ; they are all copied from life." Hoping that the reader will excuse him for introducing so many characters into his story, Woodworth pleads the "impossibility" of doing otherwise "without a violation of fact." Although *The Champions of Freedom* contains "fictitious scenes, incidents, and characters," it is nonetheless "the most correct and complete History of the recent War, that has yet appeared." Woodworth hopes that the book "will be found equally interesting, as a history or a novel" and that the "lovers of each will find themselves pleasantly led from one to another of their own favorite scenes, without a very wearisome march through those of their opponents in taste."

Woodworth (best known for writing "The Old Oaken Bucket") cannot blend history and fiction into a coherent narrative nor even discuss the possibility of doing so. After alternating historical and fictional episodes, he can only hope that his book will be read "as a history or a novel." Perhaps aware of a fundamental confusion in *The Champions*, he concludes his preface on a note of abject humility. This "is my first attempt," he writes, "and I have done the best I could. In many respects I have studied the interest of the reader alone, by making short paragraphs, and lessening the length of a chapter when the subject is dull, and increasing it when the incidents are interesting." Such a confession allows us not only to laugh but to learn. For we can understand more of what it was to write fiction in early nineteenth-century America by understanding Woodworth's imaginative problems. We can appreciate the importance of visualizing a middle ground for the making of historical romance. And, from a fresh perspective, we can see the manifold usefulness of Hawthorne's metaphor of a neutral ground in setting the appropriate conditions for his fiction.

Attaining the vantage point of a neutral ground required attention to process, to rhetorical strategies that might baffle the otherwise uncompromising pressure of the actual. So effective is this process in "The Custom-House" that "a familiar room" becomes a place where "Ghosts might enter . . . without affrighting us." The narrator of "Legends of the Province House," as we shall see in chapter 3, has a more difficult task: he must strive with the "best energy of his imagination" to throw a tinge of romance and heroic grandeur" over the subborn realities of the scene before him. In the work of Washington Irving the process takes on a formulaic quality, although it is recognizably the same. Preparing to meditate on the mutability of literature, Irving's narrator in *The Sketch-Book* alludes to "certain half-dreaming moods of mind, in which we naturally steal away from noise and glare, and seek some quiet haunt, where we may indulge our reveries and build our air-castles undisturbed." Whereas such generalized retreats as quiet haunts and "shadowy grandeurs" serve the requirements of Irving's imagination, Hawthorne characteristically makes use of detail to emphasize the process of attaining a neutral ground. Significantly, however, each writer employs a language of escape and evasion to introduce his fiction. Because many trappings of the Old World were happily "lost overboard" in voyages to the new, says a character in Sylvester Judd's *Margaret* (1845), there are "no fairies in our meadows, and no elves to spirit away our children. . . . We have no traditions, legends, fables, and scarcely a history." Writers such as Hawthorne, Irving, and Cooper sought to fashion American versions of what had been "lost overboard," to invent traditions, legends, fables, and even history by first imagining appropriate strategies of creation.

Hawthorne's neutral ground, one can say synoptically, existed for him in lieu of Irving's Crusader and Cooper's Leatherstocking. And without a ready-made, native inhabitant, it could be a nebulous region, difficult to populate, though consistently helpful in thinking about the making of fiction. Hawthorne's tendency to use terms such as "region," "precinct," and "kingdom" when talking about the neutral ground suggests a desire to literalize (or materialize) his metaphor, to define it as if it had a geographical location of its own. These terms were undoubtedly very helpful to him in setting the conditions of his fiction. But they could, on occasion, introduce problems of their own; they could lead him, for example, to overlook the fact that the metaphor of a neutral ground was a fiction for creating fiction and encourage him to look for an already existing neutral ground as a solution to his creative difficulties. His choice of Italy as a "poetic or fairy precint" in *The Marble Faun* constituted a kind of imaginative short cut which resulted in his being unable to assimilate thoroughly the various materials of that romance. At its best, Hawthorne's neutral ground functions as a state of mind.

The Haunted Mind

The quest for imaginative latitude and for a way to embody the neutral ground in a coherent work of fiction led Hawthorne to the tale rather than to the short story, to the romance rather than to the novel. Traditionally, the tale and the romance had been able to incorporate mythic and legendary material. Traditionally, these forms fostered enlargement and caricature rather than close delineation of life and incident. Hawthorne, as he well knew, did not invent the distinction between the romance and the novel any more than he invented the idea of a middle ground as a strategy for fictional creation. But he formulated such a distinction clearly and precisely to serve the requirements of his art.

Hawthorne begins his preface to *The House of the Seven Gables* by saying that when a writer calls his work a romance "it need hardly be observed that he wishes to claim a certain latitude, both as to its fashion and material, which he would not have felt himself entitled to assume had he professed to be writing a Novel." According to the conventional distinction, the novel aims "at a very minute fidelity, not merely to the possible, but to the probable and ordinary course of man's experience." The romance, on the other hand, while it must conform to artistic laws and above all to the truth of the human heart, has "a right to present that truth under circumstances, to a great extent, of the writer's own choosing or creation." The writer of romance may, for example, "manage his atmospherical medium" so as to deepen the shadows or mellow the lights of his composition; he may make use of the marvelous for special effects. Much the same thing could be said for the tale, which bears a relation to the romance similar to that which the short story bears to the novel.[5]

As studies of our literature have amply shown, a strong element of romance characterized the development of American fiction.[6] Indeed, what we regard as the best of American fiction prior to the Civil War adopts the form of the romance. And some writers in addition to Hawthorne are quite explicit about their choice of form. William Gilmore Simms, for example, in a preface to the revised edition of *The Yemassee* in 1853, insisted that the standards of romance and not those of the novel had governed its composition. Simms considers the romance to be his era's substitute for the epic. The form, of course, is altered; the material differs. Yet the "standards of the Romance . . . are very much those of the epic." The romance, Simms goes on to say, "is of loftier origin than the Novel. It approximates the poem. It may be described as an amalgam of the two." Important for Simms, as for Hawthorne, is the fact that the romance allows an extravagance of presentation: "It does not confine itself to what is known, or even what is probable"; rather, it "grasps at the possible." In Hawthorne's terms, the romance affords an entry to "the kingdom of possibilities."

Reviewing Henry James's study of Hawthorne for the *Atlantic Monthly* in 1880, William Dean Howells objected to the manner in which James failed to distinguish between the romance and the novel in speaking of Hawthorne's fiction: "No one better than Mr. James," says Howells, "knows the radical difference between a romance and a novel, but he speaks now of Hawthorne's novels, and now of his romances, throughout, as if the terms were convertible; whereas the romance and the novel are as distinct as the poem and the novel." James's criticism of the characters in *The Scarlet Letter* as being "rather types than persons, rather conditions of the mind than characters" strikes Howells as wide of the mark—a result of James's refusal to acknowledge the romance as a literary form with a particular principle of reality. For it is "almost precisely the business of the romance to deal with types and mental conditions," he explains; and Hawthorne's fiction conforms "always and essentially, in conception and performance," to the special demands of romance.

Though James may have used the terms imprecisely in his study of Hawthorne, he knew well, as Howells said, the "radical difference between a romance and a novel." In his preface to *The American* (written for the New York Edition of his work in 1908), James searched out the essence of the romance as he saw it. His considerations have a special relevance for any attempt to define what imaginative latitude, the neutral ground, and the romance meant to Hawthorne. James finds that the strange and the far are not essential ingredients of the romance; they represent simply the unknown, which the increasing range of our experience may convert to the known. Nor does a romantic temper in a character constitute an essential aspect of romance: although Emma Bovary is a romantic, nothing, James believes, "less resembles a romance" than *Madame Bovary*. The romance explores a reality that, no matter the growth of our experience, we never can know directly, a reality that "can reach us only through the beautiful circuit and subterfuge of our thought and our desire." The only "*general* attribute" of romance that James can see, the only one which fits all its cases, is the fact of the kind of experience with which it deals—experience liberated, so to speak; experience disengaged, disembroiled, disencumbered, exempt from the conditions that we usually know to attach to it and, if we wish so to put the matter, drag upon it, and operating in a medium which relieves it, in a particular interest, of the inconvenience of a *related*, a measurable state, a state subject to all our vulgar commodities.

Some relation with society is of course always maintained. The greatest intensity in a romance is evidently arrived at, James goes on to say, "when the sacrifice of community, of the 'related' sides of situations, has not been too rash." The romance, therefore, must not "flagrantly betray itself; we must even be kept, if possible, for our illusion, from suspecting any sacrifice at all." In his balloon of experience metaphor, James concludes that the art of the romancer is "insidiously"—"for the fun of it"—to cut the cable connecting the balloon and the earth, to cut it without being detected, so that we swing apart, "at large and unrelated," without realizing what has happened.

As the texture of his fiction and his explicit statements about Hawthorne's milieu demonstrate, James felt at ease imaginatively in society delineated by manners, traditions, customs of long standing. A typical situation in a James short story or novel would be "related" to, dragged upon by, society to a much greater degree than a typical situation in a Hawthorne tale or romance—there is simply more of society rendered, and more to be rendered, in James fiction. Thus, when James speaks of related or encumbered experience, he is not referring precisely to what Hawthorne would consider an insistence on actualities. The implications of James's analysis, however, illuminate the central imaginative problem of Hawthorne's career: his search to find a "region" where liberated experience (to use James's term) could be fully accommodated.

James's definition of the romance, we note, moves toward a consideration of technique, of execution, in a characteristic manner. He sets forth a theory of romance which he has come to empirically. He looks for, and finds, a unique "*general* attribute" of romance, the only one, as he says, which "fits all its cases." In the same way that James's prefaces assume the prior creation of his novels and stories,

his analysis of the romance assumes and takes critical advantage of
the fact that romances had been created by earlier writers. Hawthorne,
as we have seen, likewise availed himself of certain assumptions
concerning the romance. But his statements suggest that the romance
was for him a working, formative concept out of which a writer might
seek to create fiction and not a retrospective elucidation of the general
attributes of whatever romances he might know. Whereas James
theorizes after the fact of creation, Hawthorne theorized as a pre-
requisite of creation. He leads us, as it were, behind James's definition
of romance to a point at which the initial proposal for fiction is of
radical importance. As Hawthorne saw it, his essential problem was
to create not simply fiction but the conditions of fiction; and it led
him to confront, on a neutral ground, a kind of experience that James
identifies in retrospect (and from a different point of view) as
liberated or disencumbered.

As much as any of his explicit, prefatory statements, Hawthorne's
sketch "The Haunted Mind" describes the nature of the neutral
ground and suggests its relation to disencumbered experience. In this
sketch Hawthorne writes of an hour in the night when one starts
up suddenly and finds himself awake in a world of dreams.[7] It is
a time out of time when yesterday has vanished into the past and
tomorrow has not yet emerged from the future, "an intermediate
space where the business of life does not intrude." In an hour like
this, says Hawthorne, "the mind has a passive sensibility, but no
active strength . . . ; the imagination is a mirror, imparting vividness
to all ideas, without the power of selecting or controlling them."
Shame and guilt arising from within force one to break from "a sort
of conscious sleep" to gaze "wildly around the bed, as if the fiends
were anywhere but in your haunted mind." Embers on the hearth,
however, suggest visions of domestic comfort, which one enjoys "on
the borders of sleep and wakefulness."

"The Haunted Mind" epitomizes essential features of Hawthorne's
fiction. The horror of inner guilt, for example, and the comforting
domestic associations of the hearth, are familiar terms of his work.
But the sketch has also a larger significance: it provides a way of
discussing Hawthorne's mode of imaginative creation. It is, in a
sense, a paradigm of the creative process as Hawthorne saw that
process. Hawthorne's subject is the haunted mind, but the setting
of the sketch is a kind of neutral ground, a stage for creation, out

of time, between yesterday and tomorrow. Somewhere behind or below is the haunted mind, in which the imagination floats free, yielding up vivid but unselected and uncontrolled images. As these images—vague, horrific, and never yet encumbered—emerge onto the neutral ground, they are met by already existent actual being which swims into cognition: and the meeting of the two provides the potential instant of imaginative creation.

Any attempt to explain the creative process sentence by sentence carries with it some distortion: it has the unfortunate effect of making things seem to happen in sequence when they are happening simultaneously. Hawthorne's final statement helps to clarify what we know from attending closely to his musing dramatization of the creative process. When "indistinct horror" rises from within, one leaves a state of "conscious sleep" and searches wildly for concrete, external reality—in this case, embers on the hearth. Having brought something existing within to something existing without, one achieves a balanced enjoyment "on the borders of sleep and wakefulness." The neutral ground has been given a reality of its own—the imaginary and the actual have met and mingled.

To juxtapose the mental drama of "The Haunted Mind" with a different set of instructions for dispersing the terrors of the night gives us a surer view of the context in which Hawthorne lived and wrote. James Beattie was a Scottish moral philosopher, one of the Common Sense school which had a significant influence on American educators, clerics, and writers during the first half of the nineteenth century. In the manner of Dugald Stewart, other Common Sense thinkers, and most American critics hostile to fiction, Beattie distinguishes between memory and imagination: in remembering, he says in his *Dissertations Moral and Critical* (1783), "we revolve or revise past perceptions, with a view to our experience of them, and to their reality"; in imagining, however, "we consider the notion or thought now present in the mind, simply as it is in itself, without any view to real existence, or to past experience." From the imagination we thus get ideas "without any view to their reality." If memory yields history, the imagination yields fantasy.

At a later point in his *Dissertations* Beattie describes what he considers the most preferable way of dealing with "imaginary terrors" of the night. "By the glimmering of the moon," he writes, "I have once and again beheld at midnight, the exact form of a man or

woman, sitting silent and motionless by my bedside. Had I hid my
head, without daring to look the apparition in the face, I should have
passed the night in horror, and risen in the morning with the persua-
sion of having seen a ghost. But, rousing myself, and resolving to
find out the truth, I discovered, that it was nothing more than the
accidental disposition of my clothes upon a chair." On another occasion he was alarmed to see "by the faint light of the dawn, a coffin
laid out between my bed and the window. I started up, and recollect-
ing, that I had heard of such things having been seen by others, I
set myself to examine it, and found it was only a stream of yellowish
light, falling in a particular manner upon the floor, from between
the window-curtains."[8]

Here we have two ways of treating the imagination at its most
exacerbated. James Beattie has no place for the haunted mind: he
will move rationally to discover the facts of perception so that the
actual world—what he would call the *real* world—is reestablished
around him. If one wakes to see a stream of light as a coffin, there is
a momentary conflict between what is within the mind and what is
without. Investigation quickly proves the reality of the outer world.
In "The Haunted Mind," however, the narrator, waking suddenly,
sustains a series of images within his mind. He looks through the
partially frosted window at the wintry world outside, shivers, then
retreats head and all under the covers, for "it is too cold even for the
thoughts to venture abroad." A speculation on the luxury of living
forever like an oyster in a shell brings "in its train" a "hideous" idea—
that of the dead lying in their cold shrouds and "narrow coffins."
Having entertained these and associated fantasies, Hawthorne's narrator finally welcomes the sight of embers on the hearth because it
offsets the terrors of the haunted mind. What Beattie would banish
as a matter of course—in the name of common sense, Hawthorne
would nourish "on the borders of sleep and wakefulness"—in the
name of artistic creation.

In the terms established by Hawthorne in "The Haunted Mind,"
failure to achieve the necessary balance of the imaginary and the
actual on the neutral or border territory may come about in one of
two ways. In an overpowering daylight or wakefulness, in, that is,
the context of the insistence on actuality that James Beattie espouses,
one could not meet with the requisite conditions of imaginative
creation. Conversely, if one remains within the haunted mind, amid

its uncontrolled, unselected images, there could be no imaginative creation. Sleep, in which the haunted mind, as it were, contemplates itself, is thus no more a condition of fiction than is being wide awake. It is on the "borders" of sleep and wakefulness that the haunted mind encounters the actual world and that the primary condition of fiction is fulfilled.

Hawthorne's analysis of the haunted mind likewise bears an interesting relation to James's notion of "disengaged, disembroiled, disencumbered" experience. We recall that James's discussion concerns execution, that it assumes and is subsequent to the creation of romance. And we see once again that Hawthorne's concern differs: characteristically, he focuses on the *conditions* of imaginative creation, on an aspect of the creative process prior to that of execution. The difficulty of creating fiction in the "broad and simple daylight" of his native land (where experience, no matter how limited, would be engaged and encumbered) encouraged Hawthorne to cultivate the resources of the haunted mind which gave him access to a potentially frightening world of disengaged experience. In his terms, the problem in making fiction became one of blending the imaginative and the actual (on a neutral ground—here the borders of sleep and wakefulness) so that the creation of romance would be possible. To say that disengaged experience came from the haunted mind is of course to employ James's term to describe the exigencies of the creative situation as Hawthorne saw them. But some distinction should be maintained between such different attitudes toward the romance. It is, I believe, more precise to define the "haunted" experience which Hawthorne would hope ultimately to shape into fiction as *pre*encumbered, *pre*engaged. As he presents it in "The Haunted Mind," it is genetically liberated, of its very nature presocial. James, on the other hand, speaks of *dis*encumbered or *dis*engaged experience—experience liberated from its social relatedness into the unrelated state of romance by the "insidious" craft of the artist. Although Hawthorne died in 1864 and James's first story appeared in 1865, the two authors have traditionally been taken to represent two distinct periods in American literary history. Perhaps nowhere is their difference in time and point of view—as well as their continuity of interest—more apparent than in the kind of concern each has for the romance.

Hawthorne's final admission that "the Present, the Immediate, the Actual" had proved too potent for him singles out his need to attenuate the American insistence on actualities as the primary and perennial difficulty he faced as a writer. His metaphor of a neutral ground, as we have seen, served to describe (and structure) reality in a way that made fictional creation seem to him not only possible but viable. On the neutral ground the actual would meet and interpenetrate with experience yielded up by the uncontrolled imagination. Once each kind of reality had imbued itself "with the nature of the other," the obstacles of the wide-awake world would be overcome, the dangers of the dream world averted. To that end Hawthorne employed as appropriate forms the tale and the romance, using them at times experimentally and always in his own way. His achievement testifies to a concern for form as a means of establishing a relationship between his art and the world and thereby vindicating the creative process.

Chapter Three

The Tales:
Method and Achievement

The prefaces to Hawthorne's romances are indeed significant statements of his attitude toward fiction and reality. Long before he turned his energies to the romance, however, he had confronted the problem of how to bring his fiction into being in the form of the tale. His tales, which appeared over a period of twenty years, reveal both the struggle and the achievement of a writer who had to establish the *conditions* of his fiction in the very act of creating that fiction itself.

As he himself acknowledged, Hawthorne did not improve steadily as a writer of tales. Some of his best work came surprisingly early: "My Kinsman, Major Molineux," "Young Goodman Brown," and "The May-pole of Merry Mount" were first published in 1832, 1835, and 1836, respectively. Slight tales appeared in the same year as major tales. *Twice-Told Tales* (1837) was considered superior as a collection to *Mosses from an Old Manse* (1846) by Poe, Melville, and most later critics. Yet "Rappaccini's Daughter" (1844) and "Ethan Brand" (1851) clearly attempt and achieve more than do, say, "Mrs. Bullfrog" (1837) and "The Lily's Quest" (1839). The movement of Hawthorne's short fiction, indirect and often unsure, is toward *The Scarlet Letter*. But it took twenty years of striving before his triumph in *The Scarlet Letter* transformed the tale into the romance. During those years Hawthorne worked continually to set the proper conditions for his fiction. At times his method may amount to little more than a variation of a conventional literary device; again, though original, it may be flagrant and awkward; yet again, it may explore the fundamental question of how far one may entrust oneself to the imagination. At its best, the method disappears into the fusion of form and content which constitutes the final articulation of a tale. Always, however, it will seek to present a world free from the insistence on actualities which Hawthorne regarded as inimical to his fiction.

The Conditions of Fiction

Hawthorne opens "The Hollow of the Three Hills," his first published tale, with an abrupt evocation of a Gothic past: "In those strange old times, when fantastic dreams and madmen's reveries were realized among the actual circumstances of life, two persons met together at an appointed hour and place." Under this rubric, time functions as place; the phrase "strange old times" serves as a neutral ground in the manner of a poetic or fairy precinct. Hawthorne has begun, in a very direct manner, by denying any distinction between the real and the fantastic. If there were such a time, we see immediately, when "fantastic dreams and madmen's reveries" (the very stuff of the haunted mind) occurred among the actual conditions of life, then surely there could be no setting more congenial to Hawthorne's fiction. Without asking us to grant the possibility of such a time, Hawthorne simply postulates its existence as the condition of his tale, then uses the latitude he thereby achieves to relate a story of domestic tragedy from a thoroughly nondomestic point of view.

The aged crone of "The Hollow of the Three Hills" functions as part of the Gothic machinery of the tale.[1] By means of the crone's powers, with their suggestion of Satanic darkness, the lady of the tale can look back into her life to see the tragic consequences of her actions. She has wrung the hearts of her parents, betrayed her husband, and "sinned against natural affection" by leaving her child to die. Amid a setting redolent of witchcraft and evil, the lady experiences her visions of society. After each vision Hawthorne makes a studied transition back to the hollow, thereby reinforcing the reality principle of the tale. For this is where the lady's sins against the heart and against natural affection (heinous offenses always in Hawthorne's fiction) have led her. She must consort with witchcraft and deviltry if she is to have even a glimpse of society. She must make use of powers antithetical to love and trust if she is to measure the extent of her isolation. From the moral wilderness of the hollow she achieves a threefold vision of domestic chaos and social castigation and dies with her head in the lap of the unconcerned crone. Hawthorne has turned the world as we know it inside out. Taking advantage of the setting assumed in and achieved by his abrupt opening sentence, he has adopted a point of view by means of which we see society only in fragmentary visions. He has, moreover, managed the form of his tale so that it embodies in a unique way a theme characteristic of his work.

The opening sentence of "The Hollow of the Three Hills" constitutes a Hawthornesque variation of the time-honored opening of the fairy tale. It was a method of getting his fiction immediately under way which Hawthorne would use repeatedly. "The Great Carbuncle," for example, begins "At nightfall, once in the olden time. . . ." In "The Lily's Quest," this has become "Two lovers, once upon a time. . . ." And in "Earth's Holocaust," Hawthorne begins with "Once upon a time—but whether in the time past or the time to come is a matter of little or no moment. . . ." By adopting the convention of the fairy tale, Hawthorne achieves at a stroke the imaginative freedom he requires. And most often he shapes the ensuing tale into a modern fable complete with a moral regarding human wisdom or folly. The lesson of "Earth's Holocaust" is that reform will fail if the human heart is not first purified. "The Great Carbuncle" points up the wisdom of rejecting a jewel which would dim "all earthly things" in favor of the "cheerful glow" of the hearth. "The Lily's Quest" spells out laboriously the idea that happiness is predicated on eternity. Wrought with a greater discipline, "The Hollow of the Three Hills" does not offer a moral refrain. What it says about human guilt and woe is implicit in the stylized drama of the tale, which stands as the best evidence of what Hawthorne could realize in fiction by adopting the method of the fairy tale to the uses of his imagination.[2]

Emerson complained that Hawthorne "invites his readers too much into his study, opens the process before them. As if the confectioner should say to his customers, 'Now, let us make a cake.' " With his usual shrewdness, Emerson was right; though one need not endorse his criticism, there can be no doubt that Hawthorne frequently assembles the materials of a tale and prescribes the proper recipe befor the reader's eye. Both "David Swan" and "Fancy's Show Box," for example, move explicitly from the statement of an idea to its illustration. Of numerous events that might have had a momentous influence on our lives we are totally unaware, says Hawthorne in "David Swan": "This idea may be illustrated by a page from the secret history of David Swan." Are we guilty in thought as well as in act, Hawthorne asks in "Fancy's Show Box": "Let us illustrate the subject by an imaginary example." In "The Threefold Destiny," Hawthorne's workshop method is even more clearly exemplified. "I have sometimes produced a singular and not unpleasing effect," he begins,

so far as my own mind was concerned, by imagining a train of incidents in which the spirit and the mechanism of the fairy legend should be combined with the characters and manners of familiar life. In the little tale which follows, a subdued tinge of the wild and wonderful is thrown over a sketch of New England personages and scenery, yet, it is hoped, without entirely obliterating the sober hues of nature. Rather than a story of events claiming to be real, it may be considered as an allegory, such as the writers of the last century would have expressed in the shape of an Eastern tale, but to which I have endeavored to give a more life-like warmth than could be infused into those fanciful productions.

Such a statement obviously serves as an unannounced preface. Indeed, Hawthorne's later and more widely known prefaces grow out of his workshop method, which characteristically defines the mode of fictional creation at the outset as a way of making what I have called the conditions of his fiction understood.

Any writer who faces the necessity of establishing his own conventions will feel a concomitant need to explain processes and intentions to his reader. And such a writer will pay a price for doing so much: he will necessarily spend much creative energy experimenting to gain "effects"; he will, perhaps, endeavor to blend the old with the new, the strange with the familiar, sometimes (as in "The Threefold Destiny") to little purpose. To succeed as an artist he will have to do the work of generations in a single lifetime and incorporate the mistakes, false starts, and indirections that ordinarily dwarf careers into the broad investment of his genius. Hawthorne would probably have written fewer slight tales had he worked with the legacy of an older literature. Alternatively, he might well have achieved less; for there would simply have been less to do.

In keeping with Hawthorne's stated intention, "The Threefold Destiny" is subtitled "A Fairy Legend." And it is not alone among Hawthorne's tales in having this kind of subtitle. "Fancy's Show Box" is "A Morality"—"David Swan" is "A Fantasy." Such subtitles are neither elaborations of the main title itself nor do they function as alternative titles in the manner of many subtitles in eighteenth- and early nineteenth-century novels. In "Night Sketches: Beneath an Umbrella" and in "Egotism; or, the Bosom-Serpent," to take but two examples, Hawthorne did use subtitles in these conventional ways. But "A Morality" and "A Fantasy," as well as "A Parable" (for "The Minister's Black Veil"), "An Imaginary Retrospect" (for "The Village Uncle"), "An Apologue" (for both "The Man of Adamant" and "The Lily's Quest"), and "A Moralized Legend" (for "Feather-top")—such subtitles are descriptions of the *form* of the tales. They tell not what the tale is about, but what the tale is. They are explicit indications of the *kind* of fiction Hawthorne is endeavoring to write.

"The Threefold Destiny," for example, Hawthorne's "Fairy Legend," presents the story of Ralph Cranfield, who, "from his youth upward, had felt himself marked out for a high destiny." This, in Jamesian terms, is the *donnée* of the tale; indeed, it is virtually the *donnée* of James's "The Beast in the Jungle" in which John Marcher, too, feels that he is marked out for a special destiny. But the difference in form between the two stories is immense, and crucial. John Marcher waits and watches for years with May Bartram to see what special destiny fate has reserved for him; with a subtle twist, James makes the waiting itself Marcher's destiny. He has missed life thoroughly, utterly, irrevocably; he has become the man of his time to whom nothing ever happened, as he realizes when he throws himself face downward in a futile embrace of May Bartram's grave. Hawthorne's Ralph Cranfield feels, very much in the style of a hero of fairy legend, that his destiny is threefold: he will discover the one maiden on earth who can make him happy; he will find wealth; and he will assume a position of great authority and power. In each case, his destiny will be fulfilled only after the appearance of a special sign. For ten years Ralph Cranfield has wandered in search of his high fate. Wearied and somewhat discouraged, he returns to visit his mother's cottage in the village of his birth. There the appropriate signs are given; there Ralph's destiny will be fulfilled. He will wed Faith Edgerton, his childhood sweetheart; will reap the rich "products of the earth around his mother's dwelling"; and will "rule over the village children" in the position of schoolmaster. In this tale, visions of grandeur have been domesticated. The "Fairy Legend" has exorcized itself, as it were, after providing the necessary contours for the telling of the tale.

Hawthorne often uses twilight as an analogue of the neutral ground to achieve his imaginative effects. "The white sunshine of actual life," he says in "The Hall of Fantasy"—and elsewhere, as we have seen—is antagonistic to the imagination, which requires access to a region of mystery and shadow if it is to function creatively. Young Goodman Brown begins his shattering journey into the knowledge of evil at sunset. "The Great Carbuncle" begins at nightfall. After the prefatory paragraph in "The Threefold Destiny," Hawthorne begins the tale proper by invoking "the twilight of a summer eve." Even in describing the Genesee Falls (in "Sketches from Memory," series 2) where the dare-devil Sam Patch "took his last leap, and alighted in the other world," Hawthorne pictures the "catastrophe out of dusk and solitude," drawn to a "legend" he believes "will become poetical in the lapse of years, and was already so to me." Despite rumors of his mysterious survival Sam Patch will never be seen again, Hawthorne avers, unless his ghost, "in such a twilight as when I was there, should emerge from the foam, and vanish among the shadows that fall from cliff to cliff." In this instance, what I have called imaginative strategies stand revealed as simple rhetorical habits. That they may be at bottom the same thing, of course, is their strength and their significance.

Twilight is the middle time, between the noon of actuality and the midnight of dream. It corresponds to the point between yesterday and tomorrow that constitutes the setting of "The Haunted Mind." But just as it is difficult to remain on the borders of sleep and wakefulness, so the twilight atmosphere can be difficult to sustain. Before the legends themselves are told, the narrator of "Legends of the Province House" draws "strenuously" on his imagination in an effort to invest a contemporary tavern with romantic associations from the past. While concerns of past grandeur and present-day banality remain with Hawthorne's narrator in the outer framework, the four inner tales move expansively in a twilight of legend. At the end of one tale the narrator strives to sustain the illusion it has created; but a spoon rattling in a tumbler of whiskey punch, a schedule for the Brookline stagecoach, and the *Boston Times*—couriers of "The Present, the Immediate, the Actual"—quickly defeat his efforts. "It is desperately hard work," he concludes, "to throw the spell of hoar antiquity over localities with which the living world, and the day that is passing over us, have aught to do."

In his legends of the province house and in other tales as well, Hawthorne equates revolutionary tendencies with the democratic aspirations of the people: colonial history comes to prefigure the spirit of the American Revolution. Wearing old Puritan dress, the Gray Champion answers the cry of an oppressed people. Typically, as a figure evoked onto a historical neutral ground by a stroke of the imagination ("There was once a time" are the opening words of Hawthorne's story), he stands between the colonists and the British soldiers in an "intervening space," with "almost a twilight shadow over it"; when he disappears, some think he has melted "into the hues of twilight." But he will be at Lexington in the next century, says Hawthorne (choosing "twilight" to inaugurate both a day and the nation's history), "in the twilight of an April morning." For the Gray Champion is "the type of New England's hereditary spirit," opposed equally to domestic tyranny and to the step of the invader.

Endicott's defiance of English authority in "Endicott and the Red Cross" is presented explicitly as a rehearsal for the American Revolution. "We look back through the mist of ages," Hawthorne writes, "and recognize in the rending of the Red Cross from New England's banner the first omen of that deliverance which our fathers consummated after the bones of the stern Puritan had lain more than a century in the dust." Hawthorne's portrayal of the colonists' defiant spirit suggests that they were preserving independence at this early date: perceiving the danger from England, they "were resolved that their infant country should not fall without a struggle. . . ." Brooding over the meaning of American colonial history, perhaps predisposed to select a certain kind of dramatic event for his fiction by the tradition of Major William Hathorne's defiance of an order of Charles II, Hawthorne came to formulate a continuity in the American revolutionary spirit. At a time when American writers labored under the constraints of a lack of tradition, he thus employed the colonial past as one effective way of discovering the imaginative latitude he required. In his tales of colonial times, Hawthorne's imagination withdraws into history, then returns to the present with meaning distilled from the past; he makes Americans see what they had been as a way of showing them more fully what they are.[3]

Hawthorne's sense of the past, one should note, is complex, resistant to oversimplification. If the Puritans embody a spirit that was to find ultimate patriotic expression in the American Revolution, they are also, in Hawthorne's presentation, harsh, unyielding, and cruel, blind to all liberties but their own. His description of the crowd in "Endicott and the Red Cross" notes some whose ears have been cropped "like those of puppy dogs," others with brands on their cheeks in the form of "initials of misdemeanors," one with his nostrils slit and seared, and one who must wear a halter continually about his neck. "There was likewise a young woman," says Hawthorne, as he dwells on the symbol that was to become *The Scarlet Letter*, "with no mean share of beauty, whose doom it was to wear the letter A on the breast of her gown, in the eyes of all the world and her own children. And even her own children knew what the letter signified. Sporting with her infamy, the lost and desperate creature had embroidered the fatal token in scarlet cloth, with gold thread and the nicest art of needlework; so that the capital A might have been thought to mean Admirable, or anything rather than adultress." The stern justice of the Puritans can also be seen in the whipping post, "that important engine of Puritanic authority," in the figure of a suspected Catholic "grotesquely encased" in the stocks, and that of a man standing on the steps of the meeting house, wearing a sign that proclaims him to be a Wanton Gospeller.

But Hawthorne is careful not to let such descriptions breed a sense of superiority in the reader. "Let not the reader argue from any of these evidences of iniquity," he says, "that the times of the Puritans were more vicious than our own, when, as we pass along the very street of this sketch, we discern no badge of iniquity on man or woman. It was the policy of our ancestors to search out even the most secret sins, and expose them to shame, without fear or favor, in the broadest light of the noonday sun. Were such the custom now, we might find materials for a no less piquant sketch than the above." We are all implicated in the description—we are all deserving targets of Hawthorne's irony.

By means of the Wanton Gospeller, Hawthorne provides one of the finest strokes of ambivalence in the tale. When the minister, Roger Williams—and that detail carries its specific irony—brings news of the king's edict, Endicott fumes against what he sees as royal despotism prior to cutting the cross from the flag of England. He makes an impassioned speech to the crowd, asking why they came to such a howling wilderness, why they underwent suffering and hardship, why they toiled unstintingly for their food, why—if not for the enjoyment of civil rights and "for liberty to worship God according to our conscience." At the high point of Endicott's rhetoric, the Wanton Gospeller interrupts by asking, "Call you this liberty of conscience?" While a "sad and quiet smile" flits across the face of Roger Williams (who was later banished from the colony for independence of mind), Endicott roars, in effect, "Shut up!" and proceeds with his pious and wrathful exhortation.

Almost parenthetically, the point has been made: Endicott can resist oppression in one breath and show himself a raging zealot in the next. Intolerant, blinded by his sense of righteousness, he stands exposed to the question of the Gospeller and ridiculed by his own reply. Yet Hawthorne proceeds to honor the name of Endicott for breathing the spirit that would culminate in the American Revolution. Refusing to simplify, he has presented in Endicott a portrait of the hero as tyrant. (In a more covert way, as Ursula Brumm has shown, he fashioned his legendary Gray Champion out of the regicide judge William Goffe.)[4] "Let us thank God," Hawthorne wrote later of the Puritans in "Main-street," for having "given us such ancestors; and let each successive generation thank Him, not less fervently, for being one step further from them in the march of ages." His ambivalence toward the Puritans is a consequence of his ambivalence toward the institutions of the past and present. Democracy is both necessary and glorious; but to have it, one must eliminate the king.

The Importance of Being Human

In two of what I have termed his "processionals," those assembled pieces set perhaps in a vague banquet hall or on an undefined prairie, Hawthorne considers explicitly the values and dangers of the imagination in human life. "A Select Party," for example (praised by Melville as "the sweetest and sublimest thing that has been written since Spenser wrote"—and perhaps unequaled by Spenser), describes an "entertainment" given by a man of fancy "at one of his castles in the air." Many on earth are not worthy to attend because they lack "imaginative faith" and cannot perceive the high truths of the spirit. Lighted by meteors covered with evening mist, the castle glows with "the brilliancy of a powerful yet chastened imagination." "Beings of crude imagination" known in visionary youth and "forms of dim terror" from childhood are here termed unrealities, as are the "creatures of imagination" formed by means of an ironic vision—"an incorruptible Patriot," for example, "a Scholar without pedantry," and "a Reformer untrammelled by his theory." Hawthorne seems to be saying that an art which indulges itself with such irony or youthful crudity deals only with "creatures of imagination," which are denied reality even in this castle in the air. The Master Genius of the age who will fulfill the literary destiny of his country is a more admired guest, as is Posterity, who advises all to live for their own age if they wish to gain lasting recognition. An oncoming thunderstorm brings an abrupt end to the party. The lights are blown out, and great confusion results. "How, in the darkness that ensued," says Hawthorne, "the guests contrived to get back to earth, or whether the greater part of them contrived to get back at all, or are still wandering among clouds, mists, and puffs of tempestuous wind, bruised by the beams and rafters of the overthrown castle in the air, and deluded by all sorts of unrealities, are points that concern themselves much more than the writer or the public." He concludes with the admonition that "people should think of these matters before they thrust themselves on a pleasure party into the realm of Nowhere."

Innocuous as it seems initially (Melville judged from the title that it might concern a party of people eating pumpkin pie), "A Select Party" evinces a complex attitude toward the imagination. As defined by Hawthorne, "imaginative faith" would seem to be a highly desirable trait; those who lack it are bound heavily to the earth. The presence of the Master Genius and of Posterity seems to add ballast to the more fanciful "creatures of imagination"—such as a cadaverous figure who is in the habit of dining with Duke Humphrey (that is, not eating at all) and several who "had no existence except as voters in closely contested elections." The prevailing tone is jocular, proper for a sportive occasion. Yet at the end there is the sudden doubt that the partygoers can get back to earth. In a context of frivolity, Hawthorne's final admonition comes as a joke. And it is indeed a joke—on the reader as well as the partygoers. We begin to laugh, then realize that the guests, confused and misled, may be lost in the realm of the imagination. But there is more to our realization; for in reading the tale, we, too, have been seduced, artistically sandbagged (for this is, after all, Hawthorne's "select" party, and we are the guests), forced to learn a sobering lesson about the imagination when we expected only entertainment.

In "The Hall of Fantasy," Hawthorne ponders the "mystic region, which lies above, below, or beyond, the actual." Although successive ages may modify and repair the Hall, it "is likely to endure longer than the most substantial structure that ever cumbered the earth." Arrayed in its rooms are busts and statues of those who have been "demigods in the realm of imagination"—Homer, Dante, Shakespeare, Milton, Bunyan, Scott, and (Hawthorne's tribute to Charles Brockden Brown) "in an obscure and shadowy niche . . . the bust of one of our own countrymen, the author of Arthur Mervyn." The Hall has obvious dangers: some mistake it for "actual brick and mortar"; others live there permanently "and contract habits which unfit them for all the real employments of life." Still, the narrator concludes, despite "all its dangerous influences, we have reason to thank God that there is such a place of refuge from the gloom and chillness of actual life." Those who never find their way into the Hall possess "but half a life—the meaner and earthlier half," just as those who never find their way out of the Hall "waste all their days" among unrealities. But the imagination has a final value, crucial and unambiguous. In "The New Adam and Eve," Hawthorne's thesis is that we have lost the means of distinguishing between the workings of nature and those of art. An important kind of vision has become blurred. "It is only through the medium of the imagination," the narrator goes on to say, "that we can lessen those iron fetters, which we call truth and reality, and make ourselves even partially sensible what prisoners we are." Implicit here, in its largest and most general manifestation, is the motif of withdrawal and return basic to Hawthorne's fiction. One withdraws into the realm of imagination, views the rigorous confinement of life, then returns to the world with a fuller understanding of the human condition. The ultimate function of the imagination is thus to serve as a unique and judicious critic of reality.

The role of fiction is the product of the role of the imagination. At their best, Hawthorne's tales—public proof that the author has returned from his private journey into the imagination—lessen the fetters of reality so that we may see "what prisoners we are." At their best, the tales invite us to consider the difficulties man faces if he cannot face his humanity. The tales tell us that man must acknowledge his dependence on (even as he should rejoice to participate in) "the magnetic chain of humanity." The alternative is abstraction, a preference for idea, which breeds pride, isolation, and ultimate self-destruction.

The cancer of obsession threatens any Hawthorne character—scientist, man of religion, artist—who prefers an idea to a human being. Hawthorne's men of idea are well known: in the romances, Roger Chillingworth, Judge Pyncheon, and Hollingsworth; in the tales, such characters as Ethan Brand, Rappaccini, and Aylmer. Ethan Brand embarks on a blasphemous quest which casts him into despair; his heart no longer participates "in the universal throb." Rappaccini, according to his rival, Baglioni, "would sacrifice human life, his own among the rest, for the sake of adding so much as a grain of mustard seed to the great heap of his accumulated knowledge." Aylmer, in "The Birth-mark," rejects the best the earth can offer when he experiments upon his wife, Georgiana, and kills her in a vain attempt to make her perfect.

Hawthorne's presentation of Aylmer illustrates his characteristic manner of dealing with a man of science who rejects humanity as it is because of his idea of what he might make it. "The Birth-mark" is set vaguely in "the latter part of the last century," at a time when the recent discovery of electricity made science seem almost miraculous. It is, in a sense, a love story, or, rather, a portrayal of what can happen when a love story concerns a Man of Idea. Prefiguring the theme of his tale, Hawthorne writes that it was not unusual in those days "for the love of science to rival the love of woman in its depth and absorbing energy." Devoted absolutely to his science, Aylmer marries the beautiful Georgiana. A potential source of conflict in this situation would be the contest of Aylmer's two loves—for science and for a woman—to predominate. But such a conflict, we see, is not Hawthorne's concern nor part of his conception of the story. He tells us at the outset that Aylmer "had devoted himself . . . too unreservedly to scientific studies ever to be weaned from them by any second passion. His love for his young wife might prove the stronger of the two; but it could only be by intertwining itself with his love of science, and uniting the strength of the latter to its own." Aylmer's love of science is a constant in the story, in terms of which his love for Georgiana will be defined.

Focusing upon his central symbol, Hawthorne tells us how it became an obsession, "the central point of all," to both Aylmer and Georgiana. To Aylmer the birthmark—a diminutive hand upon her

cheek—represents his wife's "liability to sin, sorrow, decay, and death."
As the tale progresses, the dire significance of the birthmark becomes
a monomania for him. He is thus delighted when Georgiana, unable
to stand his brooding concentration on the symbol of her imperfection, proposes that he attempt to erase it from her cheek. She is,
clearly, lending herself to his science, and Aylmer is appreciative;
after a period of intense thought and labor, he thanks her for having
led him "deeper into the heart of science." Since science in Hawthorne's fiction stands opposed to the heart, this remark is indeed
anomalous; it reveals the terrible confusion of both values and
reality which makes Aylmer's obsession possible. Moreover, Aylmer's
science is artificial, foreign to the processes of nature: in order to
set and sustain the proper circumstances for his experiment in perfection, he must exclude all sunlight from his apartment. And while
he strives to make her conform to his idea of perfection, Georgiana
reads the history of Aylmer's failures in other great experiments, learns
that he has always fallen short of his greatest conceptions, but nonetheless loves him for what he is.

The pride underlying Aylmer's monomania flashes forth when, in
reply to Georgiana's profession of worship for him, he says that
should he succeed he will deem himself hardly unworthy of her
worship. Of course he fails, or, rather, succeeds only at the price of
Georgiana's life. With keen perception and a concomitant eagerness
to martyr herself to her husband's love of science, Georgiana hopes
that for a single moment "she might satisfy his highest and deepest
conception"; she knows that his spirit is "ever on the march, ever
ascending," each instant requiring "something that was beyond the
scope of the instant before." Aylmer's moment of high satisfaction is
not only brief but illusory: when Georgiana wakes momentarily after
the final experiment, he proclaims with unwitting irony, "You are
perfect." Georgiana, however, does not blame him for causing her
death. As she is dying, she comforts her "poor Aylmer," saying that
he has "aimed loftily" and "done nobly." "Do not repent that with
so high and pure a feeling, you have rejected the best the earth could
offer." Georgiana has intertwined herself with Aylmer's love of
science; she has sacrificed herself to his idea; and she dies with words
of tenderness that make the extent of his loss the more apparent.

With a profounder wisdom, says Hawthorne, Aylmer need not have
been seized with a monomania for perfection. But "the momentary

circumstance was too strong for him; he failed to look beyond the shadowy scope of time, and, living once for all in eternity, to find the perfect in the present." A dabbler in alchemy, Aylmer is a character whose goal is noble, but nonhuman; he is bound to destroy, just as a man insisting on perfect truth or perfect justice in this world would be bound to destroy. For, by definition, imperfection must be destroyed or eliminated if one is to have perfection. As explicitly as a tale can, "The Birth-mark" tells us that to be is to be imperfect, that the price of human existence is imperfection.

Hawthorne likewise portrays characters who insist on a religious idea to the detriment or exclusion of humanity. For Richard Digby, in "The Man of Adamant," the only acceptable prayers are those which are not "mingled with the sinful supplications of the multitude." Digby's religion is unique, consisting of the one idea that of all the people in the world only he has the key to salvation. But the Shakers, for Hawthorne, champion a view hardly less extreme: the basic tenet of their religion amounts to a communal renunciation of "the magnetic chain of humanity" out of a deluded concern for salvation.

In "The Shaker Bridal," for example, Father Ephraim relinquishes the rule of his village to Adam Colburn and Martha Pierson, hoping "that the time may hasten on, when the mission of Mother Ann shall have wrought its full effect—when children shall no more be born and die, and the last survivor of mortal race, some old and weary man like me, shall see the sun go down, never more to rise on a world of sin and sorrow." To long for the extinction of the human race because it has bred "a world of sin and sorrow" is a brutal twisting of human aspirations in the context of Hawthorne's fiction. Unsympathetic to the Shakers, Hawthorne characterizes the membership of the sect in this tale as being "generally below the ordinary standard of intelligence." The title, as ironic in its way as is "The Wedding-Knell," juxtaposes the ideas of marriage and death; just before the ceremony Martha is "so pale that she looked fitter to be laid in her coffin." And, indeed, whereas Adam Colburn folds his arms "with a sense of satisfied ambition," Martha dies: significantly, "her heart could endure the weight of its desolate agony no longer." Hospitable though they may be, the Shakers deny the heart and try to place human life on the high desolate plane of idea.

Thus, in "The Canterbury Pilgrims," Miriam and Josiah make their decision to go into the world in the face of both irresponsible and judicious advice to the contrary. Their desire for life and their confidence in love bring them to reject the "cold and passionless security" which the Shakers substitute for "mortal hope' and fear, as in that other refuge of the world's weary outcasts, the grave." The travelers to the Shaker village are committing a suicide of the heart which testifies to the kind of world they are leaving behind. But the direction of Miriam and Josiah, of the tale, and of Hawthorne's fiction is into life—into the imperfect, sin-burdened world where mortals grope for love and understanding.

Hawthorne's most thoroughly dramatized and effective portrayal of the dehumanizing effects of a religious idea comes in "The Gentle Boy." In this tale, both Puritan severity and Quaker fanaticism are at fault, and Hawthorne handles his materials so that each contributes to the existence of the other: persecution, he says, was at once the "cause and effect" of Quaker extravagance.[5] To combat the fanaticism of the Quakers, the Puritans have executed two members of that sect, one the father of Ilbrahim—the gentle boy in search of a home. Puritan intolerance continues to exert its pressure on Ilbrahim and the Pearsons, reaching an emotional height when the band of Puritan children (whose destructive impulse strikes Hawthorne as even worse than adult severity) falls upon Ilbrahim. The treachery of the boy whom Ilbrahim shyly counted on as a friend constitutes an insidious rejection of human kinship, a tacit acceptance of the fact that Ilbrahim is an object for scorn and punishment. Throughout the tale, Hawthorne's portrayal of the Puritans is rigorous and unsentimental; at best, the Puritans are victims of their own unrelenting system. When Catherine embraces her son Ilbrahim in the Puritan meeting house, the scene, Hawthorne tells us, "did not fail to move the sympathies of many who mistook their involuntary virtue for a sin." Hawthorne posits an antagonism of human instinct and Puritan moral habits which becomes a reflexive criticism of the Puritans themselves.

But Catherine is similarly victimized by her fanaticism; no more than the Puritans can she see her actions for what they are. In the pulpit of the meeting house she gives vent to a flood of malignity which, as Hawthorne says, she mistook for inspiration. Moreover, in "following the dictates of a wild fanaticism," Catherine has, as she herself knows, "ill performed a mother's part." She has embraced an idea which appears noble in the abstract but is so demanding that it urges her to "break the bonds of natural affection" and martyr her love. In Hawthorne's view, Catherine neglects "the holiest trust which can be committed to a woman." She relinquishes her natural role as a mother to assume the role of a religious fanatic. There is no question but that she is sincere in her religious life; like the old Quaker who tells Tobias Pearson how he left his daughter on her deathbed in a sudden onslaught of religious zeal, Catherine believes in the necessity of what she is doing. Indeed, from the point of view of the old Quaker, a mother's heart is strong within her and "may seem to contend mightily with her faith."

But a faith that can exist only at the expense of the heart is, for Hawthorne, no valid faith at all. The Quakers, as well as the Puritans in "The Gentle Boy," deny the appeal of the heart; their vision of the world—narrow, twisted, egocentric, and abstract—lacks a sense of humanity at its center. Rejected as a human being by the prejudice and neglect of a world intent on idea, Ilbrahim must find a home in heaven. Only one person has consistently ameliorated the harshness of his existence—Dorothy Pearson, whose "rational piety" makes her neither Puritan nor Quaker, whose love and compassion for Ilbrahim lead Hawthorne to praise her as being "like a verse of fireside poetry." Dorothy Pearson's capacity for love, at once the cause and the effect of her belief in the sanctity of a human heart, stands opposed to the forces of abstraction in the tale. Ultimately, Catherine's "fierce and vindictive nature" becomes softened from living with the Pearsons. But Hawthorne is rigorous to the end: when at last Catherine died, "a long train of once bitter persecutors followed her, with decent sadness and tears that were not painful, to her place by Ilbrahim's green and sunken grave."

The artist, too, is liable in his own way to the danger of cutting himself off from humanity. Indeed, one of Hawthorne's most fundamental reasons for mistrusting the value of his profession was that it encouraged him to observe, to draw apart, to study people, to burrow with his "utmost ability"—as he said in his preface to *The Snow-Image*—"into the depths of our common nature, for the purposes of psychological romance." Hawthorne's notebooks demonstrate the kind of observation he habitually devoted to people; his fiction evidences uneasiness, if not a tinge of guilt, at the objectivity with which he considered the quality of a human life. He was, it is true, early attracted to the idea of being a Paul Pry; in "Sights from a Steeple," a sketch which conveys a sense of an author in search of vignettes, the narrator says that "the most desirable mode of existence might be that of a spiritualized Paul Pry, hovering invisible around man and woman, witnessing their deeds, searching into their hearts, borrowing brightness from their felicity and from their sorrow and retaining no emotion peculiar to him self." Miles Coverdale in *The Blithedale Romance* is cast partly from the same mold.

However attractive it might seem, the Paul Pry mode of existence demanded a distance between observer and observed that Hawthorne came to regard with ever increasing suspicion. Indeed, in the implicit value system of his fiction, it might even be called the most undesirable mode of existence. Phoebe Pyncheon upbraids Holgrave in *The House of the Seven Gables* for being a cold observer who does not care what happens to Hepzibah and Clifford just as long as he is able to watch and to know. Phoebe can only disparage such a stance of neutrality, objectivity, and disinterestedness. And, one may be sure, what Phoebe thinks is wrong, Hawthorne will think is wrong. The role of the artist seemed to Hawthorne to encourage, almost to demand, the abstraction and study of humanity. By means of art, he knows very well, one perceives more fully what it is to be a human being; but the artist risks the insidious danger of unfitting himself to take part in the very life he has understood from his artistic perspective.

In his tales Hawthorne dealt with both the power and the plight of the artist. His presentation of the painter in "The Prophetic Pictures" is a case in point. Well-mannered, talented, much sought-after, the painter, "like all other men around whom an engrossing purpose wreathes itself, ... was insulated from the mass of human kind. He had no aim—no pleasure—no sympathies—but what were ultimately connected with his art. Though gentle in manner and upright in intent and action, he did not possess kindly feelings; his heart was cold; no living creature could be brought near enough to keep him warm." Interested in painting Walter and Elinor Ludlow, he pries "into their souls with his keenest insight" and discovers prophetically that Walter has a latent inclination to kill Elinor.

The explicit moral of the tale is that despite clear warnings people pay no real attention to what fate has in store for them but live up to and deserve their destiny; grafted onto that moral is the theme of the solitary, cold-hearted painter. The two themes are not effectively integrated, and the story suffers accordingly. Indeed, the theme of the artist virtually subordinates all other concerns to its own uses. Hawthorne seizes his opportunity in this tale to say of the artist what he says elsewhere concerning the pathology of isolation: "It is not good for man to cherish a solitary ambition. Unless there be those around him by whose example he may regulate himself, his thoughts, desires, and hopes will become extravagant, and he the semblance, perhaps the reality, of a madman." In "The Prophetic Pictures," the painter (who is never named but left with a professional and generic identity), adept as he is at "reading other bosoms with an acuteness almost preternatural," fails to see "the disorder of his own."

Owen Warland's difficulties and ultimate success are much more central to "The Artist of the Beautiful" than is the role of the painter to "The Prophetic Pictures," and "The Artist of the Beautiful" is also a better tale. But there is an ominous split in Owen Warland's life: when he tends to his matter-of-fact business, to his occupation of fixing watches and keeping the clocks of the community in working order—when, that is, he performs his jobs as community timekeeper, he can accomplish nothing on his experiment in creation; his idea of the beautiful virtually evaporates. And, when he labors at his creation of the beautiful, he utterly neglects his ordinary work. He cannot bring the two aspects of his life together in any fashion; his art is divorced from the world around him. Much of the fault in this tale lies of course with the world, or with the representatives of the world whom we see. Robert Danforth, the blacksmith, threatens the delicate tenor of Owen's creative life by his sheer physical mass and brute force. Obviously incapable of understanding what Owen is trying to do, Robert Danforth's instinctive respect for the practical makes Owen see his dream as "vain and idle" whenever they meet. "Thus it is," says Hawthorne, "that ideas, which grow up with the imagination and appear so lovely to it and of a value beyond whatever men call valuable, are exposed to be shattered and annihilated by contact with the practical."

Annie Hovenden, unfortunately, is likewise incapable of understanding Owen's devotion to a dream. She lacks imaginative perception, and she therefore disappoints Owen when, alone and in need of sympathy, he begins to idealize her as his perfect audience of one. But it is Annie's father, Peter Hovenden, intelligent and capable of scorn, who adds the greatest burden to Owen's difficulties. In his case, too, Hawthorne invokes the idea of a lack of perception; before his eyes failed, Peter Hovenden held the job Owen now holds, though he performed it very differently. "There was nothing so antipodal" to Owen's nature "as this man's cold, unimaginative sagacity, by contact with which everything was converted into a dream except the densest matter of the physical world."

Opposition to his artistic endeavor virtually surrounds Owen. But the fragility of his art intensifies his need of holding it protectively away from the world. The very character of Owen's mind "was microscopic," says Hawthorne, "and tended naturally to the minute, in accordance with his diminutive frame and the marvellous smallness and delicate power of his fingers." An insistence on the diminutive scope of Owen's art and on the nonhuman nature of his creation undoubtedly saves Hawthorne from many problems. It would have been an altogether different story had Owen created a giant butterfly or a tiny man. The fragility of the beautiful as Owen creates it, however, contributes to the dichotomy between art and life in the story.

Perhaps because Owen Warland's genius is artistic in nature Hawthorne constructs the tale so as to free him at the end from the idea which has engrossed him. But Owen has many of the characteristics of the Hawthorne figure who cuts himself off from the magnetic chain of humanity in favor of an idea. The "absorbing dream of his imagination" is "sacred" to him; he works to create "the one idea to which all his intellectual activity referred itself." Toward the end of the tale, however, Owen refuses to allow his beautiful butterfly to return to his hand: "Not so! not so! ... Thou hast gone forth out of thy master's heart. There is no return for thee." A creation of the heart rather than of the head, the butterfly meets a speedy end in the hand of Annie's and Robert's baby, the combination of all elements of opposition. Owen's capacity to separate himself from his dream— his ability to transcend that dream—saves him from disaster. The apparent ruin of his life's labor "was yet no ruin. He had caught a far other butterfly than this. When the artist rose high enough to achieve the beautiful, the symbol by which he made it perceptible to mortal sense became of little value in his eyes while his spirit possessed itself in the enjoyment of the reality." Owen has won a victory not merely over forces antagonistic to the imagination but over himself as well. Whether he goes on to repair clocks cheerfully we do not know. But, as an artist, he still faces a world full of problems; for art and life remain fundamentally distinct after (and even as a result of) all his labors.

In historical tales, too, Hawthorne's concern for humanity is evident. The terms of his presentation change: tyranny and oppression represent abstraction, the insistence on idea; the will of the people—democracy—represents humanity. The Gray Champion resists oppression, which Hawthorne defines as "the deformity of any government that does not grow out of the nature of things and the character of the people." For all his irritability and iron nature, Hawthorne's Endicott stands likewise for the people: thus, he can legitimately oppose any force which seeks to abrogate the rights of the colonists as human beings. And in "Edward Randolph's Portrait," Lieutenant Governor Hutchinson risks the terror of a "people's curse" by allowing British soldiers to occupy the colonial fort.

If the oppressor seeks to abuse man in history, the reformer seeks to disabuse man of history; both dehumanize. To make mankind conform to the good as he sees it, the reformer wields his one idea like a flail. He repudiates history as the record of man's imperfection and seeks to destroy the foibles of mankind by the purity and efficacy of his idea. The spirit of reform that spreads wildly in "Earth's Holocaust" seeks to purify by fire—to burn away the follies, fripperies, and evils of the past. But these reformers, like all others, overlook the nature of the heart (that is, the nature of man). Unless the heart is purified, says the dark stranger in the tale, "forth from it will reissue all the shapes of wrong and misery—the same old shapes or worse ones—which they have taken such a vast deal of trouble to consume to ashes."

Hawthorne does not oppose progress. Apropos of Holgrave's enthusiasm for progress in *The House of the Seven Gables*, he says that every man should have a youthful zeal for reform. But experience and wisdom should teach him to consider the importance of the heart, which will only improve when, in contact with other hearts, it exists in a community of love. Such a community is, of course, a difficult thing to show convincingly in fiction; it requires not only a redemptive vision, but the ability to dramatize it. Characters who are, in a sense, redeemed in Hawthorne's tales—Roderick Elliston, or in a milder way, Ralph Cranston in "The Threefold Destiny"—seem pale beside those who founder in isolation, such as Ethan Brand or Goodman Brown. It is the old problem of its being easier to represent misfortune, sorrow, and evil than the success, happiness, and good which can be their resolution—the problem that Milton addressed when he created his figure of Satan and still had paradise to be regained, or that Dante confronted when he wrote the Inferno and had the Paradiso ahead of him. For the ultimate redemptive drama is rare. In striving for it, the artist must avoid endless clichés; any version in which redemption is bestowed by artistic fiat and not earned by means of the drama of the fictional world is hardly worth the effort. Hawthorne, with his conception of a blemished human nature, tended to focus the themes of his tales on man's capacity for spiritual self-destruction. Ethan Brand's suicide is a final gesture for many a Hawthorne character who has destroyed his humanity over a period of years.

But, although his special genius as a writer of tales lay in exploring man's capacity for damnation, Hawthorne's most fundamental attitude toward the possibilities of human existence depended upon an abiding faith in the heart as the agent of redemption. In his American notebooks, he employs one of his favorite analogies and pictures the heart as a cavern:

at the entrance there is sunshine, and flowers growing about it. You step within, but a short distance, and begin to find yourself surrounded with a terrible gloom, and monsters of divers kinds; it seems like Hell itself. You are bewildered, and wander long without hope. At last a light strikes upon you. You peep towards it, and find yourself in a region that seems, in some sort, to reproduce the flowers and sunny beauty of the entrance, but all perfect. These are the depths of the heart, or of human nature, bright and peaceful; the gloom and terror may lie deep; but deeper still is the eternal beauty.

The statement offers a paradigm of what Hawthorne wanted his fiction to be. During his years of writing tales, he found it possible—as some writers never do—to move within the cavern, into a region of guilt and "terrible gloom." Sustaining him on this journey was his faith in the human heart as, ultimately, the region of brightness, peace, and eternal beauty. The redemptive vision in which Hawthorne believed thus led to what he saw as the deepest truths, in "the depths of the heart" (or "of human nature"). And the simplest, most profound, means of articulating this vision was to write of the meaning and value of the home.

As students of Hawthorne have pointed out, houses, as well as the idea of home and hearth, bear a special place in Hawthorne's fiction. Indeed, the notion of home was virtually sacred to him; home meant Sophia, love, warmth, and understanding; by definition, it stood opposed to isolation. During his residence at the Old Manse in the early years of his marriage, Hawthorne expressed such sentiments candidly and with a sense of discovery in his notebook entries. After a summer walk in 1842 he wrote, "How sweet it was to draw near my own home, after having lived so long homeless in the world; for no man can know what home is, until, as he approaches it, he feels that a wife will meet him at the threshold." His account of a short walking trip with Emerson in the autumn of that year concludes with his return to the Manse—"the first time that I ever came home in my life; for I never had a home before." And when Sophia visited her family in the spring of 1843, Hawthorne kept a journal for her and wrote that he "wasted the customary hour at the Athenaeum, and returned home—if home it may be called, where thou art not."

These are, of course, private and personal statements; they attest to the power of love in creating a home. But the same values, more formally expressed for the public, pervade Hawthorne's sketch "The Old Manse." After an eloquent description of a trip up the Assabeth River with Ellery Channing, Hawthorne speaks of all that the homeward journey meant to him. During his outing, he says, a sense of freedom in nature appealed strongly to him: "along that shady riverbank there are spots, . . . only less sacred in my remembrance than the heart of a household fire." "And yet," he continues (though the "yet" seems curiously out of place),

how sweet, as we floated homeward adown the golden river at sunset,—how sweet was it to return within the system of human society, not as to a dungeon and a chain, but as to a stately edifice, whence we could go forth at will into statelier simplicity! How gently, too, did the sight of the Old Manse, best seen from the river, overshadowed with its willow and all environed about with the foliage of its orchard and avenue—how gently did its gray, homely aspect rebuke the speculative extravagances of the day! It had grown sacred in connection with the artificial life against which we inveighed; it had been a home for many years in spite of all; it was my home too; and with these thoughts, it seemed to me that all the artifice and conventionalism of life was but an impalpable thinness upon its surface, and that the depth below was none the worse for it. Once, as we turned our boat to the bank, there was a cloud, in the shape of an immensely gigantic figure of a hound, couched above the house, as if keeping guard over it. Gazing at this symbol, I prayed that the upper influences might long protect the institutions that had grown out of the heart of mankind.

Throughout Hawthorne's work, heart and hearth are intimately related. The mock-humorous praise of the open hearth in "Fire-Worship" has its direct and serious counterpart in "The Vision of the Fountain," in which Hawthorne stresses the importance of the fireside in domesticating the vision. Ralph Cranston, as we have seen, discovers that home is where one's destiny waits. Both "The Great Carbuncle" and "The Great Stone Face" likewise draw morals concerning the values inherent in domesticity and the futility of searching abroad for something to be found more surely at home. In "John Inglefield's Thanksgiving," home is a stable and secure institution of the heart which beckons even to the errant daughter, whose fall is measured in terms of her moral distance from home. Wakefield is an apostate from home; he leaves home and wife out of whimsy and curiosity, remains away (though only on the next block) out of stubbornness and a creeping paralysis of will, and finally becomes that most lamentable of all Hawthorne characters—the man who has lost his place in the world, the "outcast of the Universe." Reuben Bourne, in "Roger Malvin's Burial," nurses his secret into a destructive sense of guilt; he becomes obsessed with his feeling of guilt quite as much as Aylmer is obsessed with the idea of perfection. The result is an atrophy of love and understanding between him and his family and friends. The characters of "The Ambitious Guest," initially unsettled by the contagion of the young man's thirst for fame, are ironically killed by a rockslide when they rush out of their house in search of shelter; their home stands untouched. Home, clearly, is of the heart; to be heartless is to be homeless; for home is the institution to which man may safely entrust his humanity.

In Hawthorne's life, home meant Sophia. In his fiction, it came to mean characters who corresponded in crucial ways to Hawthorne's image of Sophia. Phoebe, Priscilla, and Hilda in the romances all stand for the home; as a consequence, they can serve as agents of redemption. Phoebe helps to reconcile Holgrave to humanity in *The House of the Seven Gables*. Priscilla, fragile as she seems throughout

The Blithdale Romance, supports the reformer Hollingsworth physically and morally when the drama is played out. And Hilda, in *The Marble Faun*, is, as we shall see, the household saint, who will—in answer to his plea—guide Kenyon home.

Characters such as these have struck many readers as distressingly thin for their redemptive roles. The iron rigor of her innocence has made Hilda, particularly, appear unsympathetic. We tend to prefer characters like Hester Prynne, Zenobia, and Miriam because of their capacity for passion and their instinct for the troubled avenues of human experience. The force and excitement of Hawthorne's dark women, however, dispose them to rendezvous with destruction, physical or social. His pale, blonde women, on the other hand, manage to endure. They may endure unspectacularly, but they do endure. For they are embodiments of home, maidens whose burden it is to redeem man from the depersonalizing appeal of abstraction.

In "The Gentle Boy," we recall, Hawthorne likened Dorothy Pearson to "a verse of fireside poetry." The first of his characters to embody home and love in free abundance, Dorothy Pearson offers a refuge to the gentle boy until, as Hawthorne says, death takes him to an eternal home. By happy coincidence, it was "The Gentle Boy" that played a part in bringing Hawthorne and Sophia together. Sophia seems to have reacted to the pathos of Ilbrahim's situation as did Dorothy Pearson. Whereas Dorothy gave Ilbrahim a home, Sophia drew her simple sketch of him at the grave of his father and was thus instrumental in the publication of a separate edition of "The Gentle Boy." Both the woman of fiction and the woman of life reacted from the heart. Hawthorne had imagined Dorothy Pearson; he was thus all the more prepared to fall in love with a woman whom he could see as the prototype of all his redemptive women. For Sophia gave Hawthorne, as he said, a home; and home signified for him the integrity of the human being.

From Allegory to Symbol

If the requirements of Hawthorne's imagination called initially for a neutral ground as a way of conceiving the tale (which traditionally allowed for a heightened presentation of character and event), they called also for a mode of creation that would impregnate his fiction with relevance for the moral condition of mankind. What Hawthorne had to say about sin, isolation, and the withering effects of idea came from his vision of a blemished human nature. To articulate this vision he frequently made use of an allegorical mode, shaping his materials so that they would suggest the contours of an outer and moral reality. The writer of allegory habitually seeks to indenture his fiction (be it in prose or poetry) to an extrinsic reality; his aim is to establish a relationship between the inner world of his fiction and the outer world of experience that will enable the fiction to exist in and through the acknowledged and systematic reality of that outer world. Allegory, that is, sacrifices a posture of realism in its own right in an attempt to serve the interests of an extrinsic reality. Thus understood, it has frequently been the target of critics who value fiction insofar as it assumes a sovereignty of its own, who prefer to consider the work of art as heterocosm—or world unto itself. In the hands of a master, however, allegory may serve the requirements of the outer world so memorably that a revolution of sorts takes place. Bunyan's Vanity Fair, for example, so eloquently represented the seduction of the spirit by the world to generations of readers that it came virtually to *be in itself*, rather than to represent, a moral condition.

Although his tales reflect a persistent allegorical tendency, Hawthorne was not a master allegorist. In later years he looked with disfavor on what he called his "blasted allegories" (among which he probably included his processionals), the thinness of which caused Melville to say that Hawthorne needed to frequent the butcher, that he ought to have "roast beef done rare." He frequently made use of conventional devices, giving his characters names such as Gathergold and Dryasdust, conceiving them generically as the Cynic and the Seeker, and envisioning his material so that it would illuminate a general truth of the moral world. Typically, he makes apparent his allegorical intent. He asks specifically, we recall, that "The Threefold Destiny" be read as an allegory; he notes that "Egotism; or, the Bosom-Serpent" and "The Christmas Banquet" come from "the unpublished 'Allegories of the Heart' "; and he constructs "The Celestial Rail-road" on the classic allegorical model bequeathed by Bunyan in *Pilgrim's Progress.* Perhaps most significantly, he adapts features of the allegorical mode by presenting bifurcated or fragmented characters who complement each other in the totality of an individual tale— Aylmer and Aminadab in "The Birth-mark," for example, Mr. and Mrs. Lindsey in "The Snow-Image," and the entire configuration of characters in "The Artist of the Beautiful." Such characters contribute to the kind of latitude Hawthorne persisently strove to attain even as they point up themes that define the specific nature of his work. An allegorical tradition thus afforded Hawthorne a means of access to the dimensions of the moral world.

But the symbolic mode, as distinct from the allegorical, could also involve moral considerations and at the same time offer flexibility to the writer of tales. Inheriting a penchant for symbolism from the Puritans, disposed, too, toward symbolic expression by the exigencies of the creative situation in his society, Hawthorne came to place dramatic emphasis on the symbol as a way of achieving coherent form in the tale. By means of the symbol he could invest an object with moral significance and thereby portray the ambivalence of motive and the ambiguity of experience that defined for him the texture of the human condition.

The symbol for Hawthorne promoted narrative focus and intensity even as it allowed for economy of presentation. Moreover, and with important formal consequences, it proved possible to organize a tale effectively in terms of one central symbol. A single symbol dominates "The Minister's Black Veil." The Maypole commands the focus of "The May-pole of Merry Mount." And other well known tales, written between 1836 and 1850, are structured in a similar way, among them "The Great Carbuncle," "Lady Eleanore's Mantle," "The Birthmark," and "The Great Stone Face." Finally, of course, there is *The Scarlet Letter*, the culmination of Hawthorne's efforts to adapt the form of the tale to the special purposes of his imagination.

Prior to *The Scarlet Letter*, Hawthorne's fiction had been cast exclusively in the form of the tale. It is conventional, of course, to say that *Fanshawe* represented a false start in the novel or romance and that Hawthorne turned to the tale as a result of his dissatisfaction with that early narrative. For what it may be worth, however, *Fanshawe* is subtitled *A Tale*; it was indeed a false start, but as a tale rather than as a romance. *The Scarlet Letter*, too, came into being as a tale. Hawthorne's original plan, according to his publisher James T. Fields, was to include *The Scarlet Letter* with several other tales in a volume entitled "Old-Time Legends: Together with Sketches, Experimental and Ideal." Hawthorne's design, says Fields, "was to make 'The Scarlet Letter' occupy about two hundred pages in his new book;

but I persuaded him, after reading the first chapters of the story, to elaborate it, and publish it as a separate work." How much Hawthorne "elaborated" his tale of the scarlet letter we do not know; if a central symbol was to provide meaning and coherence to the whole, however, he could hardly give it the expansiveness of his later romances. He wrote to Fields wondering if a book consisting entirely of "The Scarlet Letter" might not be too somber; the *tale*, as he called it, keeps close to its point and simply turns "different sides of the same dark idea to the reader's eye."

With its use of the past, its dependence on a single symbol, its sustained tone or manner, and its rigid economy of presentation, *The Scarlet Letter* is the end result of Hawthorne's creative efforts in the form of the tale. In *The Scarlet Letter* he extended that form until the suppressed imaginative eloquence of the narrative made it into something different. *The Scarlet Letter* marks Hawthorne's final accomplishment in the tale even as it signals the beginning of his achievement in the romance; it marks the point at which Hawthorne transformed the tale into the romance in his effort to adapt that form once again to the purposes of his imagination.

The presence of "The Custom-House" in *The Scarlet Letter* deserves a word of comment at this point. Afraid that his tale of the scarlet letter would prove too somber by itself, Hawthorne included his introductory sketch as a way of lightening the tone of the volume. As a form, the sketch had been consistently useful to Hawthorne; for it gave him a way to deal with the present, with society, with the very things he had to evade or to attenuate in order to compose his kind of fiction. Hawthorne tended to sketch what was otherwise recalcitrant to his imagination. In turn, the sketch became an avenue to the world around him, as we can see in (among other sketches) "Sights from a Steeple," in "Night Sketches," and in his extremely effective "The Old Manse." Having given a day to fancy, the narrator of "Night Sketches" finds a "gloomy sense of unreality" depressing his spirits, impelling him to venture out in order to satisfy himself that the world is not composed only of "shadowy materials." Through the medium of the sketch, he reestablishes contact with social reality.

The world of the Salem Custom House, Hawthorne tells us, was stultifying to his imagination. He could neither write fiction while he worked there nor treat fictionally of the Custom House afterward.

But he could and did sketch the life of the Custom House in a memorable way. And he wedded the sketch and the tale, the present and the past, by his claim of having found the scarlet letter in the attic of the building.

In "The Old Manse" Hawthorne had told of exploring the garret of the Manse, which was "but a twilight at the best," and finding manuscripts and other records of former generations. In "The Custom-House" he develops the fullest possibilities of the idea of finding a document and becoming an editor. His sketch served the purposes of his fiction in a new manner: it provided a way to reflect prefatorily on the past, to define the neutral ground as the basis of imaginative creation, and to introduce the fiction by claiming to have found it shunted aside into a corner of the present world.

In later years, Hawthorne's method of integrating past and present in *The Scarlet Letter* must have appealed strongly to him. He planned, for example, to preface "The Ancestral Footstep" with a sketch of his consular experiences at Liverpool; in it he would hear from a visitor the story that would constitute the romance. The "Septimius" narrative was to be prefaced with a sketch of Hawthorne's residence at the Wayside which would introduce the legend Hawthorne had heard from Thoreau of the man who would not die: "I may fable that a manuscript was found," wrote Hawthorne in a preliminary study of "Septimius," "containing records of this man, and allusions to his purposes to live forever." Finally, Hawthorne intended that "The Dolliver Romance" would begin with a prefatory sketch of Thoreau, during the course of which Hawthorne would mention the legend that was to be the theme of the romance.

During these years, when he was writing with difficulty and indecision, Hawthorne thus attempted to blend past and present as he had done so brilliantly in *The Scarlet Letter*. The form of the sketch, he hoped, would again contain and yield his fiction, just as "The Custom-House" had contained and yielded the scarlet letter. But Hawthorne in the 1860s was working at cross purposes: in the late romances, potentially symbolic objects remained devoid of meaning or else labored under a significance arbitrarily assigned; bursts of inventiveness lacked direction and were followed by periods of acute dissatisfaction; "the Present, the Immediate, the Actual" could not be made to accommodate the past, the remote, and the imaginary—and no sketch could of itself bear the full burden of creation. *The Scarlet Letter*—in which, after more than two decades as an author, Hawthorne made his greatest sketch serve the purposes of his greatest tale—remained a unique achievement, one not to be duplicated.

Chapter Four

Six Tales

The manner in which Hawthorne liberated his imagination for the purposes of telling a tale and the attitudes toward the human condition embodied in his work tell us much about the nature of his artistic achievement. But achievement, in a different sense, comes uniquely in each individual work as a result of the fusion of form and content, of the coherence of technique and material. To confront Hawthorne's tales individually is to see the processes and thematic implications of his art as functioning parts of the narrative act. Accordingly, I have selected six representative tales—not, perhaps, the six best (whatever they may be), but surely six of the best—for close analysis. A reading of these six tales suggests further the range and quality of Hawthorne's fiction by bringing it into immediate perspective.

"The Minister's Black Veil"

"The Minister's Black Veil" (1836) is the first of Hawthorne's tales in which the imaginative confronting of a central symbol generates a principle of organization and dramatic coherence. The story takes its form from the meaning and the effects of the Reverend Mr. Hooper's veil—from what it signifies about the human condition, from the efforts of the characters to account for it, and from the consequences it has on the life of the man who wears it. As much as some readers have yearned to know precisely why Mr. Hooper donned the veil, the matter is not relevant to the narrative as we have it; to know why he put it on would be to have a different story. For the focus of the tale is on the veil, not on the minister's motives. Along with his parishioners and the minister himself, the reader must ponder the central fact of the veil.

The veil itself, Hawthorne tells us, consists of two folds of crape which entirely conceal Mr. Hooper's features, "except the mouth and chin, but probably did not intercept his sight, further than to give a darkened aspect to all living and inanimate things." It is not, therefore, a kind of robber's mask which conceals the lower half of the face and muffles the voice, nor a conventional mask with eye slits; it is a veil which at once hides Mr. Hooper's eyes from the world and presents that world in a darkened aspect to his eyes. It is something which hangs between Mr. Hooper and the world.

When, for the first time, Mr. Hooper stands up in the pulpit wearing this veil, his congregation is aghast. "More than one woman of delicate nerves was forced to leave the meeting-house." Yet, says Hawthorne, "perhaps the palefaced congregation was almost as fearful a sight to the minister, as his black veil to them." His sermon is the most powerful the congregation has ever heard him preach. Its subject is secret sin "and those sad mysteries which we hide from our nearest and dearest, and would fain conceal from our own consciousness, even forgetting that the Omniscent can detect them." Each member of the congregation "felt as if the preacher had crept upon them, behind his awful veil, and discovered their hoarded iniquity of deed or thought."

On his deathbed, Mr. Hooper (now Father Hooper) refuses to let the veil be lifted from his face, even though the Reverend Mr. Clark reminds him that it has cast suspicion on his life and asks with what horrible crime on his soul Father Hooper will die. But "why do you tremble at me alone?" cries Father Hooper, looking through his veil at the circle of "pale spectators":

Tremble also at each other! Have men avoided me, and women shown no pity, and children screamed and fled, only for my black veil? What, but the mystery which it obscurely typifies, has made this piece of crape so awful? When the friend shows his inmost heart to his friend; the lover to his best beloved; when man does not vainly shrink from the eye of his Creator, loathsomely treasuring up the secret of his sin; then deem me a monster, for the symbol beneath which I have lived and die! I look around me, and, lo! on every visage a Black Veil.

Suggested at the outset, this idea that every human being wears a black veil is thus stated explicitly by Father Hooper on his deathbed. All men wear black veils behind which the world is never allowed to look; in this mortal life the veils can never be removed (though, as Mr. Hooper once tells Elizabeth, his betrothed, "there is an hour to come when all of us shall cast aside our veils"). Since men do not literally wear such veils, the moral insight afforded by this idea is metaphorical in nature. And the relation between Hawthorne's dominant metaphor and his central symbol becomes clear: to achieve his symbol Hawthorne has—simply but significantly—literalized a metaphor; he has presented a physical, observable piece of crape as a visible emblem of the human condition. The symbol embodies and takes its meaning from the metaphor of the black veil.

The complexity of the tale arises from the consequences of Mr. Hooper putting on his veil. And it is important to view these consequences as Hawthorne presents them in the tale. As readers (almost as latter-day parishioners), we have been perennially tempted to think that Mr. Hooper is guilty of some secret sin: he preaches powerfully on the subject, as we know, and there are rumors in the village that he may be guilty of such sin. Edgar Allan Poe concluded that Mr. Hooper was guilty of a dark crime against the young lady whose funeral takes place in the tale. Among others, W. B. Carnochan refers to the minister's deathbed speech as an "implied confession."[1] Hawthorne's authoritative portrait of Arthur Dimmesdale as a sinful cleric might even lead one to suspect Mr. Hooper of the specific sin of adultery. But there is no evidence whatsoever in the story that Mr. Hooper is guilty of any particular secret sin; to get caught up in such a guessing game is to deflect attention from the veil to the minister's prior life. The view that Mr. Hooper is guilty of some unspecified secret sin, while it has the appearance of greater sagacity, merely makes a point of the obvious. For the burden of the tale is that no one can show his true face to the world. When Elizabeth tells him the speculation bruited about the village concerning his veil, Mr. Hooper says: "If I hide my face for sorrow, there is cause enough . . . ; and if I cover it for secret sin, what mortal might not do the same?" Georgiana's birthmark tells us we are all imperfect; Mr. Smith's experience in "Fancy's Show Box" shows us that the mind can commit grievous sin silently, secretly, alone. As a result, "man must not disclaim his brotherhood, even with the guiltiest, since, though his hand be clean, his heart has surely been polluted by the flitting phantoms of iniquity." Thus, as a human being, Mr. Hooper hides (and in a sense proclaims) iniquity that, for all we know in the tale, is neither more nor less than that of any other man.

The dual consequence of his wearing the veil is both to isolate Mr. Hooper from humanity and to make him "a very efficient clergyman." To the community he is "irreparably a bugbear": the timid avoid him; children flee at his approach. Because he will not remove the veil, even for a moment, at her request, he loses Elizabeth. The veil separates him from mankind; from beneath it "there rolled a cloud into the sunshine, an ambiguity of sin or sorrow, which enveloped the poor minister, so that love or sympathy could never reach him." His own antipathy to the veil is well known: "he never willingly passed before a mirror, nor stooped to drink at a still fountain, lest, in its peaceful bosom, he should be affrighted by himself." But because of "his mysterious emblem—for there was no other apparent cause—he became a man of awful power over souls that were in agony for sin." "Dying sinners cried aloud for Mr. Hooper." Thus he lives a long life, "irreproachable in outward act, yet shrouded in dismal suspicions; kind and loving, though unloved, and dimly feared; a man apart from men, shunned in their health and joy, but ever summoned to their aid in mortal anguish." On his deathbed he still wears the piece of crape that throughout his life "had hung between him and the world: it had separated him from cheerful brotherhood and woman's love, and kept him in that saddest of all prisons, his own heart."

As a prisoner in the sad chambers of his own heart, Mr. Hooper does not belong to the company of those Hawthorne characters who divorce themselves from humanity out of pride. He is no Richard Digby (Hawthorne's Man of Adamant), disdainful of the multitude, convinced that he alone sees the road to salvation. He does not neglect the responsibilities of his office: to his parishioners he is always kind and generous. He has, to judge from his words, put on a veil to represent the spiritual fact that all men wear veils in this lifetime; it is a veil belonging to mortality, not to eternity. And he has accepted the kind of isolation that wearing a veil has imposed on him. As the moral preceptor of his congregation, Mr. Hooper has brought a lesson before their eyes, a parable in the form of the veil ("A Parable," let us recall, is the subtitle of the tale.) Symbol and spiritual reflector, the veil ought to remind all men and women that they too wear veils. Grim lesson that it is, it ought to draw people more closely together in the knowledge that ultimate revelations are impossible, perhaps even undesirable, in this life.

In a sense, Mr. Hooper is something of a martyr to spiritual truth. Although people will not see the lesson he puts before them, he never upbraids them or acts unkindly toward them.[2] Isolated, apart from love, he is a victim of spiritual blindness, all the more worthy because he has let people look at him instead of forcing them to look at themselves. They miss his parable; they misconstrue the meaning of the veil—just as readers do who reenact the experience of the congregation and insist that the emblem hides some secret sin that separates Mr. Hooper from mankind. But no sin sets Mr. Hooper apart. He is set apart by his explicit and obsessive recognition of man's common nature.

Mr. Hooper's deathbed speech, however, indicates that the people of the village have not regarded him as an Everyman wearing humanity's veil nor seen their own veils more clearly because of the emblem over his face. And one wonders if the people are totally at fault. What makes the evil so awful, Mr. Hooper asks, "but the mystery which it obscurely typifies." Perhaps in this final remark on the meaning of the veil, he suggests the cause of its failure: to the people it has indeed been an obscure type of they know not what. Earlier, when Elizabeth asks explicitly what the veil signifies and why he has put it on, Mr. Hooper replies that it is "a type and a symbol"—but of what he does not say. The obscurity of the symbol functions ultimately as a failure in eloquence on the part of the preacher. Mr. Hooper has not retired to the lofty citadel of the mind; but he has nonetheless cut himself off from love and happiness, if not from agony and woe, by imprisoning himself in his own heart. Separated from the life-giving heart of the community, separated more personally from the heart and love of Elizabeth, Mr. Hooper fails to communicate, fails in his veiled role to identify himself. The blindness of his congregation is obvious: but it is made possible by the obscurity of his parable.

Hawthorne's "Parable" includes that of Mr. Hooper as part of its larger dimension. In "The Minister's Black Veil" the meaning of the veil and the effect of the veil lend two different kinds of dramatic force to the narrative. The same veil that tells of the sad unity of mankind proves divisive in effect. From the opposition and tension of these two dramatic forces derives the essential ambivalence of the tale. Mr. Hooper's parable inheres in the meaning of the veil; to what it signifies, he can add nothing. But Hawthorne shows us that the minister's perception of a truth of the human condition has ended his emotional life and curtailed (even as it has intensified) the areas of human experience in which he can participate. Because he has taken the veil, Mr. Hooper is necessarily cut off. For this is the price of the veil, the ultimate cost of perceiving one of the "sad and awful" truths of human nature.

"The May-pole of Merry Mount"

"Jollity and gloom were contending for an empire," writes Hawthorne in introducing the contending parties in "The May-pole of Merry Mount" (1836). He describes the Merry Mounters, gaily dressed for a mirthful frolic, masquerading as monsters, Indians, and beasts of the forest. The spirit of May reigns among these colonists, who have decked out a pine tree in fantastic array as a perennially youthful Maypole. "Had a wanderer," says Hawthorne, "bewildered in the melancholy forest, heard their mirth, and stolen a half-affrighted glance, he might have fancied them the crew of Comus, some already transferred to brutes, some midway between man and beast, and the others rioting in the flow of tipsy jollity that foreran the change." But no wanderer is present to see the scene in this manner; the only spectators are a band of Puritans hidden in the forest. And they "compared the masques to those devils and ruined souls with whom their superstition peopled the black wilderness." Hawthorne presents the scene, describes it from the point of view of an imaginary wanderer, then from the perspective of the Puritans, the implacable foes of Merry Mount. Having mentioned the Puritans and left us in no doubt of their antipathy, he returns to a description of the Merry Mounters and the central actors in their ceremonies.

The Lord and Lady of the May, it is important to note, are emotionally estranged from the community at Merry Mount before Endicott and his Puritans destroy the settlement and take them away. In the hour before her marriage the Lady Edith is pensive. "I struggle as with a dream," she tells Edgar, "and fancy that these shapes of our jovial friends are visionary, and their mirth unreal, and that we are no true Lord and Lady of the May. What is the mystery in my heart?" Edith is saddened by their mutual feeling that nothing in the future may be "brighter than the mere remembrance of what is now passing." Once the hearts of the young lovers "glowed with real passion," explains Hawthorne, they "were sensible of something vague and unsubstantial in their former pleasures, and felt a dreary presentiment of inevitable change. From the moment that they had truly loved, they had subjected themselves to earth's doom of care and sorrow, and troubled joy, and had no more a home at Merry Mount. That was Edith's mystery," and the cause of their estrangement from the Merry Mount community.

Having touched momentarily on the Puritan view of the Merry Mount frolic and having defined the pensive homelessness of Edith and Edgar, Hawthorne proceeds explicitly to qualify the conception of an idyllic Merry Mount. The people of the community, he says, are the "sworn triflers of a lifetime." They are addicts of mirth ("the counterfeit of happiness"), votaries of the Maypole, around which they dance at least once a month. With its festive and phallic associations, the Maypole is "their religion, or their altar . . . ; it was the banner-staff of Merry Mount." To go with such a religion they have a "flower-decked priest," the very antitype of the Puritan minister.

Apparently, however, Hawthorne does not want his criticism of Merry Mount to dominate the tale. When "The May-pole of Merry Mount" was first published in the *Token* in 1836, the Merry Mount priest was addressed by Endicott as Claxton; in *Twice-Told Tales* in 1837, and forever since, his name has been Blackstone. In each case Hawthorne adds the same footnote doubting the accuracy of Endicott's identification. Now the Reverend Lawrence Claxton (or Clarkson), though he was never in the colonies, was known as a ranter and an Anabaptist who tolerated May-poles; the Reverend William Blackstone (or Blaxton), on the other hand, one of the earliest Episcopal clergymen resident in New England, was a man of learning who had no such reputation, though he did take up residence in Roger Williams's colony. With Claxton as the priest, Hawthorne's portrait of Merry Mount takes on a quality of more substantial criticism than with Blackstone. The change of names would seem to be in the interest of balance. Endicott's liability to exaggeration likewise becomes more apparent when he calls Blackstone "priest of Baal."

After his portrayal of the Merry Mounters as triflers and counterfeiters, Hawthorne brings the reader up short by adding that, "unfortunately," men of a sterner faith also lived in the new world. The Puritans are "dismal wretches" who pray, work, and pray again, who keep their weapons "always at hand to shoot down the straggling savage." They could not appear more thoroughly counterposed to the Merry Mounters: "Their festivals were fast days, and their chief pastime the singing of psalms." If a youth or maiden but dreamed of dancing, it would most likely be done around the "whipping post, which might be termed the Puritan May-pole." Chief among these apostles of severity is Endicott, "the Puritan of Puritans," the "severest Puritan of all," who makes short work of the Maypole with his sword and passes out stripes to the Merry Mounters with promises of branding and cropping of ears later.

Having undercut the frivolous, carnival-loving Merry Mounters and the stern iron-willed Puritans so that one can identify with neither side, Hawthorne tells us that "the future complexion of New England was involved in this important quarrel."[3] The alternatives, as he presents them, are two: "should the grizzled saints establish their jurisdiction over the gay sinners, then would their spirits darken all the clime, and make it a land of clouded visages, of hard toil, of sermon and psalm, forever. But should the banner-staff of Merry Mount be fortunate, sunshine would break upon the hills, and flowers would beautify the forest, and late posterity do homage to the Maypole." Taken out of context, this passage would certainly seem to indicate a preference for the gaiety of Merry Mount rather than for the gloom of the Puritans. But, we recall, if the Puritans are "most dismal wretches," the Merry Mounters are the "sworn triflers of a lifetime." Furthermore, in this struggle for an empire between "jollity and gloom," there is most immediately at stake the empire of two young hearts, which is, at the moment the Puritans rush forth, in a state of sadness and doubt.

Hawthorne has integrated the elements of his tale by bringing the clash between the Puritans and the Merry Mounters to a climax at the very moment that the true love of Edith and Edgar, now blessed in valid marriage by the Merry Mount priest, has wrought their emotional and moral estrangement. The former Lord and Lady of the May are homeless, subject now to "doom, . . . sorrow, and troubled joy." It is almost as if their graduation from folly has evoked a stern adult world—as if the clash of Puritans and Merry Mounters is an imperial context for their emotional initiation into life. For at twilight, from their hiding place, rush the Puritans, whose "darksome figures were intermixed with the wild shapes of their foes," making the scene a version of the haunted mind—"a picture of the moment, when waking thoughts start up amid the scattered fantasies of a dream." The dream of Merry Mount has ended; Edith and Edgar must now contend with the waking world. Hawthorne has played out the drama of their maturation in the context of tensions inherent in New England history, just as he has played out a drama of New England history in the more intimate context of awakening love.

The somber vision of happiness held out by the end of the tale enforces Hawthorne's moral.[4] Confronted by the love of Edith and Edgar, even Endicott, "the iron man," is softened; he smiles at the "fair spectacle of early love." With an apparent knowledge of the ever-darkening contours of life, he almost sighs "for the inevitable blight of early hopes." He orders that Edith and Edgar be dressed in more decent attire; he commands that Edgar's hair be cropped "in the true pumpkin-shell fashion." And he lifts the wreath of roses from the Maypole he has destroyed and throws it, "with his own gauntleted hand, over the heads of the Lord and Lady of the May." It was, says Hawthorne,

a deed of prophecy. As the moral gloom of the world overpowers all systematic gayety, even so was their home of wild mirth made desolate amid the sad forest. They returned to it no more. But as their flowery garland was wreathed of the brightest roses that had grown there, so, in the tie that united them, were intertwined all the purest and best of their early joys. They went heavenward, supporting each other along the difficult path which it was their lot to tread, and never wasted one regretful thought on the vanities of Merry Mount.

The resolution of the tale, deliberate and unequivocal, leaves no room for sentimentality or empty wishes. At its conclusion, the term of natural innocence leads one to a life of sorrow and troubled joy. But innocence artificially protracted becomes a mockery of itself, a delusion by means of which the forced gesture of mirth passes for happiness. In their particular milieu, the Lord and Lady of the May must walk the stern path of the Puritans, wasting no regrets on a life from which their doubts and their love had alienated them even before the Puritans arrived, but with the "flowery garland'" bestowed by Endicott as a token of mutual joys that have made them what they are.

"Young Goodman Brown"

To judge from the title, wrote Herman Melville in his review of
Mosses from an Old Manse, one would suppose that "Young Goodman Brown" (1835) was "a simple little tale, intended as a supple-
ment to 'Goody Two-Shoes.' Whereas it is as deep as Dante." Readers
since Melville's time have agreed that "Young Goodman Brown"
is one of Hawthorne's most profound tales. In the manner of its
concern with guilt and evil, it exemplifies what Melville called the
"power of blackness" in Hawthorne's work. The thrust of the narrative is to move the protagonist toward a personal and climactic
vision of evil which leaves in its aftermath an abiding legacy of
distrust.

"Young Goodman Brown" takes in a strict if surprising sense the
form of a story of initiation; ritual and ceremony dominate the central
scene in which Goodman Brown is invited to become an initiate into
the community of evil proclaimed by the devil. And although the
ritual of initiation is perforce left incomplete, Goodman Brown is
ruined for life by all that the devil shows him. In the course of one
evening he is given such a monstrous perception of the scope, depth,
and universality of evil that he is forever blind to the world as it
normally presents itself. As David Levin reminds us in his discussion
of "specter evidence" in "Young Goodman Brown," however, the
focus of the story remains steadily on the protagonist. The tale is not
about the evil of other people in Salem village—Goody Cloyse, for
example, or Deacon Gookin, or Goodman Brown's father and grandfather; it is, rather, "about Brown's doubt, his discovery of the *possibility* of universal evil."[5] So corrosive is his experience that anything
contrary to the vision he has seen he considers a fraud. Just as surely
as if he had ascended to the heavenly choirs and achieved a mystic
comprehension of the destiny of all things, he has experienced what
is for him an ultimate vision.

What Goodman Brown sees in the forest persuades as well as
corrodes; in a scene shuddering with woe yet stabilized by the dignity
of fallen grandeur, he hears that the human race is immersed in guilt,
that evil is the nature of mankind. "Welcome, my children," says the
dark and majestic figure of the devil, "to the communion of your race.
You have found thus young your nature and your destiny." Although
at this point Goodman Brown is standing beside his wife Faith, he is

unaware of her presence. In the assembly behind them, continues the devil, are all those whom they have

reverenced from youth. . . . This night it shall be granted you to know their secret deeds. . . . [You] shall exult to behold the whole earth one stain of guilt, one mighty blood spot. Far more than this. It shall be yours to penetrate, in every bosom, the deep mystery of sin, the fountain of all wicked arts, and which inexhaustibly supplies more evil impulses than human power—than my power at its utmost—can make manifest in deeds. And now, my children look upon each other.

In such an unhallowed atmosphere Goodman Brown and Faith exchange glances, while the dark figure addresses them again in a "deep and solemn tone, almost sad with its despairing awfulness, as if his once angelic nature could yet mourn for our miserable race": you have depended upon one another's hearts, says the devil, you have hoped that "virtue were not all a dream. Now are ye undeceived. Evil is the nature of mankind. Evil must be your only happiness. Welcome, again, my children, to the communion of your race." And the assembled worshipers repeat the welcome in a cry of "despair and triumph."

There is an element of finality in the scene. Goodman Brown has traveled to the end of a journey from which he can return but never recover. He stops short of the ultimate step of infernal baptism, which would, of course, bring the story to a much different resolution. As he and Faith look at each other, they cannot make the decision which would allow each to see the hidden springs of guilt in the other: "What polluted wretches would the next glance show them to each other, shuddering alike at what they disclosed and what they saw!" Offered the power to pierce the veil that (as the Reverend Mr. Hooper knew) covers every human personality, the husband and wife cannot bear the idea of spiritual nakedness. Suddenly Goodman Brown cries out, "Faith! Faith! . . . look up to heaven and resist the Wicked One." Faith's allegorically appropriate name allows here, as elsewhere, for a masterful and openhanded ambiguity of effect. Goodman Brown is obviously addressing the image of his wife, urging her to resist the devil. At the same time he is exhorting himself to have faith, to look heavenward, to withstand the infernal eloquence of the Wicked One. And his cry has a miraculous effect; it obliterates the fiery theatrics of the scene along with the entire cast of demonic characters. "Hardly had he spoken" when he finds himself alone "amid calm night and solitude, listening to a roar of the wind, which died heavily away through the forest." At the beginning of the scene the minister and Deacon Gookin had escorted Goodman Brown to a "blazing rock." Now he staggers against the same rock and feels it "chill and damp; while a hanging twig, that had been all on fire, besprinkled his cheek with the coldest dew."

Assumed in "Young Goodman Brown" is a distinction between dream and reality that one must understand in the terms of Hawthorne's presentation. The question proposed to Goodman Brown is into which of these categories good and evil belong. At the outset of the story, Faith asks her husband to postpone his journey until sunrise and sleep in his own bed that night: "a lone woman," she says, "is troubled with such dreams and such thoughts that she's afeard of herself sometimes." Mulling over the guilty purpose that has brought him into the forest, Goodman Brown recalls Faith's talk of dreams; he wonders if he detected trouble in her face, "as if a dream had warned her of what work is to be done tonight." In the forest he goes through a dreamlike experience, marked by a series of abrupt transitions and sudden apparitions. The devil introduces a further notion of a dream by saying that Goodman Brown and Faith "had still hoped that virtue were not all a dream." Thus, the counterpoised terms, dream and reality, are shown to depend for their application upon one's prior attitude toward the moral nature of the world. And it is precisely because of Hawthorne's presentation of spectral or counterfeit evidence that such absolute distinctions founder—along with a protagonist (or reader) who would seek to apply them. For, as Levin demonstrates, the tale offers a choice "between dream and a reality that is unquestionably spectral."[6] In the manner of witnesses at the Salem witchcraft trials in 1692, Goodman Brown fails to distinguish between the specter or shape of a person and the person himself, between appearances (fashioned by the devil) and realities (created by God). Hawthorne's language is insistent: Goodman Brown sees "figures," "shapes," "visages" that appear in the guise of those he knows. He hears the voices of invisible travelers (on invisible horses) that, "he could have sworn," sound like those of the deacon and the minister. He gazes at a cloud that hurries across the sky, although "no wind was stirring." At an early point in the journey the devil discourses "so aptly, that his arguments seemed rather to spring up in the bosom" of Goodman Brown than "to be suggested by himself." And of course that is the case if Goodman Brown has internalized the source of evil. Michael J. Colacurcio is surely right in saying that according to Hawthorne's "psychological scheme Brown's suspicion and distrust and the Devil's wiles" are two ways of describing the same phenomena.[7]

For the devil, of course, virtue must be a dream, evil the only reality. And once Goodman Brown sees the "evidence" for that idea, he can never rid himself of it. It rises within him to cast a shadow over the apparent realities of his life in Salem village that he once took as visible (and comforting) evidence of sanctity:[8]

On the Sabbath day, when the congregation were singing a holy psalm, he could not listen because an anthem of sin rushed loudly upon his ear and drowned all the blessed strain. When the minister spoke from the pulpit with power and fervid eloquence, and, with his hand on the open Bible, of the sacred truths of our religion, and of saint-like lives and triumphant death, and of future bliss or misery unutterable, then did Goodman Brown turn pale, dreading lest the roof should thunder down upon the gray blasphemer and his hearers. Often, awakening suddenly at midnight, he shrank from the bosom of Faith; and at morning or eventide, when the family knelt down at prayer, he scowled and muttered to himself, and gazed sternly at his wife, and turned away. And when he had lived long, and was borne to his grave a hoary corpse, followed by Faith, an aged woman, and children and grandchildren, a goodly procession, besides neighbors not a few, they carved no hopeful verse upon his tombstone, for his dying hour was gloom.

His spectral experience in the forest has affected Goodman Brown as the most dismal, the most horrible, and, withal, the most intransigent experience of his life. Since he cannot believe in Faith, no other reality can modulate the gnawing gloom of a persistent doubt. He has journeyed into the dreamworld of the forest, into the haunted mind now functioning with the full force of history, and confronted a world steeped in guilt (whether projected by his fantasies or conjured by the devil) that makes his return to the village a pilgrimage into hypocrisy. But just as the experience has been personal, so has the effect. Goodman Brown alone is changed. He alone brings the dark vision of the forest to bear on the moral life of the community.

He alone, "from the night of that fearful dream," as Hawthorne says, becomes "a stern, a sad, a darkly meditative, a distrustful, if not a desperate man."

It is difficult to say precisely why Goodman Brown leaves Faith to spend his night in the forest. As we have seen, she asks him to put off his journey and tarry with her; he replies that this night of all nights in the year he must tarry away from her. He does not say what his purpose is, but conveniently uses her term: "My journey, as thou callest it, forth and back again, must needs be done 'twixt now and sunrise." And he chides her for doubting him when they are but three months married.

But he does go on his journey with a guilty conscience, leaving Faith with her pink ribbons behind. His heart tells him he is a wretch to leave Faith, "a blessed angel on earth," on "such an errand." He resolves that "after this one night" he will "cling to her skirts and follow her to heaven." Clearly, Goodman Brown wants "this one night." His journey into the forest can be defined as a kind of indeterminate allegory, representing man's irrational drive to leave faith, home, and security temporarily behind, for whatever reason, and take a chance with one (more?) adventure onto the wilder shores of experience. Our protagonist becomes an Everyman named Brown, a "young" man, who will be aged in one night by an adventure that makes everyone in this world seem a fallen idol. But our protagonist is also, and specifically, a seventeenth-century Puritan, a "young" man only three months joined to Faith, whose belief in the value of visible moral evidence becomes inverted rather than discredited. He has made a covenant to meet the devil, who has come from Boston to Salem village in fifteen minutes for the occasion. The simplicity of Goodman Brown's statements to the devil help to measure the extent of the change he will undergo in the forest. "Faith kept me back awhile," he says to explain his tardiness; "That old woman taught me my catechism," he remarks of Goody Cloyse ("and there was a world of meaning," Hawthorne writes, "in that simple comment"); finally, when he beholds a pink ribbon fluttering down from above he cries out, "My Faith is gone." At that frenzied and faithless moment he embraces the devil's premise that evil constitutes the only reality in the world.

Faith has been Goodman Brown's last resource. But the process of consigning people to the devil—or of instantly crediting reports of their wrongdoing—has its genesis in his brittle commitment to the world in which he lives.[9] He has learned with some wonder that the devil knew his father and grandfather. With amazement he has heard the devil claim that the governor and council are firm supporters of his interest. And quickly he dissociates himself: the governor and the council have their own ways, he reasons, "and are no rule for a simple husbandman like me." That Goody Cloyse consorts with the devil—who momentarily assumes the figure of Goodman Brown's grandfather and thereby demonstrates his mastery of appearances— is a blow that strikes closer to home. Again Goodman Brown dissociates himself, this time with the vehemence necessary to cast off one who has earned his respect: "what if a wretched old woman do choose to go to the devil when I thought she was going to heaven: is that any reason why I should quit my dear Faith and go after her?" He even decides to return to Salem Village and applauds himself greatly for his resolution; then, "conscious of the guilty purpose that had brought him hither," he hides when he hears the sounds of horses approaching. The discovery that Deacon Gookin and the old minister are likewise part of the devil's brotherhood shakes him deeply, although his conviction depends on the flimsiest of aural evidence: Goodman Brown cannot see them nor discern "so much as a shadow." The point is that he immediately believes in their perfidy and looks "up at the sky, doubting whether there really was a heaven above him."

Once again, Goodman Brown dissociates himself from persons he has reverenced. Bereft now of saintly company, of father and grand- father, of governor and council, of Goody Cloyse, Deacon Gookin, and the minister, he can make one final resolution: "With Heaven above, and Faith below, I will yet stand firm against the devil." Gone is all sense of community. Already having doubted the existence of heaven, Goodman Brown stands alone, crying out "in a voice of agony and desperation" for a Faith he has deliberately left behind. At that point (let us note Hawthorne's language carefully) "something flut- tered lightly down through the air, and caught on the branch of a tree. The young man seized it, and beheld a pink ribbon." From a heaven he already doubts comes "something" that this man shouting for Faith sees as a "pink ribbon." Since the pink ribbons of her cap are intact the next morning when Faith bursts into joy at the sight of Goodman Brown, what we have here is best seen as a final,

Faith-testing, instance of spectral evidence. Having converted "something" to a "pink ribbon" by an ultimate projection of his guilt, our protagonist is at first "stupified," then "maddened with despair." He speaks the obvious truth when he says his Faith is gone. He reveals his virtual solipsism when he concludes that "there is no good on earth."

As he rushes through the "haunted forest" to join the devil's congregation, Goodman Brown becomes "the chief horror of the scene." "In truth," writes Hawthorne, holding out the possibility that we might have been witnessing a specter undone by spectral evidence, "there could be nothing more frightful" in the forest "than the *figure* of Goodman Brown" (my italics). But Brown at the beginning and end of the tale is presented as a character, not a specter. He has (in a far more serious way than Wakefield) deliberately left his place in the moral universe and returned with a perspective that converts everything to evil and hypocrisy. From his dream vision or spectral adventure in the forest, he has received a paralyzing sense that the brotherhood of man is possible only under the fatherhood of the devil. His vision is absolute, unalterable; it turns his world inside out and compels him to live and die in a gloom born of his inverted sense of moral reality.

"Rappaccini's Daughter"

"Rappaccini's Daughter" (1844) is replete with symbols and symbolic allusions. Its principal setting is a fantastic garden filled with lush vegetation and poisonous flowers, in the center of which is a broken fountain. Numerous references to Eden, to Adam, and to Dante fill the tale with overtones which add to the complexity of its texture. The structure of the tale involves two mutually dependent stories—one contained and given fuller meaning by the dimensions of the other. Though his focus is on Beatrice as she is seen by Giovanni, Hawthorne's story of this young man and woman is folded within the contours of Baglioni's rivalry with Rappaccini. To take full account of the inner story, one must attend to the implications of the outer.

Hawthorne sets his tale "very long ago" in Padua, Italy, and makes an early reference to Dante: Giovanni Guasconti, a youth of "remarkable beauty of person" who has come to study at the University and is "not unstudied in the great poem of his country," recalls that one of the ancestors of the family in whose ancient palace he takes lodgings "had been pictured by Dante as a partaker of the immortal agonies of his Inferno." Such associations, "together with the tendency to heartbreak" natural to a young man for the first time away from home, cause Giovanni to sigh heavily. Sensing his mood, his landlady bids him look out the window, and it is thus that he takes his first look at Rappaccini's garden.

The reference to Dante, as one comes to expect in Hawthorne's best work, is more than decorative; it serves to point up the significant contrast between Dante's Beatrice and Rappaccini's daughter Beatrice. In Dante's poem, Beatrice is the activating agent of grace; lost in the dark wood of error, Dante could not begin his arduous pilgrimage were it not for her intercession in heaven; she is, moreover, his guide when Virgil and the light of reason can lead him no farther. Dante's Beatrice is thus an instrument of redemption. But Hawthorne presents a trapped and poisonous Beatrice, who herself needs a special kind of redemption: a prisoner in the garden, her body nourished by poison, she nonetheless belongs to God in spirit; her spirit, indeed, "craves love as its daily food." There is no question in the tale of her physical escape from the garden into, say, the streets of Padua. But a very large concern of the tale is that this imprisoned and poisonous Beatrice stands in need of love for spiritual sustenance and liberation.[10]

Giovanni stumbles quite by chance into the role of redeemer or rescuer, the bringer of love. And he fails miserably, not through intent, not out of a conscious desire to do ill, but simply because he is a very ordinary and limited young man whose limitations are pointed up all the more explicitly by the exigencies of a role that demands what he cannot give. When Beatrice first sees him from her garden, he is looking out from a window above; she beholds his beautiful head—"rather a Grecian than an Italian head, with fair, regular features, and a glistening of gold among his ringlets—gazing down upon her like a being that hovered in mid-air." The golden haired Giovanni, appearing, as it were, in mid-air, is endowed physically with all the attributes of the godlike hero who rescues the fair maiden from distress. Instinctively, "scarcely knowing what he did," he throws down to her a bouquet of flowers which he has purchased (instinctively?) shortly before.

In the terms set up by the narrative, Giovanni's first gesture toward

Beatrice is natural and commendable. Though Beatrice lives among the flowers in her garden, and though Giovanni's bouquet seems to be withering quickly as she disappears into her house, the bouquet is not redundant. Without knowing the secret of her poisonous garden world, Giovanni has bestowed with his fresh flowers a token antidote of the heart. But this is one of the few gestures of the heart that he ever makes to Beatrice.

Repeatedly, Hawthorne tells us of his shallowness and affectation. He "had not a deep heart, or, at all events, its depths were not sounded now; but he had a quick fancy." Allowed into the garden, Giovanni wonders momentarily if his intense interest in Beatrice "were not delusory"; could his interest, asks Hawthorne, be "merely the fantasy of a young man's brain, only slightly or not at all connected with his heart?" Again, Giovanni seems less in love than in the throes of "that cunning semblance of love which flourishes in the imagination, but strikes no depth of root into the heart." When, after an interview with Baglioni, Giovanni buys a second bouquet of flowers, it is with the express purpose of testing Beatrice to see if she is what his senses proclaim her to be. And, before he goes into the garden for his final, fateful interview, he pauses to gaze at himself in a mirror, "a vanity to be expected in a beautiful young man, yet, as displaying itself at that troubled and feverish moment, the token of a certain shallowness of feeling and insincerity of character."

Giovanni, in short, lacks the depth of heart necessary to tender to Beatrice the love to which her spirit could respond. He vacillates between faith and doubt, between the promptings of the heart and those of the fancy—and his alternating moods comprise the essential dramatic movement of the tale. He is not so much tricked or deluded as limited by his fancy, which blurs any profounder vision and makes it impossible for him to believe in Beatrice's spiritual beauty even though he has perceived its manifestations. Had he trusted in the heart rather than in the fancy he would have been reassured "that all this ugly mystery was but an earthly illusion," that despite the "mist of evil" surrounding her the real Beatrice was "a heavenly angel." But Giovanni is "incapable ... of such high faith." When Beatrice says she had been lonely until heaven sent him, he turns angrily upon her, burying her with invective, calling her "a world's wonder of hideous monstrosity." And when she sadly explains the truth of her situation, a contrite Giovanni betrays the poverty of his

heart one final time. Perhaps, he thinks, he can yet lead "the redeemed Beatrice" from the garden; putting his faith not in the heart
but in a scientific antidote, he ministers the potion given him by
Baglioni, and—compounding his emotional blindness—promises that
it is "almost divine in its efficacy."

By listening to the advice of Signor Pietro Baglioni, Giovanni becomes unwittingly involved in the rivalry between this friend of his
father and Rappaccini. Certainly the advice seems well meant; but
in this tale things are not often what they seem. Rappaccini is a
brilliant scientist, admits Baglioni, as good as any in Italy, "with perhaps one single exception." Although this cryptic qualification is
never explained, there can be little doubt that the "exception" is
Baglioni himself. Baglioni goes on to expound Rappaccini's theory
of medicine, to admit that with his vast knowledge of poisons Rappaccini undeniably "does less mischief than might be expected," and
to admit further, albeit grudgingly, that he has, "now and then, . . .
effected, or seemed to effect, a marvellous cure."

Then, in a statement that reflects heavily on the attitude of the
speaker, he gives Giovanni his private opinion: Rappaccini "should
receive little credit for such instances of success,—they being probably
the work of chance,—but should be held strictly accountable for his
failures, which may justly be considered his own work." The statement is so grossly onesided as to be humorous. And Hawthorne reinforces the certainty of bias by saying that Giovanni "might have
taken Baglioni's opinions with many grains of allowance had he
known that there was a professional warfare of long continuance
between him and Dr. Rappaccini, in which the latter was generally
thought to have gained the advantage." Yet this same Baglioni formulates what has come to be virtually the standard judgment of the
mighty scientist: Rappaccini "cares infinitely more for science than
for mankind," says Baglioni; his patients interest him only as subjects
for experiments; and—most famous description of all—"he would
sacrifice human life, his own among the rest, or whatever else was
dearest to him, for the sake of adding so much as a grain of mustard
seed to the great heap of his accumulated knowledge."

We have tended to accept, with at best token qualifications, part
of Baglioni's opinion of Rappaccini while discounting his absurd and
irrational views relative to the doctor's successes and failures. What
we tend to accept are those phrases which fit Hawthorne's basic mode

of describing the dehumanized scientist who neglects the heart in favor of the head and who cuts himself off from the magnetic chain of humanity. It is of course impossible to view Rappaccini as a normal, fun-loving devotee of the heart. His garden is both terrible and unnatural; what Baglioni says of him may be only an exaggeration of a sinister truth. But from what we see in the tale Baglioni's descriptions fit himself as much as they do Rappaccini. Baglioni cares more about vanquishing his rival than he cares for the welfare of Giovonni and Beatrice; out of his conviction that Rappaccini is using Giovanni for an experiment, he tries to counter the doctor by doing the same. Baglioni precipitates the sacrifice of a human life, and there is reason to suspect that the sacrifice will add something to his accumulated knowledge. Finally, Baglioni appears at Giovanni's window above the garden at the climactic point of the tale and calls "loudly, in a tone of triumph mixed with horror, to the thunder-stricken man of science: 'Rappaccini! Rappaccini! And is *this* the upshot of your experiment?' " As a major force of the envelope story, Baglioni contributes to Giovanni's failure of love and implicates himself in the death of Beatrice. By doubling the role of scientist, Hawthorne has set the heart in a more poignant solitude.

Although we see relatively little of Rappaccini in the tale, it is possible to construct a portrait of him apart from Baglioni's descriptions. He is indeed a twisted genius, but with a motive for his actions which Baglioni does not comprehend. Hawthorne describes Rappaccini as "a tall, emaciated, sallow, and sickly-looking man, dressed in a scholar's garb of black." Intellectual cultivation is stamped on his face, which had never shown much warmth of heart. Rappaccini has created the poisonous garden and made his daughter poisonous so that she can live in it. Such is his power that his garden suggests an "adultery of various vegetable species," a production "no longer of God's making, but the monstrous offspring of man's depraved fancy, glowing with only an evil mockery of beauty." This garden is his world, although its poison would be fatal to him. And Rappaccini, as he tells Beatrice, has subtly filtered this poison into Giovanni's system: "he now stands apart from common man, as thou dost, daughter of my pride and triumph, from ordinary women. Pass on, then, through the world, most dear to one another, and dreadful to all besides!"

Rappaccini's motive for these acts is of special importance: in a twisted and prideful way, he has done all that he has done for what he sees as the welfare of his daughter. When Beatrice asks why he has inflicted such a "miserable doom" upon her, he is astonished: "Dost thou deem it misery to be endowed with marvellous gifts, against which no power nor strength could avail an enemy? Misery, to be able to quell the mightiest with a breath? Misery, to be as terrible as thou art beautiful? Wouldst thou, then, have preferred the condition of a weak woman, exposed to all evil, and capable of none?"

Rappaccini, a grotesque figure of the mad scientist as overly protective father, has thus rendered his daughter poisonous to defend her against the evils of the world. He has poisoned Giovanni to give her a companion in this inverted paradise, this "Eden of the present world." And just as Baglioni has precipitated Beatrice's death by his concern to outmaneuver Rappaccini, just as Giovanni has failed to evince the potent magic of love that could have been the true antidote to Rappaccini's scientific skill, so Rappaccini, warped apostle of the head that he is, has never seen that Beatrice "would fain have been loved, not feared." She is, we recall from his boast, the daughter of his pride and triumph, not the daughter of his heart.

In his lengthy final scene, Hawthorne integrates the already interrelated elements of his narrative by bringing together for the only time the characters of his inner and outer stories. With different motives, the two scientists have used Beatrice and Giovanni as pawns in their own games: Rappaccini to insure the perverse welfare of his daughter, Baglioni to thwart Rappaccini. When Giovanni plays into their hands by putting his faith in science, the narrative envelope collapses. The inner story of Giovanni and Beatrice, which depended on the heart for its continued existence, is, in effect, rejected by one of its principals, the would-be redeemer. In the terms of Hawthorne's tale, there is no redemption for Beatrice in this world. Doubt and skepticism (bred by power and pride, jealousy and revenge) prove to be the ultimate poisons of the heart. What they measure is an insufficiency of love.

"Ethan Brand"

In "Ethan Brand" (1850) Hawthorne articulates most explicitly the theme of a man of idea that had run through his fiction for almost twenty years. The definition and focus of the tale bring us face to face with a man whose obsession with a single idea has made him absolutely committed to its realization. The head has completely vanquished the heart, turning it to marble. Yet "Ethan Brand" was apparently not conceived as a tale. It bears the subtitle "A Chapter from an Abortive Romance." And there are several references in the narrative to episodes that have supposedly taken place at an earlier time. Hawthorne presents us with a conclusion, a final chapter; and incomplete as it may be with reference to the original conception of his romance, it has a ring of finality, the authority of a literary work that embodies an author's basic theme purely, simply, classically.

In a notebook entry in 1844, Hawthorne recorded the idea of an investigator searching for the Unpardonable Sin and finding it at last "in his own heart and practice." After a brief entry concerning the reflection of trees in a river, he took up his idea again, pondering the possible nature of such a sin. "The Unpardonable Sin," he wrote, "might consist in a want of love and reverence for the Human Soul; in consequence of which, the investigator pried into its dark depths, not with a hope or purpose of making it better, but from a cold philosophical curiosity,—content that it should be wicked in whatever kind or degree, and only desiring to study it out. Would not this, in other words, be the separation of the intellect from the heart?"

Hawthorne also drew extensively on other notebook entries for the writing of "Ethan Brand." During his stay at North Adams in 1838 he had recorded many details of his surroundings. The lime kiln, the local topography dominated by Graylock, the German Jew with his diorama, the dog chasing his tail, and such characters as the doctor and Lawyer Giles all appear in the notebook and are transmuted to the fictional world of "Ethan Brand." And the "investigator" who searches for the Unpardonable Sin finds a fictional embodiment in the character of Ethan Brand. The resolution of Ethan Brand's quest brings the discrete phenomena of Hawthorne's experience and imaginative speculation into coherent dramatic form.

In the course of time, the term Unpardonable Sin has come to be applied to the evil purposes of a number of Hawthorne's characters. It is common practice to say that such characters as Aylmer, Rappaccini, Roger Chillingworth, Jaffrey Pyncheon, and Hollingsworth commit the Unpardonable Sin. All of these characters victimize other human beings by a programmatic use of the intellect divorced from the heart; their actions correspond in varying degrees with the tentative definition of the Unpardonable Sin as Hawthorne entered it in his notebook in 1844. In Hawthorne's fiction, however, the term occurs only once—in "Ethan Brand." And, as Hawthorne reveals the nature of this sin in his abortive romance, it takes on an additional dimension which makes Ethan Brand's Unpardonable Sin, though similar in many ways to other sins of the head, unique to him as it is unique to the tale in which he appears.

Aylmer, Rappaccini, and other characters certainly exhibit a fatal lack of "love and reverence for the Human Soul." In each case, however, a finite intention motivates and goads them to their actions. Aylmer wants Georgiana to be perfect; Rappaccini desires to protect Beatrice from an evil world by giving her a monstrous power; Judge Pyncheon betrays Clifford and threatens Hepzibah for the sake of wealth; and Hollingsworth wants Blithedale for his scheme of reforming criminals. These characters ravage the hearts of others in an effort to realize the Idea that glows solitary in their minds. But in each case, the goal—material or psychological—is within the realm of human conception; reform, wealth, revenge, protective power, and perfection are dreams perhaps never absolutely attainable, but they are nonetheless human dreams.

As the *sine qua non* of his quest, however, Ethan Brand attempts to conceive of a sin so vast that God could not forgive it. According to the local legend, he would evoke a fiend from the furnace of the lime kiln "night after night, in order to confer with him about the Unpardonable Sin; the man and the fiend each laboring to frame the image of some mode of guilt which could neither be atoned for nor forgiven." No matter the naiveté of such a legend—the significant fact is that Ethan Brand devotes himself to the idea "of extending man's possible guilt beyond the scope of Heaven's else infinite mercy."

Now a man who could commit a sin so great that God could not forgive it would, by that very fact, have outreached God. His sin would demonstrate that "Heaven's else infinite mercy" was indeed finite and limited. The genesis of Ethan Brand's career is thus an attempt to conceive of a way to extend heavenly mercy beyond its capacity. Whereas other Hawthorne characters would be godlike, Ethan Brand would be God. He sets out deliberately, with no intermediate purpose, to defeat God.[11]

As he muses by his lime kiln (appropriatedly capable of being pronounced "lime kil," with the final *n* silent), Ethan Brand can think of no specific act with such infinite implications. Then, for eighteen years, he travels throughout the world searching for a way to commit a sin that is unpardonable. His ultimate aim is always to overreach his Creator. He has, for example, with "cold and remorseless purpose," made a young girl "the subject of a psychological experiment, and wasted, absorbed, and perhaps annihilated her soul, in the process." The worst feature of this deliberate act of destruction is that, for Ethan Brand, it is incidental to his purpose; he uses the girl as a means to an end. One can of course (and should) argue that Aylmer uses Georgiana as a means to an end; he sacrifices her to an idea of perfection. By implication, Aylmer challenges God through His creation. But Ethan Brand alone challenges heaven directly, immediately and totally. Ethan Brand alone sets out with the avowed intention of demonstrating a greater capacity for sin than God has for forgiveness. And "Ethan Brand" alone, of all Hawthorne's tales, is imaginatively conceived for the purpose of confronting the Unpardonable Sin.

The narrative purpose of "The Birthmark" directs our attention to the terrible price of failing to see that to be human is to be imperfect; "Rappaccini's Daughter" dramatizes the disaster of a heart beset with overprotectiveness, revenge, and a failure of faith; but in "Ethan Brand" there are no human considerations through which one insults heaven. The search is direct, as if only two beings, God and Ethan Brand, existed in the universe. Thus, Ethan Brand can injure human beings with maximum impersonality; the victory of head over heart is absolute. His is a mighty sin of presumption (which prefigures his final despair); the quest itself, which incorporates the evil actions of eighteen years, is the Unpardonable Sin.

Sitting once again by his old lime kiln, Ethan Brand recapitulates the stages of his journey from presumption to despair. Years before, he was "a simple and loving man":

> He remembered with what tenderness, with what love and sympathy for mankind, and what pity for human guilt and woe, he had first begun to contemplate those ideas which afterwards became the inspiration of his life; with what reverence he had then looked into the heart of man, viewing it as a temple originally divine, and, however desecrated, still to be held sacred by a brother; with what awful fear he had deprecated the success of his pursuit, and prayed that the Unpardonable Sin might never be revealed to him. Then ensued that vast intellectual development, which, in its progress, disturbed the counterpoise between his mind and his

heart. The Idea that possessed his life had operated as a means of education; it had gone on cultivating his powers to the highest point of which
they were susceptible; it had raised him from the level of an unlettered
laborer to stand on a star-lit eminence, whither the philosophers of the
earth, laden with the lore of universities, might vainly strive to clamber
after him. So much for the intellect! But where was the heart? That, indeed, had withered,—had contracted,—had hardened,—had perished! It
had ceased to partake of the universal throb. He had lost his hold of the
magnetic chain of humanity. He was no longer a brother-man, opening
the chambers or the dungeons of our common nature by the key of holy
sympathy which gave him a right to share in all its secrets; he was now
a cold observer, looking on mankind as the subject of his experiment, and,
at length, converting man and woman to be his puppets, and pulling the
wires that moved them to such degrees of crime as were demanded for
his study.

Human creation is basically irrelevant to Ethan Brand, important only
as a means to the commission of the Unpardonable Sin. Quite naturally, as Nina Baym observes, his quest "drives him into a self-enclosed
universe."[12] From the moment he decides to outreach God, he forfeits
his place in the magnetic chain of humanity, which is, after all, made
up of God's creatures.

The stage-agent, the lawyer, and the doctor are precisely the kind
of human beings antipodal to the nature of Ethan Brand. A "flavor
of brandy-toddy and tobacco smoke" impregnated the ideas, the expression, and the person of the stage-agent. The lawyer turned soap-
boiler is "a maimed and miserable wretch," lacking part of one foot
and an entire hand. Intemperance has accelerated his downfall. Yet
he is a man "whom the world could not trample on, and had no right
to scorn, . . . since he had still kept up the courage and spirit of a
man, asked nothing in charity, and with his one hand—and that the
left one—fought a stern battle against want and hostile circumstances."
The village doctor, possessed by brandy as by "an evil spirit," is likewise a broken man. But so great is his skill at healing "that society
caught hold of him, and would not let him sink out of its reach. So,
swaying to and fro upon his horse, and grumbling thick accents at the
bedside, he visited all the sick-chambers for miles about among the
mountain towns, and sometimes raised a dying man, as it were, by
miracle, or quite as often, no doubt, sent his patient to a grave that
was dug many a year too soon."

Apparent nonentities, derelicts, human debris, these three characters have never lost touch with humanity. The inherent self-respect of the lawyer allows him still to be a man. The drunken and erratic skill of the doctor is still in the service of humanity. When they offer Ethan Brand a drink from a black bottle in a gesture of drunken comradeship, he orders them away angrily. These men he cannot tolerate; "no mind, which has wrought itself by intense and solitary meditation into a high state of enthusiasm, can endure the kind of contact with low and vulgar modes of thought and feeling to which Ethan Brand was now subjected."

As one might expect, Ethan Brand is most comfortable alone. The old man asking for news of his daughter causes Ethan Brand to quail momentarily at the enormity of what his quest has led him to. The Jew with his diorama annoys him; the two have met before, and the Jew can apparently represent the Unpardonable Sin to Ethan Brand by means of his showbox. Possibly seeing an analogy between himself and the dog who chases his tail, Ethan Brand laughs, and the dismal reverberations of his laugh cause the assorted company to leave. The only glimpse of sympathy for him comes from little Joe; when Bartram and Joe are retiring to their hut, the son looks back at Ethan Brand, "and the tears came into his eyes, for his tender spirit had an intuition of the bleak and terrible loneliness in which this man had enveloped himself."

The Unpardonable Sin, as Ethan Brand had told Bartram, lies within his heart, or what was once his heart. Standing erect in pride, he defines it as "a sin that grew nowhere else! The sin of an intellect that triumphed over the sense of brotherhood with man and reverence for God, and sacrificed everything to its own mighty claims! The only sin that deserves a recompense of immortal agony! Freely, were it to do again, would I incur the guilt. Unshrinkingly I accept the retribution." In the hour of his greatest despair Ethan Brand stands revealed as a success; his quest becomes a parable of how to succeed at spiritual self-destruction.

The unlettered and earthy, however, have a kind of final, anti-climactic victory in the tale. When Bartram finds the bones of Ethan Brand, with the heart intact and unmeltable, in the lime kiln, he is perplexed for a moment. Then he accepts the fact on his own terms: "At any rate, it is burnt into what looks like special good lime; and, taking all the bones together, my kiln is half a bushel the richer for him." By half a bushel, the bones of Ethan Brand contribute to Bartram's well-being. By half a bushel, Ethan Brand serves the mundane purposes of a humanity he has scorned.

"My Kinsman, Major Molineux"

"My Kinsman, Major Molineux" stands, in a sense, in two places in Hawthorne's career. First published in the *Token* in 1832, it was not included in a book of tales until the publication of *The Snow-Image* in 1851. Thus it came before the public once again at a time when Hawthorne was giving up the writing of tales, even though it was a production of his early career.

The tale blends a personal theme of initiation into the sobering responsibilities of adulthood with the historical movement of the American colonists in defiance of royal authority. To begin his tale, Hawthorne invites the reader briefly into his workshop: his opening remarks serve quite frankly "as preface to the following adventures, which chanced upon a summer night, not far from a hundred years ago." The reader is asked to dispense with details and to assume a historical situation "that had caused much temporary inflammation of the popular mind." In the context of such a situation, young Robin, country-bred and "barely eighteen," makes his first visit to town; he is looking for his kinsman, who, childless himself, has indicated a willingness to help the youth make a start in life. As the story unfolds, however, Hawthorne doubles the context of his fiction as he would four years later in "The May-pole of Merry Mount"; for it also becomes true that the popular fervor which culminates in the major's disgrace swells to its climactic point in the context of Robin's consciousness.

Hawthorne repeatedly and with gentle irony characterizes Robin as "a shrewd youth." And Robin believes innocently in his own shrewdness. At some points he is not unlike Captain Amasa Delano of Melville's "Benito Cereno" with his naive strategies of reassurance—though, of course, Hawthorne's Robin is wandering toward a point of enlightenment, whereas Melville's Delano is thoroughly encased in a situation which, happily for his physical well-being, he never does comprehend. When the first man Robin asks for directions to Major Molineux's dwelling testily orders him away, Robin, "being a shrewd youth, soon thought himself able to account for the mystery:

'This is some country representative,' " he concludes, who has never been inside the major's house " 'and lacks the breeding to answer a stranger civilly.' " If the man were not so old, Robin might hit him on the nose. He accepts the laughter from the barber's shop as being directed at him for his poor choice of a guide.

The innkeeper's solicitude for his patronage strikes him as a natural consequence of his obvious family resemblance to the major—a heavy-handed attempt to curry favor with the great. When he admits that his purse is nearly empty and states his purpose in town, the "sudden and general movement in the room" seems to him to express "the eagerness of each individual to become his guide." Warned away by the innkeeper, Robin hears "a general laugh" from those in the tavern as soon as he is outside the door. "With his usual shrewdness," he considers it strange that an empty pocketbook should have more weight than the major's name. And for the second time he thinks of physical retaliation, this time with his cudgel: "If I had one of those grinning rascals in the woods, where I and my oak sapling grew up together, I would teach him that my arm is heavy though my purse be light."

Robin's two means of expressing his identity and authority are both inefficacious and out of place in his new milieu. One, his kinship with Major Molineux, he has counted on heavily to assist him in his intro-duction to the town; the other, his oak cudgel, has come from the country where, doubtless, it was a sign that he was not to be trifled with. But if the magic of the major's name can only evoke laughter in the town, the weapon of nature, vestige of another life, is ineffec-tive in its new setting. Shortly after he leaves the tavern, Robin, fatigued and hungry, thinks he might demand "violently, and with lifted cudgel, the necessary guidance from the first solitary passenger whom he should meet." His encounter with the young woman in the scarlet petticoat puts this idea of aggression momentarily out of mind. But finally Robin brings the authority of the forest to bear on his search; he plants himself fully before a passerby, "holding the oak cudgel with both hands across his body as a bar to further passage." Futile in one sense, his crude stance of violence does bring him an answer from the man of the bulging forehead whom Robin has seen in the tavern—his face now painted half-black, half-red: wait an hour and Major Molineux will pass by.

Robin's encounter with the woman in the scarlet petticoat brings his "shrewdness" again to light. Indeed, at this point Robin plays the innocent and almost receives an initiation which he did not bargain for. His approach is indirect: " 'Pretty mistress,' for I may call her so with a conscience, thought the shrewd youth, since I know nothing to the contrary. . . ." Her assertion that "Major Molineux dwells here" makes Robin doubt "whether that sweet voice spoke Gospel truth." So he replies, "cunningly," that he is indeed in luck and will she please bring the major to the door. The scarlet woman almost prevails; "though Robin read in her eyes what he did not hear in her words, yet the slender-waisted maiden in the scarlet petticoat proved stronger than the athletic country youth." Only the appearance of the watch-man keeps him from crossing her doorstep. Asked if he will guide Robin to the dwelling of Major Molineux, the watchman does not reply; but after he rounds a corner, the sound of drowsy laughter comes to Robin's ears. And the scarlet woman titters from a window above and beckons to him. "But Robin, being of the household of a New England clergyman, was a good youth as well as a shrewd one; so he resisted temptation and fled away." Later, he tells the man who has befriended him at the church door that he, rather than his brother, was the family choice to profit from the major's generous intentions: "For I have the name of being a shrewd youth."

The town has taken on the aspects of a nightmare—a world of senseless laughter, temptation, and caricature, in which no one seems willing or able to answer a simple and straightforward question. Robin's unrelenting "shrewdness," however, repeatedly offsets the fantastic quality of appearances around him; he blindly makes sense out of what, to him, ought to be senseless. The bizarre appearance of the man with the red and black face intensifies the quality of general and mounting incoherence: "the effect was as if two individual devils, a fiend of fire and a fiend of darkness, had united themselves to form the infernal visage."

Robin's reaction to this wild and grinning figure disposes even the most sympathetic reader to join the town in laughing at him—to enact, that is, the drama of his initiation. Seating himself on the steps of the church to wait the hour for his kinsman, he spends a few moments "in philosophical speculation upon the species of man who had just left him; but having settled this point shrewdly, rationally, and satisfactorily, he was compelled to look elsewhere for his amusement." How Robin accounts "rationally" for a man running around with his face painted a grotesque black and red we are not told; that he does so, however, evidences a depth of faith in the dimension of his own (in-)experience which it would have been difficult otherwise to suspect.

During his solitary hour in front of the church, Robin grows lonely. He looks through a window into the church, but, psychically as well as physically outside, he experiences "a sensation of loneliness stronger than he had ever felt in the remotest depths of his native woods." He thinks of the hour of prayer held in the bosom of nature in front of his father's household, where even the wayfarer might "keep his heart pure by freshening the memory of home." Imagining the scene in detail, Robin watches the reverent procedures of his family until they enter the door of their house; but when he tries to enter his reverie, the latch of the door falls into place and he is "excluded from his home." With his mind vibrating "between fancy and reality," he is uncertain whether he is "here" or "there." A feeling of homelessness underlies his confused sense of reality. Locked out of the house of his memory, he has not yet been admitted to the house of his expectations. Robin occupies a middle ground, the domain of romance, where (as he sits in front of the church) "the moon, creating, like the imaginative power, a beautiful strangeness in familiar objects, gave something of romance to a scene that might not have possessed it in the light of day."

Despite his ability to rationalize the grotesque, Robin is moving toward an eruption of feeling that will be both retrospective and prospective. "I have laughed very little since I left home," he tells his new friend, hoping that the sound of merriment at a distance will pass their way. And it does, to stop squarely in front of Robin, the man with the red and black face now a "single horseman" riding in authority and giving the appearance of "war personified": "the red of one cheek was an emblem of fire and sword; the blackness of the other betokened the mourning that attends them." Accompanying him on foot are "wild figures in the Indian dress, and many fantastic shapes without a model, giving the whole march a visionary air, as if a dream had broken loose from some feverish brain, and were sweeping visibly through the midnight streets." The nightmare has indeed "broken loose" so that Robin can no longer avoid seeing it for what it is.

"Right before" his eyes, in a moment of stasis lighted by bright torch-
light and moonlight that shone "like day," sits Robin's kinsman,
Major Molineux, enshrined in "tar-and-feathery dignity" at the center
of the wild procession.

Hawthorne presents the major as a figure of natural dignity whose
pride of bearing has been shaken but not abrogated by an ordeal of
pain and "overwhelming humiliation." Perhaps the "bitterest pang"
of all, however, "was when his eyes met those of Robin; for he evidently knew him on the instant, as the youth stood witnessing the
foul disgrace of a head that had grown grey in honor." The two stare
at each other in silence, "and Robin's knees shook, and his hair bristled,
with a mixture of pity and terror."

Gradually and inevitably, Robin has been brought face to face with
the events of history, with the overthrow of authority, with the Saturnalian excesses of revolution.[13] As he stands looking at history, at a
tableau vivant staged for his edification, he undergoes the classic
catharsis of pity and terror. But history is also looking at Robin:
when the procession moves in front of him, he becomes aware that
the "double-faced fellow" is staring at him, and he is uncomfortable
at the idea that he might be made to "bear a part in the pageantry."
His idea is validated and even emphasized by Hawthorne's narrator.
Immediately before his command to halt, "the leader turned himself
in the saddle, and fixed his glance full upon the country youth." A
moment later, the major's glance meets that of Robin in recognition.

The audience of one has suddenly become the focus of the drama,
contemplated both by the new leader and by the deposed one. Indeed,
at the climactic moment of the tale, Robin finds himself the center
of attention for the crowd in general. Accordingly, when the adventures of the night pass through his consciousness, culminating in "a
perception of tremendous ridicule" that leaves him with "a sort of
mental inebriety," Robin's perspective includes a dawning recognition
of his foolish part "in the whole scene." The reprise of the laughter
that has followed him throughout the evening, carefully orchestrated
by Hawthorne, comes complete with evidence that the people are now
looking at Robin as they laugh, and that he is aware of himself as
target. Hearing the sound of sluggish merriment, Robin turns and
sees the watchman "rubbing his eyes, and drowsily enjoying the lad's
amazement." Silvery laughter accompanied by a twitch at his arm

causes Robin to turn again; "a saucy eye met his, and he saw the lady of the scarlet petticoat." The innkeeper, laughing dryly, stands "on tiptoe in the crowd" to get a better look at Robin. And the man of the "sepulchral hems," almost overcome with "convulsive merriment," gazes at Robin from a balcony across the street. The people of the town, not just those who are identified but "all who had made sport of him that night," are laughing at *our* protagonist, momentarily the central character of *their* scene. As the laughter spreads contagiously through the crowd, it finally seizes Robin, who gives "a shout of laughter that echoed through the street." Amid a chorus of uncontrollable laughter, Robin's shout is the loudest of all.

As the culmination of laughter directed at him, Robin's laugh is one of recognition and self-recognition, based on the perception that what has happened makes him a unique object of mockery. His role in this climactic scene of the drama is to outdo the crowd in laughing at him. Robin is not, it is important to note, laughing at the major. He does not, it is important to recall, join the pitiless march when the leader gives a sign to move forward. As the crowd surges on "in counterfeited pomp, in senseless uproar, in frenzied merriment, trampling all on an old man's heart," Robin remains behind in "a silent street." History has swept by him (cruel in its excesses, not to be denied in its movement), stopped briefly to demonstrate his complex relation to it, then passed on leaving Robin shaken and subdued, the sense of identity he had hoped to establish swept away beyond recall.

Significantly, Robin neither repudiates the major nor castigates the crowd. His immediate impulse, understandable and human, is to return home. With an irony made possible by his new perspective on the events of the evening, he says to his companion that thanks to him "and to my other friends, I have at last met my kinsman, and he will scarcely desire to see my face again." Robin's final words in the tale are "I begin to grow weary of a town life, Sir. Will you show me the way to the ferry?" The suggestion that he might have an alternative to going home comes from this gentleman who has befriended him: if Robin continues in his desire to depart, the gentleman will assist him on his journey in a few days. If, however, "you prefer to remain with us"—and Hawthorne archly hints at a world of meaning as he uses his characterizing word one last time—"perhaps, as you are a shrewd youth, you may rise in the world, without the help of

your kinsman, Major Molineux." With a sense of his own foolishness,
of the major's downfall, and of the mocking laughter of the crowd
swirling in his mind, Robin makes no reply. But the implications of
the gentlemen's statement are clear: if he is to succeed "in the world,"
Robin must put away his cudgel, dispense with the anticipated patronage of his kinsman, and establish his own identity in a society restively
intent upon doing the same.

Chapter Five

The Scarlet Letter

Measuring the Letter

In his study of Nathaniel Hawthorne, Henry James makes a series of comparative statements about *The Scarlet Letter* and John Gibson Lockhart's *Adam Blair* that afford an instructive context for discussing Hawthorne's romance. Pervading both narratives, James points out, are the "manners of a rigidly theological society"; in both, too, a minister commits adultery and is driven to public confession by remorse. The stories, he sees, differ greatly in tone and treatment. Lockhart "was struck with the warmth of the subject that offered itself to him, and Hawthorne with its coldness; the one with its glow, its sentimental interest—the other with its shadow, its moral interest." Whereas Lockhart delineates "the history of the passion," Hawthorne gives us "the history of its sequel." Despite such differences, however, James finds "a great deal of analogy" between the two works.[1]

James is typically perceptive in defining the narrative quality of Lockhart's novel and Hawthorne's romance. To consider the relationship of *Adam Blair* and *The Scarlet Letter* afresh, however, is to encounter some surprises regarding the fundamental basis of his comparison. A reading of *Adam Blair* reveals significant differences of plot, characterization, and structure. The first half of the novel, which leads one gradually to the moment of adultery, offers no parallels to *The Scarlet Letter*. Adam Blair, a widower-minister with a young daughter, is visited by Charlotte Campbell, a near relative of the dead Mrs. Blair, who is temporarily separated from her husband. For half the novel, and it is decidedly the better half, Lockhart prefigures the adulterous union. In this first half inheres the passion of the narrative; though he is at times merely clever, Lockhart achieves a sense of the "grossly human and vulgarly natural" of which James speaks by means of carefully arranged incident and a prose redolent with suppressed emotion.

The second half of *Adam Blair*, which one might expect to display some striking resemblance to *The Scarlet Letter*, offers little but significant differences. Immediately after the act of adultery Adam Blair falls ill; before he has fully recovered, Charlotte contracts his illness and dies. Her husband then returns and says to a trembling and contrite Adam Blair, "Sir, you are a young man, and I believe you have already repented of your offense. I forgive you,—I forgive you, freely, sir." Adam Blair proceeds without delay to a meeting of the Presbytery, makes a public confession, and resigns his pastoral office; for the next ten years he tills the soil, until, finally, he accepts a call back to his old parish, where he serves as a model of humility and holiness for twenty additional years.

The differences with respect to *The Scarlet Letter* are obvious. For one thing, the interrelationships of the characters are radically distinct from those in Hawthorne's romance. Mr. Campbell is no Chillingworth, Charlotte is no Hester Prynne, and Adam Blair's daughter is no Pearl—all of which suggests, in a manifold sense, that *Adam Blair* contains no scarlet letter. Nor is the Scottish community that of Puritan Boston; again the difference, laden with significance for any comparison of the two narratives, can be said to be the scarlet letter. Moreover, Hawthorne focuses his entire dramatic attention on a segment of experience which Lockhart subordinates to other concerns. Adam Blair's sin and illness, Charlotte's death, her husband's forgiveness, and Blair's confession follow one another very quickly. Lockhart moves rapidly to the confession scene, then to an extended treatment of Blair's years of pastoral penance. Hawthorne, beginning well after Dimmesdale's and Hester's adultery, presents a drama of exacerbated conscience, self-consuming vengeance, and protean pride which takes its special form from an inability to confess. Confession in *Adam Blair* marks an important turning point in the action; confession in *The Scarlet Letter* marks the end, the final revelation. Once again, the difference is the scarlet letter.

Even so brief an examination suggests fundamental differences between *Adam Blair* and *The Scarlet Letter*. As his remarks make clear, James examines carefully into differences of tone and treatment as a way of characterizing the special quality of each narrative. But he does perceive a substantial analogy between the two works, and one might well wonder how he arrives at and sustains that judgment. Part of the answer may be that *The Scarlet Letter* contains (among other things) such a definitive portrait of a fallen minister that any novel with a similar character is likely to suggest a comparison. More specifically, however, James perceives so great an analogy because of the way in which he reads *The Scarlet Letter*.

As James sees it, Dimmesdale is to *The Scarlet Letter* what Adam Blair is to *Adam Blair*. He reads *The Scarlet Letter* as if it were a novel entitled *Arthur Dimmesdale*. "The story, indeed," he says, "is in a secondary degree that of Hester Prynne; she becomes, really, after the first scene, an accessory figure.... It is upon her guilty lover that the author projects most frequently the cold, thin rays of his fitfully-moving lantern, which makes here and there a little luminous circle, on the edge of which hovers the livid and sinister figure of the injured and retributive husband." Because he views Dimmesdale as central to *The Scarlet Letter*, with Hester largely "an accessory figure" and Chillingworth "on the edge" of Hawthorne's circle of consideration, James is able to see a basic analogy between Hawthorne's romance and *Adam Blair*. Although he perceives that tone and manner differ, both books are to him stories of "a Calvinist minister who becomes the lover of a married woman, is overwhelmed with remorse at his misdeed, and makes a public confession of it."

What James does not see is what one might call the scarlet letterness of *The Scarlet Letter*. Or, rather, seeing it virtually everywhere he looks, he objects to it as contrived symbolism. Either way, he fails to envision the scarlet letter, in its various manifestations, as the center of Hawthorne's romance. We have since learned to read *The Scarlet Letter* with the letter itself, in the words of Charles Feidelson, Jr., as "the very focus" of the narrative; in this light, "every character, in effect, reenacts the 'Custom House' scene in which Hawthorne himself contemplated the letter...." As Feidelson says (in words that take on here an unintentional irony), "the author's *donnee*, as James would call it, is ... a symbol whose inherent meaning is *The Scarlet Letter*. The world that the writer seeks is generated by contemplation of the symbol...."[2] Hawthorne's "*donnee*" is indeed the scarlet letter— although James, as we have seen, takes another view of the matter. And because of this, *The Scarlet Letter*, as an achieved work of art, has little analogy with *Adam Blair*. Only by making Dimmesdale central to the romance or by forgetting that he takes his existence

from the totality of his fictional world can one find notable similarities
between the two narratives. Because of the way in which he reads
The Scarlet Letter, James is consistent in pointing out an analogy.
Because of the way in which we have come to read *The Scarlet Letter*,
we cannot accept his conclusion. At the center of *The Scarlet Letter*
stands the letter itself, pervasive and all-important, defining the dramatic contours of the narrative.

The implications of Hawthorne's "finding" the scarlet letter in
the Custom House are of considerable importance to the narrative
and to the symbolic status of the letter itself. For, in claiming to
have found the letter prior to the story, Hawthorne is of course
claiming to have found it after the story. The letter has supposedly
survived the world which brought it into existence and gave it
meaning: two hundred years have passed since the day of Hester
Prynne, Arthur Dimmesdale, and Roger Chillingworth; gone are
the royal governors, the magistrates, and the Puritan divines; gone,
too, are the scaffold, the marketplace, and the church in which Arthur
Dimmesdale delivered his great election sermon. The people and
the things are dead. But the letter—as a physical object—remains.
Hawthorne notes this "affair of fine red cloth, much worn and faded,"
notes the old fashioned stitching and the remains of gold embroidery,
and tells us that "by an accurate measurement, each limb proved to
be precisely three inches and a quarter in length." He begins, in
short, by emphasizing the literal existence of the letter—its palpable,
physical reality, its very measureableness. Like any effective symbol,
the scarlet letter achieves its symbolic status not in spite of but by
reason of its literal texture. Before anything else, Hawthorne seems
to say, this is a scarlet letter; because of that, it is capable of further
meaning. The letter will have to carry the burden of the tale. And
Hawthorne has taken a first step to insure its capacity to do so by
making it seem more real than any other part of his story.

Only after establishing and emphasizing the literalness of the
letter (an emphasis sustained throughout the narrative itself) does
Hawthorne in "The Custom-House" hint at the "deep meaning, most
worthy of interpretation,... which, as it were, streamed forth from
the mystic symbol" and refer to his "absorbing contemplation" of the
letter. Having found, examined, measured ("precisely"), and contemplated the letter, he can begin. And he begins, as we know, by

focusing immediately on the bright and brilliant letter worn for the first time by Hester Prynne and seen for the first time by the people of Boston. The scarlet letter serves as a vestige of a world that was and thereby as the entry to a world that will be.

The Scaffold Scenes

At the beginning, middle, and end of *The Scarlet Letter* stand Hawthorne's three scaffold scenes. Much emphasis has been placed upon them, and justly so; to know these scenes well is to have a purchase on a romance which is remarkable for its synthesis of elements. Of large structural and thematic significance, each of the scaffold scenes brings together in a moment of moral, emotional, and psychological tension the major characters and forces of the story; concomitantly, each scene centers attention in a dramatic manner on the scarlet letter.

The first scaffold scene, we recall, takes place at midday. For this, as the beadle proclaims, is "the righteous Colony of the Massachusetts, where iniquity is dragged out into the sunshine." As Hawthorne constructs the scene, Hester Prynne stands on the scaffold holding her infant, the people stand below, and the leaders of the community—civil officers, magistrates, ministers—stand above on a balcony. The inhabitants of Boston are thus divided for this scene—the leaders apart and above; and such a division serves Hawthorne's purpose in characterizing both the officials and the people as component parts of this drama.

The officials, clearly, have authority in the matter. Earlier, a group of women outside the jail have muttered about the leniency of Hester Prynne's sentence; in assembly in the marketplace, however, established authority is unchallenged. The leaders of the community—notably Governor Bellingham, the Reverend Mr. Wilson, and the Reverend Mr. Dimmesdale—feel the responsibility of exhorting, commanding Hester to confess the name of her partner. Doubtless, says Hawthorne, these are good men, "just and sage." But out of all humanity, he continues, "it would not have been easy to select the same number of wise and virtuous persons, who should be less capable of sitting in judgment on an erring woman's heart, and disentangling its mesh of good and evil, than the sages of rigid aspect

towards whom Hester now turned her face." Indeed, Hester seems
convinced "that whatever sympathy she might expect lay in the
larger and warmer heart of the multitude."

The idea that sympathy and warmth come from the "people" is,
as we have seen, at the very center of Hawthorne's democratic and
artistic faith. Committed to a belief in the value of humanity, he
would respect the "universal throb" of the human heart and regard
the "magnetic chain of humanity" as virtually sacred. But it is the
feelings rather than the ideas or perceptions of humanity that are to
be trusted. As Hawthorne says in *The Scarlet Letter*: "when an un-
instructed multitude attempts to see with its eyes, it is exceedingly
apt to be deceived." But when it forms its judgment, "as it usually
does, on the intuitions of its great and warm heart, the conclusions
thus attained are often so profound and so unerring, as to possess the
character of truths supernaturally revealed."

Strong language, this, expressing Hawthorne's fervent commitment
to the collective heart of humanity as a fundamental source of wisdom. But, as Hawthorne sees and often says in his tales of colonial
times, this was "not an age of delicacy." The Puritans are stern,
somber, and repressive; their children belong "to the most intolerant
brood that ever lived." In portraying a Puritan multitude, Hawthorne
faces the problem of characterizing sternness and somberness while
at the same time remaining true to his faith in humanity. He sports
with the Puritans in his description of the Election holiday, saying
that they compressed their mirth and public joy into this festal
season and thereby so far dispelled their customary gloom that for
one day "they appeared scarcely more grave than most other com-
munities at a period of general affliction." Still, despite the lack of
popular merriment on this holiday, "the great, honest face of the
people smiled, grimly, perhaps, but widely too." Hawthorne sees
through Puritan severity to a fundamental humanity; he may castigate
or sport with the Puritan posture of grimness, but he cannot repudiate
(he can do nothing but admire) the essential humanity that lies
under the sad-colored garments of those he is describing. The public is
despotic in its temper, he says, incorporating the specific example of
the Puritans under this general principle; "it is capable of denying
common justice, when too strenuously demanded as a right"; but
when, "as despots love to have it," an appeal is made to its generosity,
the public frequently awards "more than justice." The seat of gen-

erosity is the heart. And in perhaps no other place does Hawthorne repeat so insistently his faith in the great, warm heart of the people as in *The Scarlet Letter.*

The center of attention in the first scaffold scene is, of course, the letter worn by Hester Prynne. "The point which drew all eyes, and, as it were, transfigured the wearer," says Hawthorne, was the "SCARLET LETTER, so fantastically embroidered and illuminated upon her bosom." In this scene the community officially discovers the letter; given the moral imperative that iniquity should be "dragged out into the sunshine," the stares of the townspeople, the "thousand unrelenting eyes . . . concentred" on Hester's bosom, constitute a kind of public meditation on the nature of sinfulness and guilt. Toward the end of the scene the Reverend Mr. Wilson, carefully prepared for the occasion, preaches a discourse on sin, "in all its branches, but with continuous reference to the ignominious letter. So forcibly did he dwell upon this symbol," writes Hawthorne, that it assumed new terrors in the people's imagination "and seemed to derive its scarlet hue from the flames of the infernal pit." The letter dominates the scene; it sets Hester apart to such an extent that those who had known her previously "were now impressed as if they beheld her for the first time"; it has the effect of "a spell" which puts her in a "sphere by herself."

As Hester stands on the scaffold, tall, "lady-like," with "dark and abundant hair," the crowd notes with some astonishment that her beauty shines out and makes a halo of her misfortune. From the beginning of her exposure to public view, Hester bears her ordeal with haughty agony. Undeniably she flaunts the letter; yet Hawthorne seems to sympathize with the emotional understanding shown by the youngest matron outside the jail when she says that the pang of the letter will be always in Hester's heart. Alone in the world with the symbol and consequence of her sin, Hester dons an armor of pride that is also a mantle of suffering.

In this initial scene Roger Chillingworth appears on the outskirts of the crowd in a motley civilized and savage costume and soon after experiences an unsettling shock of recognition. Once Chillingworth has recognized Hester on the scaffold, "a writhing horror" twists across his face "like a snake"; for one moment his features are visibly convulsed by a powerful emotion which he quickly controls by an effort of will. Then "the convulsion grew almost imperceptible, and finally subsided into the depths of his nature." When he sees that he is recognized by Hester, "he slowly and calmly raised his finger, made a gesture with it in the air, and laid it on his lips."

Chillingworth has repressed his instinctive emotional response to the situation. The snakelike convulsion that expressed his feelings has been pushed deep into his being where it remains as the source of monomania and revenge. And his first message to Hester Prynne is the time-honored gesture of silence and secrecy, the finger raised to the lips. Thus, from the beginning Chillingworth has possessed himself of "the lock and key" of Hester's silence. From the beginning, apparently, he has "resolved not to be pilloried beside her on her pedestal of shame."[3]

On the scaffold with the other leaders of the community stands Arthur Dimmesdale, whose role as Hester's pastor and spiritual mentor forces him to address her and to ask for the name of her partner in sin. In the terrible ambivalence of his position Dimmesdale wants Hester to name him even as he does not want to be named. He would have her pin the letter on him, but he will not reveal his partnership in it. "Be not silent from any mistaken pity and tenderness," he says to Hester; though your partner in sin

were to step down from a high place, and stand there beside thee, on thy pedestal of shame, yet better were it so, than to hide a guilty heart through life. What can thy silence do for him, except it tempt him—yea, compel him, as it were—to add hypocrisy to sin? Heaven hath granted thee an open ignominy, that thereby thou mayest work out an open triumph over the evil within thee, and the sorrow without. Take heed how thou deniest to him—who, perchance, hath not the courage to grasp it for himself— the bitter, but wholesome, cup that is now presented to thy lips!

To the multitude, Dimmesdale's appeal seems powerful beyond withstanding. Proof against such emotional eloquence, however, is the man who has it in him to frame the appeal. Even in the first scaffold scene Hawthorne shows forth the deep ambivalence of Dimmesdale's position: the minister would like to be named and known for what he is, an adulterer. Thus, when he speaks the above words to Hester Prynne, the words themselves are true, pathetically so. Being named would bring shame and disgrace, but also the relief of standing clear in one's own identity; moreover, in this community, this "righteous" colony, there is an undeniably correct course of action for Dimmesdale to take—sin and iniquity, he knows, ought to be dragged out into the broad light of noonday. His appeal to Hester is thus pathetically sincere; he is asking her to help him in a way he cannot help himself.

But we gradually come to see why he cannot help himself. For, with all his physical and psychological debility, which makes him seem weak and gives him the posture of a moral invalid deserving of pity (or perhaps contempt), Dimmesdale is afflicted with a devious pride. He cannot surrender an identity which brings him the adulation of his parishioners, the respect and praise of his peers. His contortions in the guise of humility only add to the public admiration which, in turn, feeds an ego fundamentally intent on itself.

After the appeal of Dimmesdale and the harsher stricture of Mr. Wilson have failed to make Hester speak, Chillingworth moves closer to the scaffold and imperiously bids her to name the father of her child. " 'I will not speak!' answered Hester, turning pale as death, but responding to this voice, which she too surely recognized. 'And my child must seek a heavenly Father; she shall never know an earthly one!' " After gesturing first for silence, Roger Chillingworth has thus spoken in this first scaffold scene, lending his voice, for personal reasons, to the communal desire for Hester to name her partner. But the gesture of silence has fitted Hester's mood—*The Scarlet Letter* will develop amid the dry regions of silence.

The first scaffold scene concludes (at the end of chapter 3) with a final emphasis on the letter. When Hester is led back to prison, those who peered after her whispered "that the scarlet letter threw a lurid gleam along the dark passage-way of the interior." The Reverend Mr. Wilson has put Hester's letter at the center of his formal discourse; Dimmesdale and Chillingworth have spoken to Hester, overtly and covertly. And the private drama, depending for its form on the silence of the actors, has begun in the midst of communal meditation and a public demand for confession. Thus the terms of the private drama stand opposed to the efforts of the community to have everything immediately out in the open. Those who see the community as a source of all wrong in the romance forget that silence—breeding pride, hypocrisy, and vengeance—is the imposition and the condition of the private drama. But, of course, only in this particular community would silence invoke such subterranean suffering.

Hawthorne's second scaffold scene, which comes precisely at the middle of his romance, turns the moral structure of the first inside out. This is Dimmesdale's scene, staged at midnight rather than at midday. In terms of Puritan orthodoxy it can be nothing but a scene of pseudo-confession, a "mockery of penitence," in Hawthorne's words, a "vain show of expiation." Again Hawthorne emphasizes the letter, this time by stressing Dimmesdale's infatuation with his own guilt. During one of his nights of penance, the thought of going to the scaffold has come over Dimmesdale. Attiring himself with "as much care as if it had been for public worship, and precisely in the same manner," he makes his way to the deserted marketplace. Alone on the scaffold, he feels that the entire world is gazing at the scarlet letter over his heart. His shriek of agony, a good deal more modulated than at first it seems, awakens Governor Bellingham and Mistress Hibbins; but neither sees him on the scaffold. The Reverend Mr. Wilson, returning from the deathbed of Governor Winthrop, walks slowly by the scaffold without noticing Dimmesdale. For darkness is not the medium in which the Puritans recognize sin. Darkness corresponds to secrecy; the midnight scaffold scene is an extension of the private drama. Accordingly, it involves Dimmesdale, Chillingworth, Hester, and Pearl in a unique and lurid confrontation.

Returning homeward with Pearl from the same errand which has brought the Reverend Mr. Wilson and Roger Chillingworth to minister to the final spiritual and bodily needs of Governor Winthrop, Hester is summoned onto the scaffold by Dimmesdale. As he stands with Hester and Pearl, the minister feels the vitality of life other than his own, but he shrinks back from Pearl's request to stand thus together in the broad light of the following noon. The meteor that then lights up the sky bathes them "in the noon of that strange and solemn splendor"; but it is, of course, a false noon, unnatural, lacking moral efficacy.

Hawthorne puts his meteor to good use. It leads him to refer to the New England habit of reading history as God's Providence— of interpreting natural phenomena as signs of special meaning from God to his chosen people. But the massive self-projection of Dimmesdale's guilt also finds embodiment in the meteor. What shall we say, asks Hawthorne, when one man "discovers a revelation, addressed to himself alone," written across the sky: "In such a case, it could only be the symptom of a highly disordered mental state, when a man, rendered morbidly self contemplative by long, interior, and secret pain, had extended his egotism over the whole expanse of nature, until the firmament itself should appear no more than a fitting page for his soul's history and fate." Thus Dimmesdale sees a great scarlet *A* in the sky; cosmic ego evokes cosmic evidence of guilt. But Hawthorne does not dispense with his meteor without a final touch that corroborates Dimmesdale's sense of its shape by illustrating the collective ego of the community. People in the town, Dimmesdale hears the next day, have likewise seen the *A*. "As our good Governor Winthrop was made an angel this past night," the sexton tells him, "it was doubtless held fit that there should be some notice thereof." Hawthorne provides the meteor; history and conscience do the rest. And the public and the private worlds in the romance remain apart and opposed.

The same glance that reveals to Dimmesdale the great letter in the sky discloses Chillingworth at the foot of the scaffold. Lighted by the meteor, Chillingworth's features take on a new expression, or, as Hawthorne says, perhaps "the physician was not careful then, as at all other times, to hide the malevolence with which he looked upon his victim." In a setting suggesting to Hester and Dimmesdale the day of judgment, Chillingworth seems "the arch-fiend" himself, come to claim his own. So intense is Dimmesdale's perception of Chillington that, when utter blackness succeeds the vivid light of the meteor, the smiling and scowling face of the physician seems somehow to remain, "painted on the darkness," the only reality in an "annihilated" world. "Come good Sir, and my dear friend," says Chillingworth: "let me lead you home." "I will go home with you," replies Dimmesdale. Thus he goes "home" with the man he fears and hates, the man who has discovered the secret of the scarlet letter and whose principle of being has come to depend on its remaining a secret. The nadir of Dimmesdale's moral struggle stands as the moment of triumph for the avenging Chillingworth.

Hawthorne prepares for his third and final scaffold scene by refocusing attention on Hester's scarlet letter. After seven years it has become an object of familiarity in the town. But in the marketplace on Election day are many people from the country who have heard exaggerated rumors about the letter without ever having seen it. They throng about Hester Prynne "with rude and boorish intrusive-

ness." Noting the curiosity of the crowd, sailors "thrust their sun-
burnt and desperado-looking faces into the ring" and Indians fasten
"their snake-like black eyes on Hester's bosom." Lastly, their interest
in a "wornout subject languidly reviving itself, by sympathy with
what they saw others feel," the people of the town torment Hester
Prynne, "perhaps more than all the rest, with their cool, well-acquainted
gaze at her familiar shame." Thus, just prior to the scaffold scene,
"the burning letter . . . had strangely become the centre of more
remark and excitement, and was thus made to sear her breast more
painfully than at any time since the first time she put it on."

The ensuing scene takes its form unexpectedly, amid the wonder
of the spectators. Dimmesdale again takes the initiative, this time
at midday; he beckons Hester and Pearl to ascend the scaffold with
him. Hester's strength is necessary if he is to be "guided by the
will which God hath granted" him. At the hour of his greatest public
success and triumph ("Never, on New England soil, had stood the
man so honored by his mortal brethren as the preacher!"), Arthur
Dimmesdale, the spiritual darling of the people, ascends the scaffold
with Hester and Pearl. Once again, Roger Chillingworth is present:
in the first scaffold scene, he would know the name of Hester's partner; in the second, he does know; and, in the third, he tries desperately
to keep others from knowing. Do not perish in dishonor, he whispers
in savage fear to Dimmesdale; "I can yet save you." But Dimmesdale
repudiates Chillingworth as the tempter, and with the help of God
(and Hester) moves toward the freedom of the scaffold. "Hadst thou
sought the whole earth over," says Chillingworth, quite in keeping
with the dramatic logic of the narrative, "there was no one place so
secret,—no high place nor lowly place, where thou couldst have escaped
me,—save on this very scaffold!" And Dimmesdale thanks God, as-
sures a doubting Hester that he is doing God's will, and reveals his
own scarlet letter to the astonished multitude.

In contrast to the second scaffold scene, which Chillingworth comes
to dominate, this final scene remains under the control of Dimmesdale. Perhaps convinced by the towering eloquence of his Election
Day sermon, he insists on viewing the world as the creation of a
merciful Providence.[4] He cannot agree with Hester when she hopes
they may meet in eternity, having "ransomed one another" with all
their woe. Only God knows, says Dimmesdale, returning to the subject of his own spiritual drama,

and He is merciful! He hath proved his mercy, most of all, in my afflictions. By giving me this burning torture to bear upon my breast! By sending yonder dark and terrible old man, to keep the torture always at red-heat! By bringing me hither, to die this death of triumphant ignominy before the people! Had either of these agonies been wanting, I had been lost for ever! Praised be his name! His will be done! Farewell!

The paradox of mercy by affliction thus makes possible the "triumphant ignominy" of Dimmesdale's death. Thankful for the *A*, for Chillingworth, and for the scaffold, the minister has projected an intense religious odyssey, with himself in the heroic central role.[5] His statement that he is "the one sinner in the world" attests to the fusion of guilt and ego that has characterized his life even as it proclaims the omnipotence of the God who can save him. A curious mixture of theology and self, Dimmesdale's ascending faith distances him from Hester and leaves him assured of his own salvation.

Ambivalence and Achievement

The special quality of Hawthorne's achievement in *The Scarlet Letter* derives from the essential duality or ambivalence of his fictional world and its component parts. In a number of tales, of course, Hawthorne had explored modes of ambiguity and ambivalence. Goodman Brown's adventure with evil and Mr. Hooper's black veil resist any consideration that does not take their complexity into account; "The Wedding-Knell" and "The Shaker Bridal" counterpose—even in their titles—the ideas of marriage and death as aspects of the same ceremony. In *The Scarlet Letter*, however, Hawthorne sustains a vision of the ambivalent nature of reality beyond all he had done before and in a way he was never to do again. Hester, Dimmesdale, Chillingworth, the scarlet letter itself—all signify more than one thing; all must be considered in more than one way. To some readers, Hester Prynne seems a virtual saint, a woman who walks in humility and patience; to others, she is an unbending woman of pride, who glories in her sin. Hawthorne provides material for both portraits. He dramatizes the double (or multiple) nature of every important character, thing, and event in his romance. And one must take this doubleness into full account, must see that the coherence of Hawthorne's narrative emanates from duality, that only in terms of ever-deepening ambivalence is experience possible in the world of this romance. As a literary document which stands at a particular place in Hawthorne's career, *The Scarlet Letter* has all the finality, all the completedness, of a fact. As a masterpiece of literary art, however, it generates meaning by a technique of dynamic interrelationships, meaning that is for the reader in a perpetual state of becoming.

The duality of experience in *The Scarlet Letter*—embodied in language, character, and theme—takes frequently the forms of paradox and irony. Hester Prynne, as we have seen, stands in the marketplace with a "burning blush, and yet a haughty smile"; her beauty shines out and makes "a halo of her misfortune"; on the scaffold she takes refuge in public exposure. Moreover, she has embroidered her letter fancifully; she has adorned the symbol of her sin almost as if she were parading that symbol and that sin before the public. Yet the young matron outside the jail whispers meaningfully that "not a stitch in that embroidered letter, but she has felt it in her heart." Hester, one sees, glories in her letter and suffers in her glory; and only by seeing the relationship between her suffering and glory does one do justice to Hawthorne's characterization of her.

Again, Pearl is said to be "the direct consequence of sin." As the scarlet letter incarnate, Pearl brings both pain and pleasure to Hester. "She is my happiness—she is my torture," says Hester; "she is the scarlet letter, only capable of being loved, and so endowed with a million-fold the power of retribution for my sin." The child, says Dimmesdale in the governor's palace, was meant for a blessing and for a retribution. And in the child may be seen perpetuated the "warfare of Hester's spirit." For the child's mother bears herself in town with what "might be pride, but was so like humility" that it softens the public attitude toward her. The "emblem and product of sin," the "scarlet letter in another form," the "unpremeditated offshoot of a passionate moment," Pearl cavorts through the romance embodying the seamless garment of joy and suffering that is the fate of Hester Prynne. Only when the drama is played out can Pearl enjoy in some far-off land the happiness of a normal—and apparently domestic—existence.

The penance imposed by the community has an ironic effect on Hester, changing her life "in a great measure, from passion and feeling, to thought." Alone and independent by decree, Hester's mind ranges widely, questing and probing into areas of thought concerning which the Puritan world would allow small latitude. Indeed, says

Hawthorne, "she assumed a freedom of speculation, then common enough on the other side of the Atlantic, but which our forefathers, had they known of it, would have held to be a deadlier crime than that stigmatized by the scarlet letter. In her lonesome cottage,... thoughts visited her, such as dared to enter no other dwelling in New England." The place of women in society, the "dark question" of the woman and the world concern her mightily. But she wanders "without a clew in the dark labyrinth of mind," beset by problems which arise because her heart "had lost its regular and healthy throb." Hawthorne suggests the quality of Hester's confusion and despair by saying that at times "a fearful doubt strove to possess her soul, whether it were not better to send Pearl at once to heaven, and go herself to such futurity as Eternal Justice should provide." Then, with the emphasis of a one-sentence paragraph, he says: "The scarlet letter had not done its office."

Hester, clearly, cannot hate her sin. And because of that she can only embrace all that the letter brings to her—suffering and joy, solitude, challenge, and a resulting independence of spirit. Meant by the community to have a single signification, to be an emblem of adultery, the letter takes on additional meanings which both reflect and contribute to the ambivalence of Hester's total experience. Moreover, "by making the letter beautiful," Nina Baym points out, the artist in Hester denies its literal meaning and subverts "the intention of the magistrates who condemn her to wear it."[6] As a symbol of an adultress, the *A* ought to constitute a penance that will be the handmaiden of penitence—certainly that is the official Puritan hope. And Hester seems to undertake a life of penitence: "the blameless purity of her life, during all these years in which she had been set apart for infamy" is "reckoned largely in her favor," as is her uncomplaining submission to the dogged uncharitableness of the public. Without complaint she assists the victims of poverty, even though her payment for food and clothing is a bitter taunt or sarcastic jibe. And at times of general or individual sorrow, Hester, "the outcast of society," responds warmly and naturally:

She came, not as a guest, but as a rightful inmate, into the household that was darkened by trouble;... There glimmered the embroidered letter, with comfort in its unearthly ray. Elsewhere the token of sin, it was the taper of the sick-chamber. It had even thrown its gleam, in the sufferer's hard extremity, across the verge of time. . . . In such emergencies, Hester's nature showed itself warm and rich; a well-spring of human tenderness, unfailing to every real demand, and inexhaustible by the largest. Her breast, with its badge of shame, was but the softer pillow for the head that needed one. She was self-ordained a Sister of Mercy; or, we may rather say, the world's heavy hand had so ordained her, when neither the world nor she looked forward to this result. The letter was the symbol of her calling. Such helpfulness was found in her,—so much power to do, and power to sympathize,—that many people refused to interpret the scarlet A by its original signification. They said that it meant Able; so strong was Hester Prynne, with a woman's strength.

The world has ordained her a Sister of Mercy; to the world the *A* might mean Able or even Angel. But despite all these acts of helpfulness, despite a tenderness and sympathy unqualified in any way by Hawthorne's language, Hester is not contrite: "The scarlet letter," as he says, "had not done its office." The iron grace of Hester's life for seven years, a discipline bred on suppressed emotion, leads directly to the forest interview with Arthur Dimmesdale. The letter *A*, we see, might also stand for Arthur—which would double its meaning of adultery and the ambivalence of Hester's attitude toward it. The community has pinned the initial of her lover on her breast, then wondered for seven years who he might be.[7]

In the forest scene Hester must lend her strength to Dimmesdale; and, in the lending, we see that seven years of public penance have not touched the image she has of her action with him: "What we did had a consecration of its own. We felt it so! We said so to each other." Believing this, Hester has no grounds for penitence; her act with Dimmesdale was different, she affirms, uniquely consecrated and hence not within the province of ordinary law. We see (and the perception goes a long way toward an understanding of the basis of Hawthorne's characterization of Hester) that seven years of penance have not been efficacious because they have fallen wide of the mark; Hester has lived through these years with unshaken faith in the passion which won for her—in the eyes of the public—a badge of dishonor. She has worn her letter with all the strength, determination, and ambivalence of a person punished by the many for a wrong that only the few can see as a higher, freer good. Made to live according to the letter of the law, she remains aloof and, ultimately, becomes opposed to the spirit of the law. Hester believes, as lovers have always believed, in the supremacy of her passion. And it is Hawthorne's achievement to make her appeal to passion seem fresh, to lend it an emotional eloquence rendered all the more persuasive by the desert places of suffering through which she has lived in uncomplaining silence. In the forest Hester removes her symbolic *A* (no need for the symbol when Arthur is alone with her, when they will redefine the very act by agreeing to run away), lets her dark hair tumble down, and demonstrates that seven years of ignominy have left her a resolute priestess of a private cult. Dimmesdale, the public priest, is seduced (perhaps again); tempted by winds of heresy, he enters again the private world of passion in a final psychic grab at identity.

Hester's decision to accompany Dimmesdale marks the culmination of a lengthy process in her life. For seven years, says Hawthorne, she has wandered "without rule or guidance, in a moral wilderness; as vast, as intricate and shadowy" as the gloomy and untamed forest in which she and Dimmesdale are deciding their fate. She has roamed freely, as it were, criticizing human institutions, "whatever priests or legislators had established." Shame, despair, and solitude had been her stern and wild teachers; "and they had made her strong, but taught her much amiss." Thus, concludes Hawthorne (with a characteristic qualification which forces certitude into a posture of appearance), "we seem to see that, as regarded Hester Prynne, the whole seven years of outlaw and ignominy had been little other than a preparation for this very hour."

The consequences of the letter as penance are thus just the reverse of what the Puritan community thought they would be. A sin of passion, nursed by the memory of its sacredness, has blossomed into a sin of purpose. Hester, as we have seen, has virtually been preparing for such a moment of decision; but Dimmesdale, broken and ensnared by hypocrisy as he is, has never contemplated such a step in his wildest dreams. He embraces his sin once again, now willfully, with all the ardor of a convert to a new faith.

The ambivalence of Dimmesdale's position is part and parcel of the total ambivalence of the romance. Because of his sin, he has undergone excruciating penance; if Chillingworth lives to torture him, Dimmesdale lives to be tortured. Yet the fundamental falseness of his position yields an idiom of anguish that stands him very well in his professional life. His sermons, for example, are models of efficacy: the more he reviles himself as a sinner (in general terms, from the

security of the pulpit), the more his congregation elevates him to
new heights of spirituality and thinks comparatively of its own un-
worthiness. His anguish is convincing, compelling, and genuine, although it springs from and compounds his hypocrisy—even because
of his knowledge that it springs from and compounds his hypocrisy.
The irony is that Dimmesdale's sermons give spiritual assistance to
everyone but himself. On the morning after his midnight vigil on
the scaffold, he preaches a sermon "which was held to be the richest
and most powerful, and the most replete with heavenly influences,
that had ever proceeded from his lips. Souls, it is said, more souls than
one, were brought to the truth by the efficacy of that sermon." Among
these souls, as we know, is that of the pure young maiden whom
Dimmesdale is sorely tempted to shock upon his return from the forest
interview with Hester Prynne.

The idea that sin may have beneficial consequences—and the implications of that idea—are more central to the theme of *The Marble
Faun* than to that of *The Scarlet Letter*. But the idea contributes to
the ambivalence of Hawthorne's masterpiece, especially in his characterization of Dimmesdale. Dimmesdale knows the manner in which his
vague pulpit confessions will be taken; he knows that they will em-
bellish the image of his spirituality in the public mind; yet he makes
these confessions, conscious that his very awareness of their power
makes them all the more false, conscious, too, that he is punishing
himself all the more and that his words will introduce people, by
whatever devious route, to the road of spiritual awareness and truth.
He goes so far as to wonder if a sinful man might have a mission to
remain in sin out of a zeal for the glory of God, if he saw that his
efficacy depended on his sinfulness. But Chillingworth, to whom he
speaks, can refute this argument in Dimmesdale's own terms (the
irony is that he should be called upon to do so): these men deceive
themselves, says Chillingworth; "Wouldst thou have me to believe,
O wise and pious friend, that a false show can be better—can be more
for God's glory, or man's welfare—than God's own truth?" And Dimmesdale drops the subject rather than make an overt case for hypocrisy.

Dimmesdale clearly suffers from an excess of self. His weakness
and suffering throughout most of the romance, as I suggested earlier,
have tended to blur for some readers the fact of his pride, which, like
his scarlet letter, lies beneath and gives special form to his mask of
saintliness. Self-condemnation, self-abnegation, and self-loathing are

the stimulants of Dimmesdale's psychic life; they constitute, as well, the price he must pay if he would not abdicate the self reverenced by the public. And that self—formed out of a communal wish to admire a young, pious, and learned minister—he cannot bring himself to renounce. That his private suffering contributes to the public mask of spirituality is a kind of masochistic dividend for him. Weak and proud, false and efficacious, the minister thus stumbles ever deeper and ever more self-consciously into thickets of hypocrisy. Perhaps the most telling example occurs during the forest interview when Dimmesdale inquires of Hester when the ship on which they now plan to sail is scheduled to depart and considers it "most fortunate" that it will not leave for four days. With a posture of reluctance, Hawthorne interprets the minister's thoughts—in order "to hold nothing back from the reader." Dimmesdale considers the departure date "very fortunate" because in three days he is to preach the Election Day sermon, "and, as such an occasion formed an honorable epoch in the life of a New England clergyman, he could not have chanced upon a more suitable mode and time of terminating his professional career. 'At least, they shall say of me,' thought this exemplary man, 'that I leave no public duty unperformed, nor ill performed!' " Hawthorne laments the fact that the minister could be "so miserably deceived": "We have had, and may still have, worse things to tell of him; but none, we apprehend, so pitiably weak; no evidence, at once so slight and irrefragable, of a subtle disease, that had long since begun to eat into the real substance of his character." To wear one face in private and another in public for a considerable period of time, Hawthorne concludes, leaves a man finally "bewildered as to which may be the true."

As the final step in a developing process, Hawthorne has shown us an absolutely stunning doubleness in the minister's character. Having chosen to breathe "the wild, free atmosphere of an unredeemed, unchristianized, lawless region," having undergone a "total change of dynasty and moral code," Dimmesdale reaffirms to himself (he does not mention it to Hester) the importance of the Election Day sermon. He wants to have it both ways, to leave, but to leave with his "public duty" well performed—which is to say, with the congregation marveling at their saintly and inspired minister. Let us note that Dimmesdale's motive here is characteristically secret. No sooner is he converted to Hester's romantic cult than he has an immediate private life outside it which gives him latitude to plan by himself, for himself. The psychological keenness informing Dimmesdale's transformation is of a high order. No matter what "religion" the minister professes, he serves ultimately the interests of one master—himself. Thus, in keeping with the brilliant economy of *The Scarlet Letter*, the moment at which Dimmesdale commits himself consciously to deadly liberating sin becomes the moment at which he secretly wishes to cap his public life with a final burst of eloquence on the most important occasion the Puritan community can offer.

Dimmesdale and Chillingworth, we may say, make each other possible in *The Scarlet Letter*. If Chillingworth were not present, it would almost be necessary for Dimmesdale to invent him. Conversely, with no Dimmesdale there could be no Chillingworth as we know him; the avenger requires the victim to make him what he is, just as the victim requires the avenger.

Chillingworth has made the torture of Dimmesdale the very principle of his existence. The minister's perception in the forest interview with Hester seems accurate: Chillingworth is the worst sinner of all; he has violated in cold blood the sanctity of a human heart—the great sin of all Hawthorne antagonists. He has used his skill as a physician to keep Dimmesdale alive so that he can continue to punish him spiritually and psychologically. On the seashore with Hester Prynne, Chillingworth agrees readily that it would have been better for Dimmesdale to die at once than to have survived seven years of suffering. For never, he says, "did mortal man suffer what this man has suffered. And all, all, in the sight of his worst enemy!" Chillingworth wreaks a terrible revenge upon Dimmesdale: seven years of consummate torture; seven years of willful, malicious, treacherous vengeance. And from the relationship of avenger and victim comes the only real passion of the narrative aside from that shown by Hester Prynne in her forest interview with Arthur Dimmesdale. When, after months (perhaps years) of intense observation, Chillingworth advances into Dimmesdale's room, stands directly in front of the sleeping minister, lays "his hand upon his bosom, and thrust[s] aside the vestment that, hitherto, had always covered it even from the professional eye," he climaxes an act of psychic rape on the passive minister. This is a moment of private revelation (like all instances of revelation in the romance it takes place at noon); Chillingworth has virtually overpowered Dimmesdale and taken the knowledge he wants. It throws him into rapture and ecstasy, into uncontrollable and frenzied gestures, into Satanic postures. An act of unholy passion has been perpetrated.

The ambivalent consequences of Chillingworth's revenge derive from the change in its pattern and motive. Precisely where the change occurs would be difficult to say; perhaps Chillingworth's discovery in Dimmesdale's chamber marks a moment of transition. But Chillingworth begins his search for Hester's partner in adultery, as he imagines, "with the severe and equal integrity of a judge, desirous only of truth, even as if the question involved no more than the air-drawn lines and figures of a geometrical problem, instead of human passions, and wrongs inflicted on himself." As he proceeds, however, "a terrible fascination, a kind of fierce, though still calm, necessity seized the old man within its gripe, and never set him free again, until he had done all its bidding." Shortly before his quest penetrates to the naked bosom of the sleeping minister, Chillingworth feels that "were it only for the art's sake, I must search this matter to the bottom."

After that episode, a stance of objectivity seems less evident; Chillingworth's revenge becomes more intense, more involved, more personal. And, like Dimmesdale's hypocrisy, it comes to fester and feed upon itself. When Hester asks if he has not tortured Dimmesdale enough, Chillingworth replies "No!—no!—He has but increased the debt." Chillingworth cries out against Dimmesdale in recognition of what his revenge has done to himself. He has been transformed from an earnest, studious, thoughtful man to a fiend whom Hester Prynne observes with a feeling of shock and wonder. Hawthorne leaves us in no doubt of the radical change: Chillingworth was "a striking evidence of man's faculty of transforming himself into a devil, if he will only, for a reasonable space of time, undertake a devil's office." He had "effected such a transformation by devoting himself, for seven years, to the constant analysis of a heart full of torture, and deriving his enjoyment thence, and adding fuel to those fiery tortures which he analyzed and gloated over."

But the point is that all this has, as Chillingworth himself says, "increased the debt." The arch-sinner of *The Scarlet Letter* has victimized himself, has caught himself on a vicious blade of revenge which cuts two ways. Though there can be no getting even for Chillingworth, he must constantly intensify his torture; yet the more he intensifies his torture, the more he destroys himself. To shield himself from the bruising reality of the situation, he recalls his "old faith, long forgotten," which explains the entire action as a drama of "dark necessity." Yet Chillingworth, for all his evil, admits to Hester that his was the first wrong—it was a mistake, he sees, to attempt to warm his heart and his hearth with a marriage to a young girl after commiting himself to a life of solitude and thought. The mistake has terrible consequences, but since it arose from a sense of loneliness and incompleteness, from a human longing for warmth, Hawthorne cannot help providing a context for understanding it. Chillingworth, too, takes the first step to break down the silence and secrecy among the characters by releasing Hester from her promise of concealing his identity. Chillingworth personifies the Hawthorne antagonist in all his essential pride and monomania; but he comes into the romance trailing clouds of weakness; we understand his villainy (in all its complexity) all the more by seeing in him betrayed vestiges of humanity.

The complex interrelationships of Hester Prynne, Dimmesdale, Chillingworth, and the community yield a rich texture to the classic formal structure of *The Scarlet Letter.* T. S. Eliot has praised Hawthorne for being the only American writer before Henry James whose characters are aware of one another.[8] With respect to *The Scarlet Letter* that observation is not fully accurate, but it suggests the importance of both consciousness and context in the romance. Hester, Dimmesdale, and Chillingworth, each of whom goes through much of the romance thinking fundamentally about himself, are what they are because of the uniqueness of the total dramatic situation. Each character takes his identity from the identities of the other characters and the community even as each contributes his identity to the identities of others and the community. One cannot discuss Hester, for example, at least with impunity, as if she were somehow liberated from the context out of which she takes her existence and to which she contributes. The same is true, of course, of any fully realized work of art. But the economy and complexity of *The Scarlet Letter* bring home the lesson with special clarity.

Taking its form in Hawthorne's imagination, the total context of *The Scarlet Letter* inheres in the letter itself. Invented by the community to serve as an unequivocal emblem of penance, the letter has

frozen Hester into a posture of haughty agony, has brought Dim-
dale to a death of "triumphant ignominy" on the scaffold, has victi-
ized the victimizer—Chillingworth. Hawthorne begins and ends with
the letter, which encompasses and transcends all its individual meanings, which signifies, totally and finally, *The Scarlet Letter* itself.

The House of the Seven Gables

Hawthorne begins *The House of the Seven Gables* with an essay on the Pyncheon family that is virtually an evocation of the past. We learn of Colonel Pyncheon, iron of purpose, inflexible of will, whose portrait shows him at his most characteristic with a Bible in one hand and an uplifted sword hilt in the other—and of his part in the execution of Matthew Maule. We see superstition and gossip brewed into a species of homely truth: Colonel Pyncheon would build his house over an unquiet grave; even more ominously, "his home would include the home of the dead and buried wizard." But the colonel proves to have more ambition than superstition. Despite the gossip, he builds his house, "a little withdrawn from the line of the street, but in pride, not modesty." He does his best, as Holgrave later says, to plant a family. But he dies on the very day of his housewarming, and both his death and his ambition become part of the family legacy.

A later Pyncheon, as we know, betrayed his daughter because of his desire to fix a claim on the lands to the East. Another became a royalist at the time of the Revolutionary War and repented just in time to save the house from confiscation. Still another, sorely in need of money, opened a shop in one corner of the mansion, the same shop that Hepzibah reopens. Does the family ever require legal tenure, asks Hawthorne, or does Maule's curse continue to haunt them all? Should the latter be true, he wonders if "each inheritor of the property—conscious of wrong, and failing to rectify it—did not commit anew the great guilt of his ancestor, and incur all its original responsibilities." Supposing such to be the case, it would seem correct to say that the Pyncheons had inherited a great misfortune. Their heritage, contaminated at its source, becomes a kind of private, familial, original sin. One wealthy, eccentric, and melancholy old bachelor, it is true, "greatly given to rummaging old records and hearkening to old traditions," was thinking of giving the house and the land back to the

Maules. But this is the man whom Clifford is supposed to have murdered.

Holgrave sums up the Pyncheon past by saying that under this roof over a portion of three centuries "there has been perpetual remorse of conscience, a constantly defeated hope, strife amongst kindred, various misery, a strange form of death, dark suspicion, unspeakable disgrace,—all, or most of which calamity I have the means of tracing to the old Puritan's inordinate desire to plant and endow a family." All seems traceable to pride and sustained by pride. Phoebe sees the relation of past to present when she recognizes Judge Pyncheon's hard, relentless look as the look of the old colonel in the portrait. Is this what has been handed down, she wonders; is this the precious heirloom? "A deeper philosopher than Phoebe," says Hawthorne, "might have found something very terrible in this idea. It implied that the weaknesses and defects, the bad passions, the mean tendencies, and the moral diseases which lead to crime are handed down from one generation to another, by a far surer process of transmission than human law has been able to establish in respect to the riches and honors which it seeks to entail upon posterity."

Tradition as Bondage

So well has Hawthorne evoked the past as it bears on the present that, when he turns to the contemporary Pyncheons, he need hardly make any transition at all. We are in the midst of what the past has engendered—pride, poverty, a decayed gentility, futile ambition, sterility. Hepzibah, upon whom Hawthorne has us attend, is what generations of Pyncheons have made her; the past victimizes her even as she embraces it. She feels a hereditary reverence for the portrait of Colonel Pyncheon; yet she trembles under its eye, "afraid to judge the character of the original so harshly as a perception of the truth compelled her to do so. But still she gazed, because the face of the picture enabled her . . . to read more accurately, and to a greater depth," the face of Judge Pyncheon which she has just seen in the street. Hepzibah, we see, studies the past as a way of knowing the present. But she is a victim of the past she cherishes and thus of the present she fears.

The Pyncheon past continues to hold the Pyncheon present in

bondage. As long as the colonel stares down from the wall, the Pyncheons must pursue his goal of establishing firm claim to the vast tract of land to the east, in Waldo County, Maine. This was the one great thing the colonel had left undone, and later Pyncheons—notably Gervayse and Judge Jaffrey—have tried in vain to find the deed that would establish their claim and stretch their wealth immeasurably. But "this impalpable claim," says Hawthorne, this search for a lost estate, "resulted in nothing more solid than to cherish, from generation to generation, an absurd delusion of family importance, which all along characterized the Pyncheons." Thus the idea of the deed helps to paralyze the family, to cast its members in attitudes of pride. And by the time of Hepzibah, the posture of pride is pathetic and ludicrous.

Hawthorne gives us only one day of Hepzibah in the shop by herself. It is enough for him to make clear the terrible difficulty of Hepzibah's establishing commerce with the world on her own initiative. Gaunt and dismal in appearance, scowling unintentionally but habitually, Hepzibah fumblingly tries to set things in their proper order minutes before she opens the door for business. She upsets a tumbler of marbles; and, while she is down on her hands and knees—literally picking up her marbles before she meets the public—Hawthorne asks us to consider her plight: a lady in "the final throes of what called itself old gentility, . . . who had fed herself from childhood with the shadowy food of aristocratic reminiscences, and whose religion it was that a lady's hand soils itself irremediably by doing aught for bread—this born lady, after sixty years of narrowing means, is fain to step down from her pedestal of imaginary rank." Broadening the social scope of his vision, Hawthorne sees "the immemorial lady,—two hundred years old, on this side of the water, and thrice as many on the other," now going to work. At first Hepzibah cannot bring herself to accept money for her wares; after Holgrave approves the opening of the shop and says she is finally joining the common struggle of mankind, she stands on her pride as a lady and gives him his morning biscuits. "Contumaciously squeamish" at the sight of money, she refuses Ned Higgins' penny and gives him a Jim Crow. Not until the boy returns for another cake, cannibalistically willing to accept Hepzibah's charity, shrewdly determined to see how far his penny will go, does she take the copper coin. Then the deed is done; "the structure of ancient aristocracy" is demolished; it is as if

Ned Higgins "had torn down the seven-gabled mansion."

Hepzibah's torture at coming into sordid contact with the world is not wholly unmitigated. She feels some novelty and some enjoyment, "the invigorating breath of a fresh outward atmosphere, after the long torpor and monotonous seclusion of her life." But the day is predominantly grim for her. Until she corrects herself, she even feels a momentary antagonism toward a lady who seems to survive in gentility while others must work. An ineffective saleswoman, she encounters impatience and wrath on the part of her customers because she has failed to stock certain staple items. She frequently gives the wrong change to her own disadvantage. Worn and tired at the end of the day, she finds in the cash drawer "perhaps half a dozen coppers, and a questionable ninepence which ultimately proved to be a copper likewise."

Clearly, Hepzibah, by herself, could never make a success of the shop. She cannot cope with the world on the world's terms. The shop seems indeed a dubious proposition as an attempt to provide a meager but independent income for Hepzibah and for the homecoming Clifford, or as an attempt to shake off or at least loosen the shackles of the past as they are exemplified in the greed and hypocrisy of Judge Pyncheon. In the romance, it serves as the first attempt to break away from the house, the curse, and the burden of family history. Modest as it is, it is all that Hepzibah can do, and Hawthorne portrays her—with all her dusty pride—sympathetically; although she may scowl and appear ludicrous, "her heart never frowned." But Hepzibah has never thought of money in terms of individual pennies or dollars, and she cannot bring herself to think in these terms. She dreams not of coppers but of fortunes drifting aristocratically her way. During the time she was planning to open her shop, "she had cherished an unacknowledged idea that some harlequin trick of fortune would intervene in her favor." Perhaps an uncle who had sailed for India fifty years ago might return and give her a fortune; perhaps the English branch of the family would bring her over to Pyncheon Hall or the Virginia branch would send her money; at the very least, perhaps the claim to the eastern lands would be admitted and she would be wealthy. Hepzibah's dreams of fortune, we see, are directed inside, not outside, the family; she looks to the past to sustain her in her gentility; only as a dire last resort, and then doubtfully, does she begin commerce with the world.

Hepzibah is thus what generations of Pyncheons have made her, and they have traditionally victimized their offspring. The entire family has been victimized by the colonel, and the final irony is that his portrait, left reverentially in its place, has for generations been hiding the deed to the eastern lands. Alice Pyncheon suffers psychic enslavement and death because of her father. Surprise at seeing young Jaffrey Pyncheon—the embodiment of the colonel—going through his papers kills the uncle Jaffrey; and, as we know, Clifford spends thirty years in jail because young Jaffrey arranges the evidence so as to incriminate him. There has indeed been, as Holgrave says, "strife amongst kindred." In his world of fear and trembling, even Clifford partakes of such an inheritance; his delicate devotion to beauty makes him unable to stand the sight of Hepzibah. Only Hepzibah, the antique victim, displays a capacity for love. But things have gone so far that when one of the wizened Pyncheon hens manages to lay a tiny egg, Hepzibah appropriates it for Clifford's breakfast: "Thus unscrupulously did the old gentlewoman sacrifice the continuance, perhaps, of an ancient feathered race, with no better end than to supply her brother with a dainty that hardly filled the bowl of a teaspoon."

The significance here is obvious: the chickens are an analogue of the Pyncheon family. Holgrave sees them explicitly as symbolic of the family, and Hawthorne comments that "the race had degenerated, like many a noble race besides, in consequence of too strict a watchfulness to keep it pure." The wise, antique aspect of the chickens suggests that they are "descendants of a time-honored race" and that they are "somehow mixed up" with the destiny of the House of the Seven Gables. Phoebe, indeed, notes a disturbing resemblance between the chickens and the family: "The distinguishing mark of the hens was a crest of lamentably scanty growth, in these latter days, but so oddly and wickedly analogous to Hepzibah's turban, that Phoebe . . . was led to fancy a resemblance betwixt these forlorn bipeds and her respectable relative." Thus, out of devotion to her brother Hepzibah offers up to him her symbolic offspring; even in kindliness, the Pyncheon family devours its young.

Observing the Past

Although the story ("horrible to say") is almost two hundred years long, Hawthorne wrote to Fields in October, 1850, "all but thirty or forty pages of it refer to the present time." Characteristically, Hawthorne focuses on the denouement of his two-hundred-year story; his interest is in the forces inherent in the narrative that will provide dramatic conflict and shape the conclusion of his romance. Clifford's return from jail draws the threads of the narrative more closely together; for Judge Pyncheon has apparently been biding his time until Clifford is once more an inmate of the family mansion; now he will move ominously into the foreground to threaten Clifford and his defender Hepzibah, and the narrative will measure the impact of his avarice and hypocrisy. As Hawthorne wrote to Evert Duyckinck in April, 1851, however, he "really had an idea" that the story of the *Seven Gables* was "rather a cheerful one than otherwise." Though the reader might be struck with the gloom of the past, he added, he himself was "illuminated" in writing the romance by a purpose of bringing it "to a prosperous close." With Hawthorne committed to a happy ending, a different narrative strand, antithetical to decay and to the past, becomes necessary. And thus Phoebe, the country cousin, enters the story, bringing the simplicity of her being into the musty home of her ancestors.

Hawthorne quickly establishes the fact that Phoebe is not in the direct Pyncheon line. "You know I have not been brought up a Pyncheon," Phoebe says to Hepzibah. And Hepzibah, the "aristocratic hucksteress," willingly resigns most of the shopkeeping to Phoebe, saying to herself, "what a nice little body she is! If she could only be a lady, too!—but that's impossible! Phoebe is no Pyncheon. She takes everything from her mother." If Phoebe is to have a chance to emanate sunshine and flowers, she must be essentially free from the family curse. Her lack of knowledge of the past, her attitude toward the present, toward the shop itself, free her to play a mighty role. She exemplifies the "new Plebeianism," which can prosper in the world better than the "old Gentility."

Images of sunshine, flowers, and angels surround Phoebe. Even more significantly, however, Hawthorne endows her with a kind of "natural magic," a "homely witchcraft," which begins to purify the house from the moment she moves in. He emphasizes her ability to make anyplace look like a home, from a hut in the forest to the house she has come to live in. The morning after Phoebe's arrival her bedchamber "had been purified of all former evil and sorrow. . . . Her dreams of the past night, being such cheerful ones, had exorcised the gloom, and now haunted the chamber in its stead." Again, Hawthorne stresses her "purifying influence" and makes it clear that "Phoebe's presence made a home about her." Not only does her fresh, maidenly figure represent "both sunshine and flowers"; she is "a religion in herself, warm, simple, true, with a substance that could walk on earth, and a spirit that was capable of heaven." Lacking the pride of a Hepzibah or an Alice Pyncheon, which derived from allegiance to family tradition; a respecter of law; the embodiment of sunshine, warmth, flowers, religion, natural magic, and homely witchcraft, Phoebe is the happiest thing that ever happened to the Pyncheon family.

Her sphere, Hawthorne tells us, is "the Actual," whereas Hepzibah's—and in a different way Clifford's—sphere is the dream. Shortly after Phoebe's arrival Hepzibah gives her a tour of the house, which is to say a lesson in family history. She tells Phoebe of the past, especially of such things as the lands to the East, a reported silver mine, a large treasure of English guineas undoubtedly hidden "somewhere about the house, or in the cellar, or possibly in the garden," saying that, if Phoebe happens to find it, they will "tie up the shop-bell for good and all!" "In the meantime," answers Phoebe, "I hear someone ringing it." This incident epitomizes their contrasting attitudes toward life and toward money: Hepzibah dreams of the fortune, the buried treasure, the pot of gold at the end of the family rainbow and subjugates the routine of the shop to the blandishments of the dream; Phoebe derives enjoyment from a sketch of the family dream, but she sets aside the imaginary for the actual as a matter of course when the shop bell rings.

Of Clifford, Hawthorne says: "With a mysterious and terrible Past, which had annihilated his memory, and a blank Future before him, he had only this visionary and impalpable Now, which, if you once look closely at it, is nothing." A dreamer and a lover of the beautiful even before his thirty years of imprisonment, Clifford returns to the House of the Seven Gables a man thwarted and maimed in spirit. "It was the spirit of the man that could not walk," says Hawthorne. By instinct a devotee of beauty, Clifford takes no pleasure in looking at Hepzibah, wrinkled, scowling, and yellow as she is, "with that odd uncouthness of a turban on her head." Hawthorne admits that Clifford owed Hepzibah nothing for all her care and devotion. A nature like Clifford's is "always selfish in its essence," he says, "and we must give it leave to be so." But Hawthorne sees the potential danger incurred by a man like Clifford, who is more suspectible to the claims of beauty than he is to those of the heart. In a statement that measures the astonishing depth of his devotion to the heart, Hawthorne admits the possibility that had Clifford possessed the means of cultivating his taste for beauty "to its utmost perfectibility" in his earlier life, "that subtile attribute might, before this period, have completely eaten out or filed away his affections. Shall we venture to pronounce, therefore, that his long and black calamity may not have had a redeeming drop of mercy at the bottom?" The possibility that Clifford's thirty-year imprisonment may have saved him from the black fate of heartlessness serves to put his suffering in a distinctively Hawthornesque perspective.

Clifford is bound to remind one in a flickering way of Owen Warland. Both are disciples of the beautiful, and Clifford's fascination with hummingbirds seems the appreciative side of Owen Warland's creation of a butterfly. But Owen Warland succeeds in a double sense, first in creating, then in rising above the destruction of his creation, whereas Clifford himself is destroyed before he has any chance to create. And there is the dark possibility that he may have developed into more of an Aylmer than an Owen Warland.

Clifford's sphere, as Hawthorne says, is the dream. For him Phoebe is "not an actual fact," but the "interpretation of all that he had lacked on earth brought warmly home to his conception; so that this mere symbol, or life-like picture, had almost the comfort of reality." Phoebe and Clifford come into the house at almost the same time, one arriving in a carriage and knocking brightly at the front door, the other arriving we know not how and making his presence known by inarticulate sounds and halting footsteps. It is as if Clifford simply emerged from the family past. Essentially, as Hawthorne reiterates, Clifford is childlike; his memory is "annihilated"; in his dreams he "invariably played the part of a child, or a very young man." His mind has undergone "a kind of new creation, after its long-suspended life," and it responds to things as does "the new mind of a child."

Except for Phoebe, who is exempted from the curse of the family past, Clifford, old and spiritually scarred, is the only kind of child the Pyncheon family seems capable of bringing forth. Though he no longer knows the family past, he is nonetheless haunted by it. When Hawthorne says that the "strong and ponderous" Judge Pyncheon "had been Clifford's nightmare," he is saying in effect that the family past, exemplified in the Judge, has terrorized Clifford. The dead Judge Pyncheon becomes "a defunct nightmare," and Clifford, as we know, responds to the Judge's death with a feeling of exhilaration and freedom that takes him and Hepzibah on a wild, impulsive train ride into the present. When they return to the house they find Phoebe and Holgrave, newly avowed in love, and the past is no more. Clifford thus has been so terribly bruised by the past that he has no further rational relation to it; committed to a dream world, his happiest fate is to exchange bad dreams for good ones, nightmares for glimpses of beauty.

It is Holgrave, the reformer, the disciple of progress, who has the most thorough and systematic knowledge of the family past. His attitude toward progress, indeed, makes him seem like an unread Jefferson espousing a revolution every generation: he objects to the "rotten Past," to "lifeless institutions" which he would like to "thrust out of the way." He thinks that houses should not be built to outlast the life of the builder and to encumber future generations, that even institutional buildings should crumble to ruin every twenty years. Hawthorne approves Holgrave's belief in progress, stating as a general principle that he possessed a sense "or inward prophecy,—which a young man had better never have been born than not to have, and a mature man had better die at once than utterly to relinquish"—a sense that the human condition can be improved. But Holgrave's fault, as Hawthorne makes clear, lies in expecting everything to come about in his own generation. For Holgrave, the House of the Seven Gables is expressive of the "odious and abominable Past" against which he declaims publicly. "I dwell in it a while," he tells Phoebe, "that I may know the better how to hate it."

To hate the past, then, one must know the past. And so Holgrave studies, observes, seems—in his relation to Hepzibah and Clifford— "to be in quest of mental food, not heart sustenance." From Phoebe's point of view he is "too calm and cool an observer." Indeed, Phoebe rebukes Holgrave severely when he admits that his impulse toward Hepzibah and Clifford is neither to help nor to hinder, but to regard, to analyze, to consider, "and to comprehend the drama which, for almost two hundreds years, has been dragging its slow length over the ground where you and I now tread." Phoebe answers indignantly: Holgrave talks as if the old house were a theater, as if the misfortunes of the family were played exclusively for his amusement. "I do not like this," she exclaims; "the play costs the performers too much, and the audience is too cold-hearted." Apparently chastened by this outburst, Holgrave still "cannot help fancying that Destiny is arranging its fifth act for a catastrophe," and Phoebe is vexed anew.

Holgrave's attitude toward the past is both personal and artistic. As a Maule, he has a family animus to bear against the Pyncheons; as an artist (a writer who has contributed to *Graham's* and *Godey's*), he has an impulse to make something of the very past which he hates. His story of Alice Pyncheon dramatizes not only the avarice and pride of the Pyncheons, but also—and significantly—the revenge and pride of the Maules. By means of his artistry and "a certain magnetic element" in his nature against which she has instinctively rebelled, Holgrave brings the past to bear on Phoebe in a way that leaves her defenseless. Her natural magic and homely witchcraft are of no avail against the compelling power he invokes from the past.

At the end of Holgrave's story of Alice Pyncheon, Hawthorne's story stands at a moment of crisis: the dead past has been made the living past, and it exercises a hypnotic effect on Phoebe. At this point the entire cycle of misfortune could be recapitulated and begun anew; new vengeance for old wrongs would signal once again the triumph of the past over the present. To his credit Holgrave does not subjugate Phoebe to his will—as his ancestor did Alice Pyncheon—though he must resist mighty temptation to do so. By refusing an opportunity for revenge, he loosens the bond of the past. Phoebe, of course, has not challenged Holgrave as Alice challenged Matthew Maule. Her innocence and lack of pride enable her to feel the power of the past without being enslaved by it. But it is Holgrave who refuses to extend the empire of vengeance.

Despite his "banditti-like associates," his wild ideas, and the picaresque quality of his life, Holgrave commands an essential respect from Hawthorne. He represents, says Hawthorne, "many compeers in his native land," in his culture and his lack of culture, in "his crude, wild, and misty philosophy, and the practical experience that counteracted some of its tendencies; in his magnanimous zeal for man's welfare, and his recklessness of whatever the ages had established in man's behalf; in his faith, and in his infidelity; in what he had, and in what he lacked."

Most importantly, however, amid the varied activities of his life,

Holgrave has "never lost his identity." He has been a country school-master, a salesman in a country store, political editor of a country newspaper, a pedlar of cologne water in New England and the Middle States; he has practiced dentistry ("and with very flattering success, especially in many of our factory towns along our inland streams"), has visited Italy, France, and Germany, has spent some time in a community of Fourierists, and has lectured publicly on Mesmerism. And he is not quite twenty-two years of age. At present, we know, he is a daguerreotypist. But although he has been basically a homeless man, moving from one job to another and adopting the exterior neces-sary to each, Holgrave has "never violated the inner-most man"—he has "carried his conscience along with him."

In the Pyncheon garden Phoebe sees "rank weeds (symbolic of the transmitted vices of society) as are always prone to root themselves around human dwellings." But, she notes, the garden has had care; the growth of the weeds has been checked by labor "bestowed daily and systematically on the garden." Since Hawthorne has spelled out the symbolic value of the weeds, we see the clear significance of the care given to the garden: Holgrave, daily and systematically, has checked the growth of "the transmitted vices of society." Unable to dispel the influence of the past, he has worked to keep it within bounds.

Breaking Away

The essential dramatic conflict in *The House of the Seven Gables* lies in the attempts to break out or away from the house itself, which are set off against Judge Pyncheon's effort to force from Clifford the secret of the missing deed. At the beginning, as we have seen, Hep-zibah's cent-shop serves to open a commerce of a modest variety between the house and the world. Hepzibah is pushed to this last extremity, as she regards it, largely because Clifford's impending ar-rival will make it necessary for her to support them both; for she is determined not to receive any assistance from the judge.

Midway through the romance, in a scene which Melville thought particularly profound, Clifford stands in the upstairs arched window watching a political procession pass by on Pyncheon Street. Over-whelmed by an impulse to be once again in contact with the mass of humanity, he attempts to jump and is restrained by Hepzibah and

Phoebe. Could he have jumped into the midst of that procession and survived, he tells Hepzibah, it might have made him another man. And Hawthorne intimates that Clifford may have been right: "He needed a shock, or perhaps he required to take a deep, deep, plunge into the ocean of human life, and to sink down and be covered by its profoundness, and then to emerge, sobered, invigorated, restored to the world and to himself. Perhaps, again, he required nothing less than the great final remedy—death!" Clifford's impulse, partly sanative, partly self-destructive, dramatizes the void of loneliness in which he has been shut up. Such an extreme gesture is not the way back into the world of men. But to the desperate man, locked in a world of bizarre logic, it may appear to be the only way back.

The cent-shop has involved Hepzibah; the arched window, Clifford. The attempt to go to church involves them both. Seeing Phoebe going off to worship, "a religion in herself," Hepzibah and Clifford long "to kneel down among the people, and be reconciled to God and man at once." If the world of man seems alien to them, the house of God, where worship of a common Father proclaims the brotherhood of the worshipers, surely will offer them a chance to pray in communion with other souls. But, dressed and ready, they cannot go; fearfully they shrink back into their solitude, more gloomy and dismal now after the thought, the glimpse, the very breath of freedom.

Hepzibah and Clifford could of course leave the house in bondage; Judge Pyncheon offers them the hospitality of his country seat. But the House of the Seven Gables belongs by right to Clifford and Hepzibah, and they are determined not to surrender it to the hypocritical judge, no matter how dismal and gloomy its atmosphere. One might wonder that the judge, the physical, emotional, and spiritual counterpart of Colonel Pyncheon, does not himself live in the house. But, we recall, the colonel never lived in the house; he moved in, only to die at the apex of his career. The judge, too, comes into the house to die, sitting in the ancestral chair, while time moves on and his chance at the governorship ticks from futurity into the past.

Taunting and caustic, Hawthorne sports ironically with the dead judge, framing the "swarthy whiteness" of his face in the twilight, picturing a fly landing on his forehead, his chin, and finally creeping over the bridge of his nose toward his "wide-open eyes" in the early morning light. "Rise up, thou subtle, worldly, selfish, iron-hearted hypocrite," mocks Hawthorne unequivocally, "and make thy choice

whether still to be subtle, worldly, selfish, iron-hearted, and hypocritical." The judge's power, great as it was when he sat in the chair,
has waned quickly; now he is so harmless that, literally, he cannot
hurt a fly.

A general sense of exhilaration pervades the story after the judge's
death. The next morning Alice's posies are in full bloom, conveying
"a mystic expression that something within the house was consummated." As embodied in Judge Pyncheon, the past is now "a defunct
nightmare." No longer need Hepzibah say, as she did to her cousin
Jaffrey, that a "hard and grasping spirit has run in our blood these
two hundred years," that "you are but doing over again, in another
shape, what your ancestor before you did, and sending down to your
posterity the curse inherited from him!" The catastrophe foreseen by
Holgrave has quietly taken place. But the reverberations pulse deeply
into the lifeblood of the narrative.

Clifford's discovery of the dead judge catapults him into a frenzied
activity. In fear and jubilation he leaves the house with Hepzibah
and takes the wild train ride which rushes him not only through space
but through time, unleashing the pent-up energies of the past, until
he alights exhausted from the train and bids Hepzibah to take command. In "The Arched Window" chapter, Clifford hears the sound
of trains and recoils from the idea of pulsating energy suggested by it.
At that point, Hawthorne says, Clifford lacks "the tragic power of
laughter." The stimulus of freedom, however, stirs him into a mood
of ebullience, crazy laughter, and fear, into an accelerated journey
through thirty years of life. Both mood and journey are transitory.
Hepzibah, who, while on the train ride, "felt herself more apart from
human kind than even in the seclusion she had just quitted," has
accompanied Clifford on his withdrawal. Now she must see to his
return. The flight of the two owls, these "time-stricken" people, proves
no more efficacious than Clifford's would-be leap into a procession of
people. Yet, as Roy H. Male points out, one thing is accomplished:
on the platform of the small station at which they alight, Hepzibah
is able to kneel in prayer, something she has been unable to do in
the house.[1]

The death of Judge Pyncheon marks the end of an avarice that
has built a dilapidated dynasty of pride. Alone in the house with the
dead judge, Phoebe and Holgrave avow their love. Phoebe has returned from her trip to the country "graver, more womanly, and

deeper-eyed" ("in token of a heart that had begun to suspect its depths") than when she first entered the house. But she has not lost her "quiet glow of natural sunshine," nor has she "forfeited her proper gift of making things look real, rather than fantastic, within her sphere." And Holgrave looks to her for direction much as Kenyon looks to Hilda near the end of *The Marble Faun*. In both cases, the direction is the same—homeward.

The Prosperous Close

The ending of *The House of the Seven Gables* has seemed unconvincing to many readers. With the evil character dead, the good characters become rich; Hepzibah, Clifford, Phoebe, and Holgrave will go to the judge's country estate, each to enjoy happiness according to his or her capacity. The chickens are there, laying eggs as if to make up for lost time; Uncle Venner will soon join the group; and Holgrave has come to equate happiness and conservatism. These final pages, says Male, "degenerate into flimsy farce." Kenneth Dauber, agreeing with the majority of critics that the ending is imposed, concludes that its "severely external" quality comes from a substitution "of wish for fact," of desire for narrative resonance. Arlin Turner goes a suggestive step farther in contending that Hawthorne sounds repeated notes of skepticism toward the end of the narrative to signal his own awareness "that the resolution is forced."[2]

But if the ending seems contrived, if Hawthorne's purpose of bringing his story to a "prosperous close" seems to have been imposed from without rather than to have arisen from the inner necessity of the narrative, the very mode of contrivance tells us a good deal about values inherent in his fiction. Holgrave's conservative views come on us quickly; even Phoebe is surprised to hear them. But there is a logic in these views which serves the thematic resolution of the romance. Earlier, we recall, Holgrave has wanted houses to be destroyed every generation; his ruling notion is that the past should in no way enslave the present. Now, however, he wonders that the judge, "being so opulent, and with a reasonable prospect of transmitting his wealth to descendants of his own," did not build his country house of stone rather than of wood. This is indeed surprising, somewhat amusing in its context, and—coming from Holgrave and at the end of this particular romance—a little appalling.

But to get the full view one must consider Holgrave's next statement: "Then, every generation of the family might have altered the interior, to suit its own taste and convenience; while the exterior, through the lapse of years, might have been adding venerableness to its original beauty, and thus giving that impression of permanence which I consider essential to the happiness of any one moment." In these terms, the exterior corresponds to the forms of the past, the interior to its fashions. The forms of the past (the things that give society its coherence of structure), Holgrave has come to believe, should be handed down from generation to generation; they should have a quality of permanence. The fashions, on the other hand, may be changed at will according to the dictates of taste and convenience; with formal stability, the fashions may be transitory. This is, of course, a compromise position for Holgrave: he has not swung from an idea of total rejection of the past to one of total acceptance. He has distinguished between forms and fashions and decided that the present ought to conserve from the past what is essential to its coherence.

This final idea of how the past and the present ought to be related emerges from the narrative as the most thoughtful, the most possible, the best that we have seen. Hepzibah's view of the past proves invalid for living in the present; Clifford's is a nightmare; Uncle Venner's, though sensible, is fragmentary and reductive. And Phoebe is substantially innocent of the past. But Holgrave finally articulates a mode of accepting the past and thus accepting the present and the future. His view helps to resolve a crucial theme of the romance. We may be surprised that he has come to such a position; but we should not be surprised that Hawthorne has brought him to it.

Holgrave's reversal of opinion serves also as a high tribute to Phoebe. Phoebe stands for the heart; and, for Hawthorne, the heart is the great agent of conservatism. Characteristically, Phoebe's impulse tempers Holgrave's intelligence—her instinct guides him home. In a perceptive comment on Phoebe, Richard Harter Fogle points out that of all the characters in *The House of the Seven Gables* she is

closest to the center of human nature. A conservative in the best sense, she represents the truth of the heart. She is the best of human ties and human feelings. She has far less moral depth than Hepzibah . . . ; she is less sensitive than Clifford, and much less intelligent than Holgrave; but Hawthorne represents her as of greater power than any of these, through an instinctive but consummate talent for everyday living. She presents a contradiction recurrent in Hawthorne: in portraying her he must condescend to some extent, although reluctantly. She has qualities which he regards as humanly perfect, but on another level he is unsatisfied and is forced to an uneasy self-restraint.[3]

Yet *The House of the Seven Gables* has come in for criticism because of Phoebe. In this romance Hawthorne tries to balance his vision of damnation with a vision of redemption. On Phoebe, who is exempted from the family curse for the purpose, rests the responsibility for redemption. Hyatt H. Waggoner, for one, believes that the burden is too great for her, that Hawthorne has not created enough of a character to play the necessary role with conviction. John Gatta, Jr., puts the matter in a larger context by demonstrating the role of "visionary history" in *Seven Gables* and Phoebe's importance in such a design. If Hawthorne, in his words, "erred in trying to superimpose an ideal, visionary narrative upon a temporal plot too clumsy and melodramatic to sustain such a purpose," then Phoebe is inadequate precisely because Hawthorne was too ambitious and conceived a romance beyond his powers as a writer.[4]

After the death of the judge, something does seem to happen to the quality of imagined reality in Hawthorne's romance. Perhaps Holgrave's statement on the best relationship of past and present has had so little attention because it is and remains a statement, and we have no sense of, no purchase on, the experience out of which such an idea must come. A segment of experience has been neglected; we are presented with the results, but left groping for the process which brought them forth. The moment of emotional transformation in the narrative comes with Phoebe's and Holgrave's avowal of love. Hawthorne's description bears attention:

And it was in this hour, so full of doubt and awe, that the one miracle was wrought, without which every human existence is a blank. The bliss which makes all things true, beautiful, and holy shone around this youth and maiden. They were conscious of nothing sad or old. They transfigured the earth, and made it Eden again, and themselves the first two dwellers in it. The dead man, so close beside them, was forgotten. At such a crisis, there is no death; for immortality is revealed anew, and embraces everything in its hallowed atmosphere.

With such an incantation, the shaping force of *The House of the Seven Gables* changes. New hope and promise supersede the grim despair of the past. "The dead man ... was forgotten," says Hawthorne; and the implications of the statement are immense. The judge is dead; the colonel is dead; the avarice, pride, and hypocrisy of the past are dead. The house itself is defunct, and Clifford and Hepzibah bid "a final farewell to the abode of their forefathers with hardly more emotion than if they had made it their arrangement to return thither at tea-time." With the death of all these things, the original imaginative conception that shaped Hawthorne's narrative focus has come to an emotional and logical conclusion. We are struck with a difference of tone and narrative authority because Holgrave, Phoebe, Clifford, and Hepzibah survive the conceptual death of the romance; as survivors, they live on outside the imaginative framework that gave them their being—live on because Hawthorne wants them to live on, wants them to be happy.

Perhaps this is why Henry James regarded *The House of the Seven Gables* as "more like a prologue to a great novel than a great novel itself," as a "magnificent fragment." The subject, the *donnée*, of the story, he wrote, "does not quite fill it out"; we receive "an impression of certain complicated purposes on the author's part, which seem to reach beyond it."[5] To consider a romance a prologue when it is as lengthy as *The House of the Seven Gables* may seem at first glance surprising; but James is correct in saying that Hawthorne's original idea does not quite fill out the story. After the judge's death one more thing is necessary—the "prosperous close." Literally and legally the surviving characters inherit wealth, but they are now bereft of purpose. So important to Hawthorne is their sense of being free that the new life seems to require little adumbration.

F. O. Matthiessen suggests that unlike Tolstoy at the end of *War and Peace* Hawthorne could not imagine an actual social existence for the characters gathered at the end of *Seven Gables*.[6] It is a perceptive observation, although it tends to blame Hawthorne for not making his romance into a novel by way of conclusion. We leave the characters in the first epilogue of *War and Peace* with a sense that the narrative—immense as it has been—is gathering for a new start; new forces are welling up, new issues confront the nation and the individual, and the lines for new conflict are being drawn. And at this late point Tolstoy brings us face to face with a new and insistent set of quotidian details—children with runny noses, Natasha cross and a little bitchy, Nicholas Rostov at times exasperating to his wife; he shows us figures who have been caught up in heroic action now surrounded by the petty nuisances of everyday life, and neither he nor they diminish the moment by lamenting their departed grandeur. In *The House of the Seven Gables*, however, the characters are virtually turned out to pasture; hope for the future remains abstract because it belongs primarily to Hawthorne and not to the narrative. Hepzibah has received a fortune from an anomalous source, but in the very way she has always dreamed of receiving a fortune; Clifford, with no more nightmares, has the means to gratify what remains of his love of the beautiful; Phoebe has returned to the country; and Holgrave has watched the "long drama of wrong and retribution" come to a conclusion. He has, he tells Phoebe, represented the old wizard Maule in this drama; but now, no longer a restless, peregrinating spirit, he formulates his view of the relation of past and present which, as we have seen, supplies the answer to essential problems raised by the narrative, but the answer as postscript. To show life as lived under Holgrave's rubric would be another story indeed.

In *The House of the Seven Gables*, Hawthorne sought to extend the limits of a talent that had already won the praise of Melville, Whipple, Longfellow, Duyckinck, and other contemporary men of letters. A theme compounded of doom, pride, and avarice might somehow yield up a final vision of happiness. It seems indeed a mighty undertaking—not only for Hawthorne, who was always chary of treating the present in his fiction—but for any writer. Perhaps his original conception, large as it was, was not large enough to encompass the death of the judge and move naturally to the dramatic rendering of prosperity; perhaps he felt that his Pyncheons and his Maule had earned a trip to the Elysian Fields.

But such appraisals should wait on the decisive judgment of success and achievement. No American novelist before Hawthorne had undertaken to meditate on the interpenetration of past and present. It was a theme rich in suggestiveness for later writers—for Henry James, for William Faulkner, for Robert Penn Warren. In exploring this theme, Hawthorne bequeathed to American literature a legacy as important to the imagination as the Pyncheon lands to the east would have been to the pocketbook. *The House of the Seven Gables* called forth from Melville the famous letter in which he said (among other things) that "there is a certain tragic phase of humanity which, in our opinion, was never more powerfully embodied than by Hawthorne." T. S. Eliot wrote that this was "Hawthorne's best novel after all." And James, gracious in the face of accomplishment, refuses to make his final word on the romance "a restrictive one": "It is a large and generous production," he says, "pervaded with that vague hum, that indefinable echo, of the whole multitudinous life of man, which is the real sign of a great work of fiction."[7]

Chapter Seven

The Blithedale Romance

Hawthorne's Narrators

Like *The House of the Seven Gables* and *The Scarlet Letter*, *The Blithedale Romance* contains elements that serve as a dramatic signature for Hawthorne's major work. Hollingsworth, for example, is one of the most firmly drawn of his men of Idea. The dark, sensual Zenobia and the light, ethereal Priscilla represent two recurrent types of women in Hawthorne's fiction. The satanic figure of Westervelt bears a relation to the numerous characters in the tales and romances who seek to hold another in bondage. And the motif of withdrawal and return, so frequently part of a Hawthorne narrative, finds an important place in *The Blithedale Romance*.

But *Blithedale* differs from Hawthorne's other romances in one significant way: only in *Blithedale* does Hawthorne use a first-person narrator to tell his story. Frequently in his sketches and at times in his tales (though not in the major ones), Hawthorne had made use of the first-person point of view. In "The Wedding-Knell," in "Dr. Heidegger's Experiment," and in "The Sister Years," his narrator is an incidental feature of the tale; in the delicate "The Vision of the Fountain" the narrator is the central but largely undefined character. Such sketches as "Sunday at Home," "The Toll-Gatherer's Day," "Snow-flakes," "Night Sketches," and "Footprints on the Sea-shore" employ a bemused narrator whose deepest concern is to fathom his relationship to the world around him. More memorably, perhaps, the narrator of "Sights from a Steeple" wonders if the "most desirable mode of existence might be that of a spiritualized Paul Pry, hovering invisible around man and woman, witnessing their deeds, searching into their hearts, borrowing brightness from their felicity, and shade from their sorrow, and retaining no emotion peculiar to himself." None of these things is possible, he realizes: if he would know "the interior of brick walls, or the mystery of human bosoms," he must guess. Seen in this light, the effectiveness of a narrator would seem to come at the expense of his personality. The narrator, that is to say, must surrender himself to his function.

Narrator Miles Coverdale of *The Blithedale Romance* has, therefore, antecedents in some of Hawthorne's earlier and lesser known work.[1] Like the narrators of the sketches, he ponders the problem of his relation to the world. Like those of some minor tales, he views his world from the outside. Unlike those narrators, however, Coverdale wants to impinge on the world around him. The role of a spiritualized Paul Pry strikes him as not only impossible but unsatisfactory; if he becomes at times little more than a materialized pryer, hiding in trees or looking into windows, it is because he cannot secure the emotional attention of the world he describes.

Although few people have taken the trouble to acknowledge it, Coverdale's problems are partly the narrative products of difficulties Hawthorne faced in writing *Blithedale*. Never before had he attempted to sustain the vision of a first-person narrator at any great length; never before had he created one who could evolve into a character in his own right. In Miles Coverdale, Hawthorne fashioned a narrator according to conventions which had defined the narrators of his sketches and minor tales. But the exigencies of the romance as a form made it impossible for Coverdale to be contained by the conventions that brought him into being. Significantly, at the outset of the romance, we see him setting out to become a formal part of the group of people at Blithedale; his initial act is one of joining. But Coverdale is released into a world which has no real need of him, and his narrative reveals his growing sense of that fact just as surely as it reveals anything else.

Dreams and Common Sense

Musing in his room on the evening before his departure for Blithedale, Miles Coverdale is "not so very confident as at some former periods that this final step, which would mix me up irrevocably with the Blithedale affair, was the wisest that could possibly be taken." He seems to have doubts about his attempt to live the better life. Indeed, Coverdale's notion that the aim of Blithedale is both generous and absurd betrays a fundamental ambivalence toward the project (and toward experience in general) which is at once the mode of Hawthorne's art and the corroding manner of Coverdale's life.[2]

Coverdale seems relatively dedicated when he departs for Blithedale in the midst of a driving spring snow storm. In the city the snow looks almost dingy to him; footprints in the snow suggest the visible "track of an old conventionalism." But when he leaves the city there is "better air to breathe": "Air that had not been breathed once and again! air that had not been spoken into words of falsehood, formality, and error, like all the air of the dusky city!" There is a sense of liberation in Coverdale's reaction, an assumption that freshness and innocence lie in the open countryside in the direction of Blithedale, whereas falsehood and error—human inventions—belong to the city. And this is an attitude toward man, society, and nature that one might expect from a Transcendentalist poet-narrator. But Coverdale's first spoken words on this trip qualify the straightforward simplicity of his enthusiasm: " 'How pleasant it is!' remarked I, while the snowflakes flew into my mouth the moment it was opened. 'How very mild and balmy is this country air!' " Determining the tone of Coverdale's remarks is the response of one of his anonymous companions: "Ah, Coverdale, don't laugh at what little enthusiasm you have left! ... I maintain that this nitrous atmosphere is really exhilarating." That Coverdale should make an ironic remark about the snow and the country air just after he has given us a passage celebrating their purity is surprising and interesting; that one of his companions should have noted, at this early point, a waning enthusiasm on Covedale's part is astonishing. Juxtaposed as they are, the ironic mode is here associated with a lack of enthusiasm. Coverdale has noticeably lost enthusiasm before he reaches Blithedale. More than anything else, his ambivalence has weathered the storm.

Whatever the state of his enthusiasm, Coverdale retains a certain respect for Blithedale and for the anonymous Blithedalers. His illness at the time of his arrival serves, as he sees, to purge him of "old conventionalisms"; it is "an avenue between two existences," a doorway into a "freer region." During the days of his illness "a number of recruits to our little army of saints and martyrs" arrive at Blithedale, most of them persons who have become disgusted with the world but have not lost their faith in the possibility of a better life. For years the idea of such a community had taken form individually in their minds. Coverdale's description is sober, analytic: "Thoughtful, strongly lined faces were among them; sombre brows, but eyes that did not require spectacles, unless prematurely dimmed by the students' lamplight, and hair that seldom showed a thread of silver." Old age and early youth have no real place in this society. But their bond, as Coverdale sees, is negative. Though they agree that a second chance at life is worth while, they are not so certain what the new system of things should be. Coverdale's hope is that "between theory and practice, a true and available mode of life might be struck out; and that, even should we ultimately fail, the months or years spent in the trial would not have been wasted, either as regarded passing enjoyment, or the experience that makes men wise."

The unavoidable fact of physical labor makes it impossible for Coverdale to think of Blithedale only in terms of theory. He is surprised on his first evening at Blithedale when Silas Foster asks who is qualified to bargain for pigs. "Pigs! Good heavens!" thinks Coverdale; "had we come out from among the swinish multitude for this?" And, when they have gone to work in earnest, Coverdale is distressed to find that their thoughts "were fast becoming cloddish," that their labor "symbolized nothing, and left us mentally sluggish." Generalizing (very much á la Hawthorne at this point), he maintains that "intellectual activity is incompatible with any large amount of bodily exercise. The yeoman and the scholar—the yeoman and the man of finest moral culture, though not the man of sturdiest sense and integrity—are two distinct individuals, and can never be melted or welded into one substance."

Yet, despite such an unequivocal statement, Coverdale does not deprecate the effects of their labor. He once says to Hollingsworth that future generations of Blithedalers will make heroes of them, and although there is an element of levity in his remark, he is expressing such an idea in the only way that is possible for him. After several weeks at Blithedale he is able to do a good day's work; he is stronger, hardier, broader in the shoulders, capable of pleasing even Silas Foster with his labor, and he feels that by tilling the soil he is doing something honest and worthwhile. When Hollingsworth once charges him with not being in earnest as a poet or as a laborer, Coverdale objects and cites his labor as proof of his earnestness. Clearly he finds a satisfaction in work, even as he laments its tendency to make thoughts "cloddish"; clearly he finds an attraction in the idea of Blithedale, even as he qualifies its attractiveness.

Despite all its reality (which Coverdale feels strongly as he returns to Blithedale from the city), Blithedale does represent a dream, a vision, a utopian venture. And at the root of Coverdale's ambivalence is the idea that dreams are noble but nonetheless destined to failure. "The greatest obstacle to being heroic," he says, "is the doubt whether one may not be going to prove one's self a fool; the truest heroism is to resist the doubt; and the profoundest wisdom to know when it ought to be resisted, and when to be obeyed." The wiser course, he acknowledges, "if not the more sagacious, [is] to follow out one's day-dream to its natural consummation, although, if the vision have been worth the having, it is certain never to be consummated otherwise than by a failure." Despite their inevitable failure, dreams are not "the rubbish of the mind"; they possess a value which is lacking "in the most ponderous realities of any practicable scheme."

Coverdale's dogged commitment to dreams is clearly distinct from the attitude of Thoreau, who advocates that one advance confidently in the direction of one's dreams. "If you have built castles in the air," says Thoreau, "your work need not be lost; that is where they should be. Now put the foundations under them." Thoreau believes in the success of dreams, Coverdale in their failure. Thoreau values dreams for their ultimate practicality, Coverdale despite their ultimate impracticality. Because Thoreau would never worry about being a fool, he would be in Coverdale's terms the kind of hero that Coverdale cannot be. *The Blithedale Romance*, says Roy R. Male, is "a kind of Walden in reverse."[3] And Coverdale, we may add, is a kind of frustrated Thoreau to the extent that dreams for him can blossom only into failure. He is not sorry that he once had "faith and force enough to form generous hopes of the world's destiny." But a faith qualified by a fear of being foolish, a hope qualified by a perception of inevitable failure, and a charity qualified, as we shall see, by a disinclination to trouble himself for others breed an ambivalence in Coverdale that defines his attitude toward Blithedale.

Contributing mightily to Coverdale's divided atttude is his persistent allegiance to common sense. In Hawthorne's fiction, common sense serves to limit imaginative perception and to cast the dreamworld into a posture of unreality. One should insist, of course, that Hawthorne saw the value of common sense in actual life; in dealing with the affairs of the everyday world, a goodly measure of common sense was both useful and necessary. Even in *Blithedale*, there is no denigration of Silas Foster as he watches the masqueraders; Coverdale sees him in his regular work clothes leaning against a tree, smoking a short pipe, doing "more to disenchant the scene, with the look of shrewd, acrid, Yankee observation, than twenty witches and necromancers could have done in the way of rendering it weird and fantastic." The antic guise withers in the presence of commonsense observation; the effect is a carefully wrought antithesis, exemplifying the double manner in which Coverdale regards Blithedale. But the limitations of Silas Foster's mode of confronting reality are thoroughly defined during the search for Zenobia's body. The emotional depth of these scenes is set off brilliantly by Foster's matter-of-factness, which strikes one as shallow and out of place. Shrewd, brittle, and limited, Foster's perception finally reduces all phenomena to cracker-barrel practicality.

For his fiction, as we have seen, Hawthorne required enchantment rather than disenchantment, magic and dream rather than common sense and practicality. In "The Artist of the Beautiful," Owen Warland struggles to realize his vision against an alliance of scorn, ignorance, shallowness, and self-doubt. But Hawthorne dramatizes the limitations of common sense most explicitly in "The Snow-Image," after Mr. Lindsey unwittingly brings the snow child in to melt beside the stove. Mr. Lindsey is depicted as "honest," "very kind-hearted," "well-meaning," and "highly benevolent." But he has "an exceedingly common-sensible way of looking at matters." As a "common-sensible individual" Mr. Lindsey insists on bringing the snow image indoors. Then "the common-sensible man" places the snow child on the hearthrug in front of the stove. It begins to droop and melt, but "the common-sensible man saw nothing amiss." When the snow image is gone, Peony says, in effect, "I told you so," and shakes "his little fist at the common-sensible man." Hawthorne leaves us in no doubt of his meaning: "This, you will observe, was one of those rare cases, which will yet occasionally happen, where common-sense finds itself at fault." The ironic understatement of this passage bursts forth in a taunting attack on Mr. Lindsey. "But, after all," Hawthorne writes, "there is no teaching anything to wise men of Mr. Lindsey's stamp. They know everything,—oh, to be sure!—everything that has been, and everything that is, and everything that, by any future possibility, can be. And should some phenomenon of nature or providence transcend their system, they will not recognize it, even if it come to pass under their very noses." The honest, kind-hearted, well-meaning, and benevolent Mr. Lindsey is thus an object of scorn at the end of the tale.

"The Snow-Image" (subtitled "A Childish Miracle") is a tale of the marvelous as perceived from two points of view. Because of her faith Mrs. Lindsey can entertain a vision of the wonderful and seek to fathom its deeper import. In one sense she was like a child, says Hawthorne: she possessed a pure heart "full of childlike simplicity and faith," which sometimes revealed "truths so profound that other people laughed at them as nonsense and absurdity." From Mr. Lindsey's commonsense point of view, however, there can be no such truths. His mode of perception blights that of his wife, reduces the marvelous to a puddle of water on the floor, and finally remains unaware that it has played the role of antagonist in a diminutive tragedy of the imagination.

Miles Coverdale is the marriage of Mr. and Mrs. Lindsey. And they are not well matched. Shortly after his arrival at Blithedale, Coverdale wonders "what, in the name of common-sense, had I to do with any better society than I had always lived in?" When Hollingsworth calls the Blithedale experiment wretched and unsubstantial, Coverdale replies, perhaps wishfully, that their "highest anticipations have a solid footing on common-sense." Again, after his dream of Zenobia, Hollingsworth, and Priscilla, Coverdale awakes with "one of those unreasonable sadnesses that you know not how to deal with, because it involves nothing for common-sense to clutch." He later attacks Hollingsworth on the grounds that the philanthropist has no "common-sense." Theodore, from Zenobia's legend, is seen to be more closely related to Coverdale when we recall that he "prided himself upon his common-sense." In the legendary terms of this inset story, Theodore experiences a failure of faith precisely because of his commitment to common sense. Hence he cannot free the veiled lady from bondage and win her for himself. In the total story Coverdale displays the same kind of failure as a part of his more complex makeup: he too refuses the veiled lady by not offering the generosity and helpfulness that could bring them together. Both Blithedale and Priscilla are most clearly to be understood by means of imaginative

faith. Since his faith is seamed with doubt and common sense, Coverdale can only muster a fitful belief in Blithedale and a retrospective
statement of love for Priscilla.

In Search of a Role

When Miles Coverdale describes himself, toward the end of *The
Blithedale Romance*, as a man who would die for a cause provided
the effort "did not involve an unreasonable amount of trouble," he
counters quickly by saying that he is exaggerating his defects. The
terms of his description are typically humorous and hyperbolic: "If
Kossuth, for example, would pitch the battlefield of Hungarian rights
within an easy ride of my abode, and choose a mild, sunny morning,
after breakfast, for the conflict, Miles Coverdale would gladly be his
man for one brave rush upon the levelled bayonets. Further than that,
I should be loath to pledge myself." With an ironic charm born of
self-knowledge, Coverdale is stacking the rhetorical deck against himself—"after breakfast" is the connoisseur's touch, worthy of a man
who is "a devoted epicure" of his own emotions.

To exaggerate a defect, however, one must first have the defect.
And Coverdale defines himself in *The Blithedale Romance* as one
who will not attempt to help others if helping involves "an unreasonable amount of trouble." His response to Westervelt during
their encounter in the forest is characteristic: "If I can do anything
for you without too much trouble to myself, say so." Coverdale has
taken an immediate dislike to Westervelt, and subsequent events justify
his feeling. But the stance of this response is of a piece with the
later, half-bantering statement about Kossuth and Hungarian rights; in
both cases he expresses a disinclination to trouble himself.

Moreover, *The Blithedale Romance* begins with a significant episode in which Coverdale displays an identical disinclination. In the
first chapter he meets old Moodie, who has heard of Coverdale's
impending departure for Blithedale. Wondering why Moodie would
be interested, Coverdale asks if he can be of service before he
leaves. "If you pleased, Mr. Coverdale," replies Moodie, "you might
do me a very great favor." At this Coverdale hesitates: " 'A very
great one,' repeated I, in a tone that must have expressed but little
alacrity of beneficence, although I was ready to do the old man
any amount of kindness involving no special trouble to myself. 'A

very great favor, do you say?'" Typically, Coverdale is afraid that a "very great favor" might involve "special trouble" to himself. Moodie, reticent, wary of rebuff, has "further thoughts." We never learn (from Moodie or from Coverdale) the substance of Moodie's abortive request; but if his favor has any relevance to the narrative, it could only be that he was planning to ask Coverdale to take Priscilla to Blithedale.

At the outset of the story Coverdale has thus refused Priscilla, who is offered to him mysteriously in the form of a "very great favor" to Moodie. Because he will not "trouble" himself, Coverdale passes up the opportunity to take Priscilla in his charge. As a consequence, he cannot make a clean break with his past life; for whether he likes it or not his refusal, in the form of Priscilla, accompanies him to Blithedale—but now in the charge of Hollingsworth.

The attempt to begin the life of paradise anew at Blithedale exemplifies the quest for the lost opportunity. Although we know little of Coverdale other than that he is a minor poet with a comfortable bachelor apartment and a taste for cigars and wine, we assume that he is sufficiently dissatisfied with life as he has heretofore attempted to live it to look for something better. And from the subsequent turn of events—including his refusal of Priscilla, her arrival at Blithedale, and his final declaration of love—it would appear that Coverdale is looking for the opportunity to have a role in life. The special narrative tension of *Blithedale*, I believe, derives from the narrator's search for a role—and specifically for a role to which he has already surrendered the right, for which he has not had faith enough to prove himself worthy. The controlling irony of the romance is that Coverdale has already declined what he is looking for.

Most often, Coverdale's role is seen as that of chorus. He himself makes the point. But his most explicit statement to this effect bears examination. After breaking off his first meeting with Westervelt, Coverdale lingers nearby "with perhaps a vague idea that some new event would grow out of Westervelt's proposed interview with Zenobia." Then, in the well-known passage:

My own part in these transactions was singularly subordinate. It resembled that of the Chorus in a classic play, which seems to be set aloof from the possibility of personal concernment, and bestows the whole measure of its hope and fear, its exultation or sorrow, on the fortunes of others, between whom and itself this sympathy is the only bond. Destiny, it may be,—the most skillful of stage-managers,—seldom chooses to ar- range its scenes, and carry forward its drama, without securing the pres- ence of at least one calm observer. It is his office to give applause when due, and sometimes an inevitable tear, to detect the final fitness of incident to character, and distil in his long-brooding thought the whole morality of the performance.

This statement would have a severely restricted application if "these transactions" referred only to the ensuing interview between Wes- tervelt and Zenobia. In that case one might expect "this transaction." If Coverdale is referring to his total relationship to the major charac- ters at Blithedale, however, he has made—as a look at the context will show—a startling and abrupt transition from the specific to the gen- eral. The substance of the passage suggests the broader meaning as the more likely of the two despite the lack of transition, and we are tacitly invited to see Coverdale's role as that of "Chorus in a classic play."

But Coverdale seems hardly "to be set aloof from the possibility of personal concernment." Indeed, on a number of occasions he evinces some dissatisfaction with a subordinate part as chorus. After noting that Priscilla talked "more largely and freely" with Hollings- worth than with Zenobia, he adds that he would have thought better of his own qualities "had Priscilla marked me out for the third place in her regards. But, though she appeared to like me tolerably well, I could never flatter myself with being distinguished by her as Hollingsworth and Zenobia were." Again, Coverdale says that he often felt lonely in the midst of cheerful society: he cannot overlook that "while these three characters figured so largely on my private theatre, I—though probably reckoned as a friend by all—was at best but a secondary or tertiary personage with either of them."[4]

When the four major characters leave Eliot's pulpit (in chapter 14), Priscilla skips off first, Zenobia and Hollingsworth follow, and Coverdale brings up the rear. Taking his cue from Zenobia's remarks, Coverdale has championed women's rights at Eliot's pulpit, only to have Hollingsworth dominate both the women and the scene. "I smiled," he says, "somewhat bitterly, it is true—in contemplation of my own ill-luck. How little did these women care for me, who had freely conceded all their claims, and a great deal more, out of the fulness of my heart; while Hollingsworth . . . seemed to have brought them to his feet!" With a conscious lack of generosity, he points out to Priscilla that Zenobia and Hollingsworth make an imposing couple; then he goes on to say that "it is an insufferable bore to see one man engrossing every thought of all the women, and leaving his friend to suffer in outer seclusion, without even the alternative of solacing himself with what the more fortunate individual has rejected."

These are not the statements one expects from a chorus; they are rather the statements of a man who considers himself to be excluded, who confronts a situation in which he has no vital role. And they involve regret rather than satisfaction or indifference. When he leaves Blithedale for the city, Coverdale humorously explains that a lack of feminine charm among the group caused him to resist the temptation to kiss all the sisters good-bye; in a telling comment he adds, "nobody, to say the truth, seemed to expect it." He gives Priscilla's hand "a pressure," which, he thinks, "she neither resisted nor returned." Her heart, he believes, "was deep, but of small compass," with room for only a few "dearest ones, among whom she never reckoned me."

Whether he is describing a scene at Eliot's pulpit, analyzing Hollingsworth's hold over women or the limited scope of Priscilla's heart, or evaluating the collective lack of glamor among the Blithedale sisterhood, Coverdale typically ends with himself. And he ends by defining himself as left out, by claiming the role of chorus because there is no other role for him to play.

The sustained metaphor of a theater, established by Hawthorne in his preface, has a special importance to Coverdale, the narrator in search of a role. Insofar as we see him fashioning his material, it is in terms of a theatrical production, a play; he realizes that a group of characters has long been upon his "mental stage, as actors in a drama," placed there by an intricate series of events, "greatly assisted by my method of insulating them from other relations." Zenobia, Priscilla, and Hollingsworth, he says, figured largely on his "private theatre." Sustained by a cluster of terms which keep it flexible, this metaphor does much to structure Coverdale's thinking about reality. Its terms are formative as well as descriptive; what they reveal is Coverdale's way of portraying to himself a world from which he is being excluded. At an early point, Zenobia's presence at Blithedale makes their "heroic enterprise'" seem to Coverdale "like an illusion, a masquerade, a pastoral, a counterfeit Arcadia, in which we grown-up men and women were making a play-day of the years that were given us to live in." He tries "to analyze this impression, but not with much success." It is simply the way things look to him. He has nothing to do in life, he tells Hollingsworth, "unless to make pretty verses, and play a part, with Zenobia and the rest of the amateurs, in our own pastoral."

Certainly an important reason for the imagery of veils and masks, which Frank Davidson examined a number of years ago, is that Coverdale sees reality in terms of the stage, where masks and roles are conventional modes of representation.[5] With meaningful ambiguity Coverdale says that a "play of passions" will evolve at Blithedale (the gentle passion, we know, is rife) and that Priscilla's imperfections affect him with "a kind of playful pathos." Zenobia once gives Priscilla a look of such murderous intensity that it "would have made the fortune of a tragic actress." The stage, Coverdale feels, would have been Zenobia's "proper sphere." Such examples—and there are dozens of others—make it clear that Coverdale sees himself in the world of a theater, where a character must have a role, must "play a part," if he is to have any right on the stage.

The action of *Blithedale* bears a structural relationship to the sustained metaphor of the theater and thus to Coverdale's search for a role. During the first half of the romance Coverdale is, in effect, on stage with the characters in the developing drama. He talks and works with them; they attend him during his illness. Gradually, however, he becomes aware of the evolving interrelationship of Zenobia, Priscilla, and Hollingsworth. These three, he says, were separated from the rest of the community in his mind "and stood forth as the indices of a problem which it was my business to solve." Involving a number of unknown quantities, the "problem" stands forth most immediately and most personally to Coverdale as a triangle. And he finds himself cast in the unenviable role of fourth side; all he can do is watch and comment. Hence he thinks of himself as a chorus, though, as we have seen, he is hardly "aloof from the possibility of personal concernment."

Coverdale's departure for the city midway through the romance comes shortly after the revealing scene at Eliot's pulpit and immediately following his break with Hollingsworth. In his lonely position Blithedale now looks different to him, arid and sunburned like the "blighted" areas of his mind. Before deciding on how to satisfy what he defines as a thirst for novelty, he withdraws to the city to judge the business of Blithedale from a distance. It strikes him as healthy, sanative, to reestablish contact with the outside world, to see it again as it is rather than as it "might or ought to be."

Coverdale's temporary withdrawal from Blithedale sets him more thoroughly at a distance from the situation developing with respect to Zenobia, Priscilla, and Hollingsworth even as it offers him a broader perspective by which to account for Westervelt. He leaves for the city only after refusing Hollingsworth's invitation to join in the philanthropic enterprise of reforming criminals. Here, indeed, would be a role with a vengeance, but one that would completely efface Coverdale in Hollingsworth's iron drama of will and inflexibility. "Be with me, or be against me!" says Hollingsworth; "there is no third choice for you." And so, declining to be a pawn, Coverdale leaves a stage that has come to be dominated by one man. In town his position of spectator becomes formalized: looking from the window of his hotel room, he sees Zenobia in the apartment across the way "like a full-length picture, in the heavy festoons of the window-curtains." Westervelt and Priscilla complete the picture. Irritated and heartsick, watching from the outside, Coverdale begins to "long for a catastrophe." He will observe ("as it seemed my part to do"); try to understand; or, failing that, try to sympathize. Then, "the curtain fallen, I would pass onward with my poor individual life, which was now attenuated of much of its proper substance, and diffused among many alien interests."

But Coverdale is once again attempting a resignation he cannot achieve. When Zenobia sees him watching, she drops the curtain in the window, and it falls "like the drop-curtain of a theatre, in the interval between acts," affecting Coverdale with "a keen, revengeful sense" of insult. Not content with being a spectator who can be shut out by the dropping of a curtain, Coverdale makes a final attempt at breaking into the drama by going directly to Zenobia's apartment. But he has nothing effectual to do or say, and Zenobia, Priscilla, and Westervelt walk out on him.

After his interview with old Moodie, Coverdale begins a new chapter of his narrative: "Well," he says, "I betook myself away, and wandered up and down, like an exorcised spirit that had been driven from its old haunts after a mighty struggle." The statement is typically exaggerated; Coverdale is no more an exorcised spirit than he is one who has made a mighty struggle. He has not been driven out. But he has been excluded. He has also wandered up and down enough to wind up in a village hall watching Westervelt's exploitation of the Veiled Lady on the stage. And here he sees an example of how, by sheer force of will, one can break into a situation in which one has no formal or conventional role. The mesmerist and his seer form a company of two; in their act there is no room for a third. Westervelt flaunts his absolute command of the Veiled Lady by challenging the audience to try, if it can, to make its presence known to her. Westervelt's demonstration affirms the supreme reality of the act itself. Thus, when Hollingsworth steps onto the stage and calls with stern confidence for Priscilla to join him, he is literally breaking up the act, tacitly denying its reality and its power in the face of a dominant will to the contrary.

When he returns to Blithedale, Coverdale is such a distance from the action that he is but an erstwhile spectator. He comes on the masqueraders while their frolic is in progress. And when he finds Zenobia, Priscilla, and Hollingsworth at Eliot's pulpit, Zenobia tells him that he has come half an hour too late and has "missed a scene" he would have enjoyed. Only when Zenobia, too, is excluded does Coverdale feel a sense of companionship. Only when the scene is emotionally set for disaster does he take over the narrative with a new kind of authority. Zenobia's suicide marks the catastrophe for which Coverdale has been longing; he is never more wedded to the action than during the grisly search for her body. Ultimately, of course, Zenobia's death precipitates the final exclusion of Coverdale: she is buried not in the spot preferred by Coverdale but in that selected by Hollingsworth; and Hollingsworth, in a final posture of guilt and dependence, stands between Priscilla and the "vindictive shadow" of Zenobia.

From Self to Solitude

The Blithedale Romance, Hyatt H. Waggoner suggests, is the story of a Happy Valley played out on the same theme as Johnson's *Rasselas* but with the plot inverted.[6] If one grants the nature of man, the impossibility of reform and the vanity of human wishes appear as two somber and undeniable facts. Hawthorne's Happy Valley has doom written into its charter. Initially, the Blithedalers are at fault in drawing apart from humanity for the purposes of reforming it. The means they choose thwart the ends they envision. As Coverdale sees, they have put themselves in competition with the world. Their view of reform is essentially myopic.

Most of the Blithedalers are nameless background figures. In the foreground are the chief characters of the romance. And the specific personalities of the principal characters hasten the doom inherent in the scheme as a whole. Zenobia's pride, passion, and fierce competitive nature collide with the single-mindedness of Hollingsworth, who is at Blithedale only to turn it to his own purpose. Inevitably, the result is disaster, the physical destruction of a self already destroyed emotionally, a crippling sense of guilt in one whose strength came from a conviction of his own infallibility. In repudiating Priscilla, Zenobia repudiates something of the essential nature of woman as conceived by Hawthorne, something, to be sure, incapable of self-definition yet perhaps for that very reason capable of surviving in a self-destructive world. In rescuing Priscilla from Westervelt, Hollingsworth forces Zenobia to confront, as his choice, the passive, uncompetitive, and indomitably innocent woman she cannot be. Given the choice between Priscilla and Zenobia, both Coverdale and Hollingsworth choose the former; for, ultimately, the choice is between life and death.

To say that Miles Coverdale cannot find a role for himself at Blithedale is of course to validate the fiction of the romance. And this is to arrive at the clarifying judgment of James H. Justus, who writes that "If Coverdale is an embarrassingly peripheral actor in the romance of Blithedale, Hawthorne makes him the leading performer in *The Blithedale Romance*." By projecting certain aspects of himself, Hawthorne created a character and bestowed on him the status of one who tells a story. Although he may shade the truth and appear at times unreliable, this narrator cannot, as Justus goes on to say, "be abstracted from the form which he encloses (the story he tells)" nor from "the form which encloses him (the story Hawthorne tells)."[7] The sensual eloquence of Zenobia and the monomania of Hollingsworth combine to make Coverdale seem weak and irresolute. Zenobia attacks his "uncertain sense of some duty to perform" as "bigotry; self-conceit; an insolent curiosity; a meddlesome temper; a cold-blooded criticism, founded on a shallow interpretation of half-perceptions; a monstrous skepticism in regard to any conscience or any wisdom, except one's own; a most irreverent propensity to thrust Providence aside, and substitute oneself in its awful place." Out of these traits, she continues, and others "as miserable as these, comes your idea of duty!" If one senses that Coverdale does not quite deserve all of this, that Zenobia looses on him a frustration engendered by Hollingsworth, the fact remains that it is Coverdale who catches the full force of her outrage. He is the victim, the fall guy, unable to respond except by saying "I wash my hands of it all" and thereby emphasizing his inability to act in and on such a world.

As the only Hawthorne narrator to tell so long a story, Miles Coverdale has a special burden to bear. He succeeds in getting the story told. But just as he has been a frustrated and cynical figure throughout, so he is a solitary figure at the end. The artist in *Blithedale* would be a man; the narrator would be a character with a role. To the human problems of the Hawthorne artist are added the technical problems of the Hawthorne narrator; the result is a partial man, lacking in generosity, unwilling to do "very great" favors for others—and a partial character, who must sit in trees to overhear conversations and peer in windows at scenes of which he is no part. Miles Coverdale's final admission of love for Priscilla is both a sad and an unsatisfactory confession, an attempt on the part of Hawthorne as well as Coverdale to make whole in retrospect a figure who has sacrificed himself to the story as pleasantly as he could.[8] When there is nothing more to narrate, when he has told us once again in his most charming manner of his disinclination to trouble himself for others, this Hawthorne narrator stands alone, contemplating his desiccated emotions.

Chapter Eight

The Marble Faun

A Different Neutral Ground

In his preface to *The Marble Faun*, Hawthorne addresses once again the problem of writing fiction which he had confronted throughout his career. Italy, he says, was chiefly valuable as the setting of his romance because it afforded him "a sort of poetic or fairy precinct, where actualities would not be so terribly insisted upon as they are, and must needs be, in America." The difficulty of writing a romance about a country which lacked shadow, antiquity, and mystery encouraged him to make use of a setting redolent with ruin and guilt, twin products of time. In Italy, Hawthorne seemed at last to have found an existing neutral ground which would give him the latitude he had long cultivated as the basic condition of his fiction.

But this particular "fairy precinct," one sees quickly in the narrative, is crowded with the relics of history, whereas Hawthorne's metaphor of a neutral ground characteristically evokes regions relatively unfurnished and unmarked by time. Set in vague, asocial worlds, "The Hollow of the Three Hills" and "The Birth-mark" are immune from history because of their intent focus on moral concerns. Tales such as "The New Adam and Eve" and "Earth's Holocaust" use apocalyptic and distancing perspectives to suggest the shallowness of social attitudes when the human heart is ignored. Hawthorne's historical tales likewise thrive on a bareness of setting. His contrasting descriptions of a Puritan meetinghouse and of a cathedral demonstrate what simplicity and grandeur can mean to his imagination. Plain on the outside, the meetinghouse in "The Gentle Boy" has "unplastered walls," "naked wood work," an "undraperied pulpit," and "rows of long cushionless benches" in place of pews. Such an "unadorned setting," as he terms it, allows Hawthorne to focus on the actions of his characters. In *Our Old Home*, on the other hand, he uses the "one set of phrases" which describe for him "all the Cathedrals in England, and elsewhere":

"an acre or two of stone-flags for a pavement; rows of vast columns supporting a vaulted roof at a dusky height"; stained glass windows, a "massive" organ, the "Bishop's throne, the pulpit, the altar." The consequence of all these trappings, Hawthorne says, is that in cathedrals the sermon, the immediate human utterance, "is an exceedingly diminutive and unimportant part of the religious services." The "magnificence of the setting," he continues, "quite dazzles out what we Puritans look upon as the jewel of the whole affair."

With its "threefold antiquity" (Etruscan, Roman, and Christian) stretching back to the mystery of the obelisks yet existing monumentally in the present, Italy in *The Marble Faun* is a cathedrallike setting, richly adorned, dazzling in its treasures, radically different from the stark new world Hawthorne had portrayed a decade before in *The Scarlet Letter.* Following the logic of his conception, the author hopes to inspire in the reader "a vague sense of ponderous remembrances; a perception of such weight and density . . . that the present moment is pressed down or crowded out, and our individual affairs and interests" become thereby less real. Rather than try to escape into the past, Hawthorne thus plans to use it to attenuate the reality of the present. Juxtaposed with "the massiveness of the Roman Past," he writes, "all matters that we handle or dream of nowadays look evanescent and visionary alike." Cast into the overwhelming shadow of the past, the present for once attracts Hawthorne as a congenial ground for romance.

But Hawthorne has difficulty making the present function as a visionary neutral ground in *The Marble Faun.* For the city of Rome presses its present-day shabbiness upon him in a decidedly unpoetic way. Despite his admiration for the "imperial city," the "city of all time, and of all the world," Hawthorne was irritated by various aspects of Roman life from the time of his arrival in January, 1858. A notebook entry in February of that year epitomizes his mood. He wishes he had kept a minute record of his

feelings and impressions during the past fortnight. It would have shown modern Rome in an aspect in which it has never yet been depicted. But I have now grown somewhat acclimated, and the first freshness of my discomfort has worn off, so that I shall never be able to express how I dislike the place, and how wretched I have been in it; and soon, I suppose, warmer weather will come, and perhaps reconcile me to Rome against my will. Cold, narrow lanes, between tall, ugly, mean-looking, white-washed houses, sour bread, pavements most uncomfortable to the feet, enormous prices for poor living; beggars, pick-pockets, ancient temples and broken monuments, and clothes hanging to dry about them; French soldiers, monks, and priests of every degree; a shabby population, smoking bad cigars,—these would have been some of the points of my description.

"Of course," he concludes, "there are better and truer things to be said. ..."

Hawthorne later wrote to James T. Fields that he bitterly detested Rome and fully acquiesced "in all the mischief that has happened to it, from Nero's conflagration downward." But his attitude at the time of leaving Italy was more complex; it reveals an uneasy combination of fascination and impatience with regard to the brilliance and squalor of the Eternal City. In his notebook he wrote that he wished never to see any part of Rome again,

though no place ever took so strong a hold of my being..., nor ever seemed so close to me and so strangely familiar. I seem to know it better than my birthplace, and to have known it longer; and though I have been very miserable there, and languid with the effects of the atmosphere, and disgusted with a thousand things in its daily life, still I cannot say I hate it, perhaps might fairly own a love for it. But life being too short for such questionable and troublesome enjoyments, I desire never to set eyes on it again. ...

The "better and truer things" of Rome evoke a problematic nostalgia that Hawthorne's disgust "with a thousand things in its daily life" disinclines him to indulge.

One senses in Hawthorne's statements a tendency to submit to the "strangely familiar" attraction of Rome all the more forcibly resisted because submitting would require a fundamental change of personality and vision. The lengthy and serious illness of his daughter Una in Italy tended, understandably, to exaggerate his vexation over petty annoyances. But Hawthorne could never rest content with "the dreariness, the ugliness, shabbiness, un-home-likeness of a Roman street." He required a personal rather than a historical sense of home which, ultimately, only New England could satisfy.[1] In Italy, he was caught up in a unique problem: assimilating experience that was and would remain alien to his temperament. Although he made a mighty

effort and produced what may well be his most challenging work of
fiction, he did not—perhaps could not—fully succeed. When he tried
by invoking the ponderous reality of the past to create a neutral ground
in the present, he could not transmute or wish away shabby streets,
dreary houses, beggars, smells, the aroma of corruption. Present-day
Rome, "a heap of broken rubbish," lay squarely in the center of his
"poetic or fairy precinct." Everywhere there was a cross, with "nastiness
at the foot of it."

Problems of Assimilation

Hawthorne's portrayal of contemporary Rome in *The Marble
Faun* is shaped by his feeling toward Catholicism and toward the
very past which, he hopes, will make the present seem "evanescent
and visionary." His distinction between the Christian and the classical past demonstrates great admiration for the latter and hardly more
than intermittent respect for the former. "As it now exists," he says,
Rome "has grown up under the Popes, and seems like nothing but
a heap of broken rubbish, thrown into the great chasm between our
own days and the Empire, merely to fill it up; and for the better
part of two thousand years, its annals of obscure policies, and wars,
and continually recurring misfortunes, seem also but broken rubbish,
as compared with its classical history." Hawthorne is not blindly romantic in his feeling for the classical past: it is possible, he believes,
that Caesar "may have trod narrower and filthier ways in his path to
the Capitol, than even those of modern Rome." Again, he speaks of
"the better civilization of Christianity" and has Kenyon bless the Middle Ages for the splendor of painted church windows and the fitness
of sculpture. Still, "to a spectator on the spot," he says in expressing
his dominant feeling, "it is remarkable that the events of Roman
history, and Roman life itself, appear not so distant as the Gothic
ages which suceeded them."

Because present-day Rome has evolved under papal authority,
Hawthorne holds the Catholic church largely responsible for the
conditions he sees. But one must make a distinction regarding his
attitude toward the church: throughout *The Marble Faun* Hawthorne seems to think of Catholicism as a masterful *idea* (or, to use
his term, "system"); he is visibly impressed by the universality of
the church, by the wealth of its spiritual resources, by its iconic

sensibility. But he objects to the human—hence imperfect and unworthy—beings who exercise its temporal authority. In a statement that measures both his admiration for the idea of the church and his scorn for the mortals who put that idea into action, Hawthorne says "it is difficult to imagine it a contrivance of mere man"; "its mighty machinery was forged and put together, not on middle earth, but either above or below. If there were but angels to work it, instead of the very different class of engineers who now manage its cranks and safety-valves, the system would soon vindicate the dignity and holiness of its origin." The priests of Rome come under special criticism. "Pampered, sensual, with red and bloated cheeks, and carnal eyes," they have what strikes him as "a grosser development of animal life than most men." Placed in an "unnatural relation with women," they have "thereby lost the healthy, human conscience that pertains to other human beings, who own the sweet household ties connecting them with wife and daughter." Yet the idea of Catholicism retains its unique and powerful appeal: must not the faith that built St. Peter's have resources for all? Hawthorne asks. If religion has a material home, is it not the World's Cathedral?

The tendency to castigate individual human beings carries over into the other aspects of Italian life portrayed in *The Marble Faun*. For paupers Hawthorne has little use: "this kind of vermin infested the house of Monte Beni worse than any other spot in beggar-haunted Italy." Beggars are "pests"—"human ones"—who hunt one out at every stage of a journey. In his notebook he writes that "the multitude of beggars in Italy makes the heart as obdurate as stone." Now, for Hawthorne, this is surprising language. In a fictional context, as we have seen, the idea of an obdurate heart would strike immediate negative connotations; if a character in a Hawthorne tale relegated beggars to the status of vermin, he would be guilty of pride and liable to exclusion from the body of humanity. Hawthorne does not choose pride in *The Marble Faun*; he does not forget the heart; but he does give way to a rhetoric of irritation that sounds angrily among efforts to assimilate and integrate the materials of his narrative. From statements such as those about beggars it seems a long way to the Election Day scene in *The Scarlet Letter*, in which, despite the severity of the Puritan community, Hawthorne can say that "the great warm heart of the people smiled, grimly perhaps, but warmly too." It seems a long way to the figures of the doctor, the lawyer, and

the stage agent in "Ethan Brand," mutilated figures all, each of whom
tries in his feeble, inept way to serve humanity. And it seems a long
way to Hawthorne's admonition in "Fancy's Show Box" that one
should not disclaim his brotherhood, even with the guiltiest. In each
case, the distance measures Hawthorne's distance from home.

When Hawthorne succumbs even momentarily to "beggar-haunted,"
"priest-ridden" Italy, his narrative runs into trouble. Perhaps he
finds too much history in Italy for the purposes of his romance and
is dismayed to see the way in which history has produced beggars
and priests. His frequent recourse in *The Marble Faun* to the techniques of the sketch suggests a problem of assimilation.[2] For Hawthorne tended to comprehend whatever was recalcitrant to the world
of his fiction according to the modes of the sketch. At the very
portals of romance, yet distinct in place and form, stands "The Custom-
House" sketch, testifying to the danger Hawthorne's imagination ran
of being inundated by the present and to the admirable stratagem
of the neutral ground which converted that danger into a special
kind of fiction. In *The Marble Faun*, Hawthorne's imagination is in
danger of losing itself in the past—and there seems to be no sure
way out. His statement that "all towns should be made capable of
purification by fire, or of decay, within each half-century" suggests
a desire to legislate the dimensions of the past; the statement is remi-
niscent of Thoreau's feeling about the necessity of periodic purification and of Holgrave's progressive ideas in *The House of the Seven
Gables*. But Hawthorne's perspective on Holgrave's ideas of reform
enables him to characterize the daguerrotypist effectively. In *The
Marble Faun*, the idea of purification characterizes nothing but Hawthorne's own troubled view.

The Transformation of Donatello

Although Hawthorne tends to blame the squalor of Rome on centuries of papal misrule, he makes significant use of the monuments
of Christianity throughout his romance. Guido's Michael, for example, helps to portray both Hilda and Miriam. And three of the most
effective scenes in *The Marble Faun* employ materials of Christian
history—the company in the catacombs, Hilda in the World's Cathedral, and the meeting of Donatello and Miriam near the statue of
Pope Julius III in Perugia.

To contrast the marketplace of Perugia with that of seventeenth-century Boston in *The Scarlet Letter* is to see the manner in which Hawthorne dramatizes the moral imagination of each society for the specific purposes of each narrative. Above the marketplace in Boston stands the scaffold, bleak and austere. In the marketplace of Perugia sits the statue of Pope Julius III, his right hand "raised and spread abroad, as if in the act of shedding forth a benediction" with serene affection. For the Puritan community, the scaffold is the formal place of public confession and punishment; simple and unadorned, it serves the intent spiritual needs of the people, whose leaders summon sinners to its pedestal of shame. For the citizens of Perugia, the bronze pontiff exemplifies a mediating influence which is part of their daily lives; the statue serves their spiritual needs by its representation of benignity and "majestic patience." It brings before them "the familiar face of generations." Whereas Hester Prynne standing "statue-like" on the scaffold is the center of public attention, Miriam and Donatello, at the foot of the pope's statue, can meet in private in the midst of a crowded square—the only attention paid them being a deferential acknowledgment of Miriam's beauty.

Hawthorne makes the pope's statue in Perugia dramatically functional for his narrative. He creates a memorable scene, one recalled by Henry James, who, in visiting Perugia, felt the statue bring Hawthorne's Miriam strongly to his mind.[3] In the context of *The Marble Faun*, the meeting of Donatello and Miriam marks an important summation of and turning point in the action. Donatello's solitary quest for self-knowledge has passed the initial groping phase; his maturation, we discover, has given a new resonance to his capacity for forgiveness, understanding, and love. The final movement of the story takes its start from the marketplace in Perugia, under the benevolent impulse of Pope Julius III.

It is doubtful if Hawthorne knew much about the pope whose statue serves his romance so well. "Murray's guidebook," he complained in his notebook while on the trip that would take him to Perugia, "is exceedingly vague and unsatisfactory along this route. . . ." The guidebook told him nothing to diminish his admiration for the statue. But although reforms in the church continued during the reign of Pope Julius III (1550–55), he was known as a man who thrived on pleasure and entertainment. According to the *Catholic Encyclopedia*, his great fault was nepotism: "Shortly after his ascen-

sion he bestowed the purple on his unworthy favourite Innocenzo del
Monte, a youth of seventeen whom he had picked up on the streets
of Parma some years previously, and who had been adopted by the
pope's brother Balduino. This act gave rise to some very disagreeable rumours concerning the Pope's relation to Innocenzo. Julius
was also extremely lavish in bestowing ecclesiastical dignities and
benefices upon his relatives." Pope Julius III, as a man, was precisely
the kind of cleric whom Hawthorne disdains throughout *The Marble
Faun*. Pope Julius III, as a statue, dispenses the aura of benignity
and universal benediction that Hawthorne recognizes and employs
for his dramatic purposes. But Hawthorne, especially the Hawthorne
of *The Marble Faun*, might well have been constrained to handle
his important scene very differently had he known the history of his
"bronze pontiff." The bronzeness of Julius III allowed Hawthorne
to treat him more charitably than most other people have.

The general tendency of Hawthorne's fiction to invest and discover meaning in what becomes a symbolic object is thus very much
a part of his technique in *The Marble Faun*. Not only does Hawthorne convert pictures, churches, and statues into metaphor; his characters likewise draw symbolic meaning from the experience around
them. Kenyon, especially, has a habit of seeing experience as emble-
matic; and although his prudishness is perhaps more thoroughgoing
than that of any other character in the book, such a habit makes him
a useful observer throughout much of the narrative.

The greatest emblem, of course, is Donatello, whose "wonderful
resemblance to the Faun of Praxiteles forms the keynote" of the
narrative. The conception of the Faun had charmed Hawthorne during his first months in Italy. In April, 1858, he saw a copy of the
Faun of Praxiteles while visiting the casino in the Villa Borghese and
thought it "a natural and delightful link betwixt human and brute
life, with something of a divine character intermingled." Two days
later he saw the original statue in the Capitol and mused again over
the possibilities of a story regarding it. In the opening chapter of
The Marble Faun he concludes a lengthy description of the statue by
prefiguring the theme of his romance: such a creature, he says, "might
be educated through the medium of his emotions." Once again, he
envisions the Faun as a kind of imaginative link in the chain of being,
"neither man nor animal, and yet no monster, but a being in whom

both races meet on friendly ground." For Hawthorne's imagination, the Faun is a true habitant of a middle, or neutral, ground.

Innocent and cheerful, incapable of guile and of good or evil, Donatello seems to Hilda to have "nothing to do with time," to have "a look of eternal youth in his face." To Miriam he appears "not precisely a man, nor yet a child, but, in a high and beautiful sense, an animal,—a creature in a state of development less than what mankind has attained, yet the more perfect within itself for that very deficiency." Throughout the first two chapters the characters sportively insist on the resemblance between Donatello and the Faun of Praxiteles—one could hardly miss the point.[4]

Traceable through a noble line at Monte Beni for a thousand years, Donatello's ancestry reaches "far beyond the region of definite and demonstrable fact" to a "region of rich poetry" in which "the rich soil, so long uncultivated and untrodden, had lapsed into a nearly primeval state of wilderness." Perhaps once in a century a "genuine Monte Beni, of the original type" made his appearance; clearly, Donatello is one of these originals. Almost literally a child of nature, Donatello is something of a moral anachronism, a premoral creature plunged into a fallen world.

Donatello's fall, his loss of a sense of identity, and his subsequent "rise" to a moral condition provide the forward thrust of Hawthorne's narrative. And Hawthorne portrays Donatello's story according to the modes established in his earlier work. After the murder of the model, Donatello experiences first an ecstatic and exhilarating sense of freedom which is much like that experienced by Arthur Dimmesdale following his forest interview with Hester Prynne. Then comes the reaction: the terrible fact of loneliness, the sense of being an alien to the world. Donatello withdraws to his ancestral home only to find that innocence is a condition of the mind rather than of a place. Finally a new Donatello returns, first to Perugia where he meets Miriam, his partner in crime, then to Rome.

Immediately after the murder, Hawthorne tells us that a "fierce energy" has suddenly inspired Donatello: "It had kindled him into a man; it had developed within him an intelligence which was no native characteristic of the Donatello whom we have heretofore known. But that simple and joyous creature was gone forever." At

Monte Beni, Donatello discovers the terrible truth that his innocence is gone. But at Monte Beni he gropes toward the self-knowledge that will validate his transformation. Kenyon, his visitor, perceives that Donatello "had already had glimpses of strange and subtle matters in those dark caverns, into which all men must descend, if they would know anything beneath the surface and illusive pleasures of existence. And when they emerge, though dazzled and blinded by the first glare of daylight, they take truer and sadder views of life forever afterwards." The result is a new restraint, a "newly acquired power of dealing with his own emotions," that indicates as much as anything the change in Donatello.

Hawthorne reinforces the pattern of Donatello's transformation by exemplifying it in complementary ways. Appropriately in a story concerned so much with art and sculpture, he alludes to "Thorwalsen's three-fold analogy,—the clay model, the Life; the plaster cast, the Death; and the sculptured marble, the Resurrection"; and the analogy seems to be verified by the "spirit that was kindling up these imperfect features [of Kenyon's bust of Donatello], like a lambent flame." Nature likewise presents a suitable analogy: though Kenyon sees what Donatello does not, their view from the tower at Monte Beni at one point shows sunshine followed by patches of ominous shadow, then a violent thunderstorm, and finally—far off in the distance—sunshine again. And although Hawthorne thinks far too much of Hilda to have her change in any essential way, her knowledge of evil gives her "a deeper look into the heart of things; such as those necessarily acquire who have passed from picture galleries into dungeon gloom, and thence back to the picture gallery again. It is questionable whether she was ever so perfect a copyist thenceforth."

Donatello's fall from innocence leads him to the kind of intelligence, restraint, and self-awareness that define the full human condition. He has matured, risen to a higher state of existence; through sorrow and remorse have come a "vivified intellect" and an altered, deepened character. His premoral innocence has given way to life in a specifically human sense. Typically, Hawthorne manages things so that he may interject a counterview; to Kenyon, on first seeing Donatello in penitential garb, the transformation "seemed hardly worth the heavy price it had cost, in the sacrifice of those simple enjoyments that were gone forever. A creature of antique healthfulness had vanished from the earth," giving way to one more "morbid and remorseful man." But such a view represents no more than a nostalgic sigh for vanished innocence. As a man—precisely because he is now a man—the new Donatello is preferable to the old.

Donatello's fall is all the more to his advantage if one considers (what seems rarely to be considered) that his original kind of freshness and effervescent innocence was doomed in any event. To the question "Could Donatello have survived in his original state?" Hawthorne supplies a somber answer: beings like Donatello tend to grow sensual and selfish as youth disappears. In saying this, Hawthorne is not discussing the ordinary Monte Benis, but those of the original type. It was indisputable, he says, that

once in a century, or oftener, a son of Monte Beni gathered into himself the scattered qualities of his race, and reproduced the character that had been assigned to it from immemorial times. Beautiful, strong, brave, sincere, of honest impulses, and endowed with simple tastes and the love of homely pleasures, he was believed to possess gifts by which he could associate himself with the wild things of the forests, and with the fowls of the air, and could feel a sympathy even with the trees, among which it was his joy to dwell. On the other hand, there were deficiencies both of intellect and heart, and especially, as it seemed, in the development of the higher portion of man's nature. These defects were less perceptible in early youth, but showed themselves more strongly with advancing age, when, as the animal spirits settled down upon a lower level, the representative of the Monte Benis was apt to become sensual, addicted to gross pleasures, heavy, unsympathizing, and insulated within the narrow limits of a surly selfishness.

Hawthorne thus confines the term of Donatello's Faun-like innocence to the period of youth: he must either be catapulted into the human condition or settle gradually ino a sensual, surly animality. Clearly, despite his new liability to sin and sorrow, to remorse and regret, Donatello's transformation cannot be lamented. Though he seems to defy age, his youth—like all youth—is transitory; and age, without humanity, would offer him nothing but a sluggish, forlorn concentration on self.

The Paradox of the Fortunate Fall

Kenyon, Hawthorne's sculptor, has two related functions in *The Marble Faun*—to observe the process of transformation in Donatello and to watch over Hilda (who can, of course, watch over herself very well). Hawthorne portrays Kenyon as a young man of quick sensibility whose love for Hilda "insulated him from the wild experiences which some men gather." At some points in the romance, I think one must in candor admit, Kenyon is a bit hard to take. When Miriam and Donatello are reunited in Perugia after their interlude of pain, Kenyon sermonizes most condescendingly, telling them that because of their crime they cannot expect a blissful future, that sorrow must temper their love. He comes to be boringly predictable on the subject of the Catholic church, "that mass of unspeakable corruption." During the carnival scene near the end of the romance, Kenyon is hit by a dewy rosebud, signifying that his bond with Hilda is intact. He is also hit by a cauliflower, "a gratuitous expression," Nina Baym observes, of Hawthorne's disgust with him as man and artist.[5] But Kenyon seems to speak for the author when he expresses a love for his native land, and Kenyon's genuine concern for the welfare of Donatello makes him consistently important in the narrative.

It is largely through Kenyon's perceptions that we follow the process of change in Donatello at Monte Beni. When he arrives at the Faun's ancestral home, Kenyon notes that Donatello's simplicity is strangely intermixed with a new measure of experience. He talks with Donatello, attempts to assuage his grief and forlornness, and perceives with wonder the change taking place in his friend: "From some mysterious source, as the sculptor felt assured, a soul had been inspired" in the young count, who now shows a deeper sense and an "intelligence that began to deal with high subjects, though in a feeble and childish way." After Kenyon suggests that Donatello might devote his life to living for others, Donatello's face becomes "elevated and spiritualized. In the black depths, the Faun had found a soul, and was struggling with it towards the light of heaven." To Miriam, the sculptor speaks of Donatello's bewilderment with the revelations of each new day: "Out of his bitter agony, a soul and intellect, I could almost say, have been inspired in him." Again, he tells Miriam that after Donatello's "recent profound experience, he will re-create the world by the new eyes with which he will regard it." Kenyon is at his best in the section of the book that takes place at Monte Beni; alert and sensitive, he does credit to the quality of perception he is supposed to have. Indeed, what he perceives provides the substance for the idea of the fortunate fall, which awaits only a more audacious temperament to give it explicit formulation.

A woman of brilliance and sorrow, Miriam Schaefer, artist in oils (as the card on her door identifies her), moves through *The Marble Faun* shrouded in mystery. When Hawthorne says that "nobody knew anything about Miriam, either for good or for evil," that she "was plucked up out of a mystery and had its roots still clinging to her," one feels that his remarks are all too true. The dark woman of the narrative, passionate and wild like Hester Prynne and Zenobia, Miriam is implicated in the murder of the model and is also primarily responsible for interpreting Donatello's experience as a fortunate fall. When, after the murder, Donatello says simply that he did what Miriam's eyes bade him to, the words strike Miriam "like a bullet." Willing death to the model, she has drawn the infatuated Donatello to do her bidding. She is numbed at the idea of being a horror in the eyes of Donatello, but on her own behalf, Hawthorne makes clear, she feels "neither regret nor penitence."

In portraying Miriam, Hawthorne's problem is to shadow her with guilt without making her actually guilty of anything prior to the murder. Before the crime, he repeatedly causes her to project her sorrow and sense of disaster into the world around her. She considers happiness, for example, to be a thin crust which covers the pit of blackness. A theme of revenge toward men runs through her paintings. She speaks of the secret of her earlier life as "no precious pearl," but a "dark-red carbuncle—red as blood." After the crime, a gem on her bosom glimmers with "a clear, red lustre." Just as Kenyon is most effective in one particular section of the narrative—when he is observing the change in Donatello—so Miriam is at her best in the particular set of circumstances when her strength yields to weakness, when it is necessary for her to appeal for human sympathy and understanding. In Miriam's hour of need, Kenyon proves suspicious and evasive; Hilda, within the citadel of her innocence, rejects her. And Miriam, alone in a vacuum of guilt, seems for once more human than mysterious.

Miriam's audacity of mind defines her as the antithesis of Hilda, who keeps a steely grip on innocence. Between the two stands Kenyon; he is outreached by Miriam's strength of mind and virtually unmanned by the unswerving devotion he tenders to the uncompromising Hilda. In advancing the idea of the fortunate fall in *The*

Marble Faun, Hawthorne, it is interesting to note, chooses to have Miriam make the initial formulation. Though she trembles at her thoughts, Miriam feels impelled to "probe them to their depths." Donatello, she says to Kenyon, has won an "inestimable treasure" from his "experience of pain." The crime in which she and Donatello were "wedded" seems to have proved a means of education. Kenyon is somewhat shaken to hear such ideas, but Miriam finds pleasure in brooding on the verge of mystery. Is not the story of man's fall repeated in the romance of Monte Beni (Hawthorne's subtitle)? Was not Adam's sin, she asks in her ultimate formulation, the destined means by which man would rise to a loftier happiness than that of the original paradise? And does not this idea "account for the permitted existence of sin, as no other theory can?"

Kenyon "rightly," says Hawthorne, feels that these meditations are too dangerous to speculate upon. For Miriam has propounded a secularized version of the fortunate fall. The original notion of *felix culpa* (or happy sin) takes its meaning from the coming of Christ, not of knowledge. Because of Adam's original sin, Christ's life and atoning death became a necessity if man were to win heaven. Only by means of grace could man attain a greater happiness than that of Eden. By himself (and by definition), he could do nothing worthy of *super*natural reward. The theological or religious idea of the fortunate fall thus assumes the life, death, and resurrection of Christ to be the central fact of all history and accounts for Adam's sin as (paradoxically) happy or fortunate in such a total context.

Miriam, however, concerns herself with the loss of innocence and the advent of knowledge. Like Adam, she says, Donatello has fallen; like Adam, he has tasted of knowledge; and like Adam, he is rising to a higher state of existence. But to make knowledge (and not Christ) the means by which man rises to a higher life and a greater happiness is to define the idea of the fortunate fall in strictly temporal terms. Compelling though it may be, seductive as it is, Miriam's interpretation of Donatello's experience is essentially secular.

Kenyon is unsettled to hear such meditations on sin and happiness. Nonetheless, he does as Miriam has asked and advances the ideas to Hilda—hypothetically, it is true, but with no sign of displeasure in them. After Hilda has rejected what seems to be Kenyon's own notion about the significance of Donatello's experience—that innocence must perish in the modern world—he says, somewhat blithely, "Then here is another moral; take your choice," and explains Miriam's idea of the fortunate fall. He concludes by asking if Adam fell so that we might rise to a far higher paradise than his. Hilda is aghast. " 'O hush,' " she cries, "shrinking from him with an expression of horror which wounded the poor, speculative sculptor to the soul. 'This is terrible; and I could weep for you, if you indeed believe it.' " The idea, she thinks, makes a mockery of religion and morality—she is "shocked beyond words." Whereupon Kenyon, habitually deferential to Hilda's opinions, replies, "Forgive me Hilda! ... I never did believe it."

The mysterious, tainted Miriam has formulated a theme for the romance. She has expounded her idea to Kenyon, who feels it to be dangerous, but neither controverts it nor rejects it. But when through Kenyon the idea reaches Hilda, the reaction is immediate and unequivocal. Virtually faced with a choice between Miriam's idea and Hilda's good graces, Kenyon quickly repudiates the idea. The mind wanders, he says, to excuse his brief flirtation with heterodoxy; he lacks a sense of direction. But with the "white wisdom" of Hilda to guide him, all would be well. "O Hilda," exclaims Kenyon, "guide me home."

Many readers find Hilda's harsh innocence objectionable. After Hilda comes to the knowledge of evil, "her dearest friend ... had no existence for her anymore." "Your judgments," says Miriam, "are often terribly severe, though you seem all made up of gentleness and mercy." Hilda's one determination is to remain innocent, whatever the cost. "I am a poor, lonely girl," she says in rejecting Miriam, "whom God has set here in an evil world, and given her only a white robe, and bid her wear it back to Him, as white as when she put it on. Your powerful magnetism would be too much for me. The pure, white atmosphere, in which I try to discern what things are good and true, would be discolored." To Miriam's charge that she is merciless, angelic, and hence, inhuman, that she needs a sin to soften her, Hilda replies, "God forgive me, if I have said a needlessly cruel word." The adverb *needlessly* measures the limited extent to which Hilda can sympathize with Miriam, or anyone else.

It is important to remember, however, that Hawthorne appears to respect Hilda's white robe of innocence immensely, even as he sees the necessity of her coming down from her tower to participate more fully in the human condition. In large part, Hilda embodies the image of what Hawthorne admired in womanhood; she possesses many of the traits that Hawthorne loved in his wife Sophia. The severity of Hilda's innocence is unmistakable; but her character takes its special form from Hawthorne's desire to protect her, to hold her aloof and unspotted amid the grimy streets of Rome and the evil pervading the city. The intensity with which Hawthorne felt the pervasive dirtiness of modern Rome, his would-be neutral ground, measures the counter intensity with which he emphasizes Hilda's innocence. For Hilda represents home, the homing instinct, and all that home connotes to Hawthorne. Hilda will guide Kenyon home. She will come down from her tower where she has tended the Virgin's shrine "to be herself enshrined and worshipped as a household saint, in the light of her husband's fireside." And all this in their native land, to which they resolve to return "now that life had so much human promise in it."

There is no doubt that Hilda has the final answers in *The Marble Faun*. Her great respect for the spiritual resources of the Catholic church leads her to question the perfection of her own faith; in St. Peter's Cathedral she finds a spiritual peace denied her elsewhere. "I have a great deal of faith, and Catholicism seems to have a great deal of good. Why should I not be a Catholic," she says to a shocked Kenyon, "if I find there what I need, and what I cannot find elsewhere." But Hilda, like Hawthorne, cannot accept the disparity between the idea of Catholicism and the imperfection of the men who represent the church. "If its ministers were but a little more than human, above all error, pure from all iniquity, what a religion would it be!" On religion as on other matters, Hilda represents the court of highest appeal. With her capacity to become a "household saint," she could represent for Hawthorne nothing less.

Although Hilda rejects Miriam's version of the fortunate fall, she has perceived Donatello's growth as surely as anyone else. When Kenyon shows her his unfinished bust of Donatello, she studies it, hardly knowing how to define her perceptions. The bust has, she says, the effect of "gradually brightening" as she looks at it; "It gives the impression of a growing intellectual power and moral sense. . . . A soul is being breathed into him; it is the Faun, but advancing toward a state of higher development." By means of this aesthetic judgment, Hilda acquiesces in the idea of Donatello's transformation. What she will not accept is the formalized and secularized theory, based on Donatello's experience, that would make sin a means of education. And, indeed, Hawthorne himself cannot rest easy with this theory; he says, we recall, that Kenyon "rightly" felt Miriam's meditations to be perilous.

Hawthorne apparently wants the theory of the fortunate fall to be both propounded and rejected; in a sense he wants to be both dangerous and safe, and with Miriam and Hilda in his romance it seems possible to play both sides. But in presenting such antithetical views, Hawthorne comes close to blurring the theme of his romance. The fact of Donatello's transformation (the English edition of the romance was entitled *Transformation*) is made to serve and even emphasize the compelling (or distressing) idea of the fortunate fall. Miriam's theory, however, tells us primarily about Miriam; Hilda's rejection of the theory tells us primarily about Hilda. In the romance, dramatization has yielded to interpretation. And so formative are the terms of the interpretive debate, so bound up in the notion of the fortunate fall is Donatello's transformation, that Hilda (and Hawthorne), in rejecting the one, might almost seem to reject the other— the very theme of the romance. Hawthorne does not throw out the baby with the bath water; he does not reject his own theme in causing Miriam's version of the theme to be challenged and repudiated by Hilda. But he does subject the idea of transformation to an interpretive issue which comes to dominate the narrative and give Hilda the last word. "What was Miriam's life to be?" he asks at the end; "and where was Donatello? But Hilda had a hopeful soul, and saw sunlight on the mountain-tops."

The Marble Faun marks Hawthorne's final attempt to win through to a redemptive vision. Life, death, resurrection; the archetypal trip through hell to earn one's reward; man's fall from innocence into the wonder of the human condition—literature has perennially celebrated such a pattern. Hawthorne endured all the aspects of Rome that he detested, all the unhomelikeness of Italy, to come to terms with this theme. But its implications disturbed him. At the end of *The Marble Faun*, Hawthorne, like Kenyon, seems to cry out to be guided home. The shrine of his "household saint" becomes the only safe place to worship. Hilda at home could be a Phoebe; Hilda in

Rome, however, becomes a devotional object, with sufficient authority
to control the resolution of the narrative. Having acknowledged the
moral complexity of the world of men, Hawthorne pays final tribute
to the Puritan maid, to her innocence, to her simplicity, to her
unerring sense of moral direction.

Chapter Nine

Furthering a Significant Legacy

A Vital Heritage

Toward the end of "The Hall of Fantasy" Hawthorne's narrator speaks with conviction of a preference for mundane, physical existence which he hopes never to relinquish. If the earth were to be destroyed, he says to his friend, his chief regret would be "that very earthiness which no other sphere or state of existence can renew or compensate." He would miss "the fragrance of flowers and of new-mown hay; the genial warmth of sunshine and the beauty of a sunset among clouds; the comfort and cheerful glow of the fireside; the deliciousness of fruits and of all good cheer; the magnificence of mountains and seas and cataracts, and the softer charm of rural scenery." He would miss, too, the manifestations of social ebullience—"country frolics," "homely humor," the "roar of laughter, in which body and soul join so heartily." Because the "material and the moral" exist together in this world, he fears their separation would bring irremediable loss.

To all of this the friend replies that the superior existence of eternity will undoubtedly allow man to re-create the joys of earth in some fashion, should he wish to. He doubts, however, if any of us will "be inclined to play such a poor scene over again." But the narrator persists: he will never forsake "our mother earth" nor be satisfied "to have her exist merely in idea. I want her great, round, solid self to endure interminably, and still to be peopled with the kindly race of man, whom I uphold to be much better than he thinks himself."

Although the terms and the context manifestly differ, this is essentially the same preference for human existence, with its joys and sorrows, its capacity for good and evil, that Odysseus hears from Achilles in Hades and that Dante expresses at the beginning of his journey into the Inferno. Achilles, Odysseus thinks, is exceptionally fortunate: he has died a hero's death, received ceremonial burial, and become a prince among the dead. But Achilles, with full knowledge of what servitude implied in his world, says that he would rather be a serf in the house of a landless man than a prince among the dead. The preference for life, human life, is clear; and it is reinforced when, at a later point in his adventures, Odysseus refuses Calypso's offer of immortality. By stressing in specific ways the importance of human existence, *The Odyssey* enacts the fundamental conviction of our literary heritage, a conviction that stands unqualified by the limitations of Homer's imagination in presenting an afterlife. Dante, of course, had a drama of supernatural dimensions available to him. From his perspective in the elaborate Vestibule of the Inferno, the overwhelmed spiritual pilgrim hears Virgil describe the souls of those who held themselves aloof from moral commitment throughout a lifetime and thus earned neither salvation nor damnation. Having lived less than human lives, they are forbidden to enter heaven or hell; their unique fate is to yearn eternally for reward or punishment, for anything that is the true consequence of being human.

Comic or tragic in vision, epic or elegiac in tone, the most significant works in Western literature have never ceased to proclaim a faith in the human condition—confused, imperfect, toil-stricken as it may be. It is to Hawthorne's credit that he furthers this significant legacy in both his major and minor fiction, shaping his sense of human experience to meet his special talent as an American writer.

The American Dimension

Hawthorne's career, like that of many writers, ended on a note of frustration. Success was something he looked back on, failure something he lived with from day to day. Themes of recovering a lost estate and of discovering an elixir of life thwarted an imagination intent on securing the future by reduplicating the past.

But Hawthorne had already secured a larger future than he knew by his way of possessing the past. At a time when the American writer struggled to compensate for the lack of a national history, Hawthorne found his way into history by exploring a local and ancestral past. At a time when the absence of antiquity, legend, and myths of origin threw the writer onto the personal resources of his imagination, Hawthorne responded by testing the relation of the imagination and society. His feat was to perceive the human issues and the artistic difficulties inherent in the history he contemplated and thereby to couple his sense of the past with a sense of community that is at times transformed into a hope for an audience.

"Alice Doane's Appeal," one of the projected "Seven Tales of My Native Land" and hence one of Hawthorne's earliest works, is perhaps the most straightforward example of his concern over the dynamic relationship of artist, audience, and narrative material. In this tale, Hawthorne renders a judgment on the sins of an epoch as they bear upon the present. More importantly, he tells a story about telling a story. The tale, as we have it now, probably exists in modified form: the added framework puts the story of Alice Doane inside a narrative envelope that makes a concern with evoking a response from an audience part of the action. Following a walk to Gallows Hill, the narrator reads the Gothic story of Alice Doane and her brother to two young ladies. Throughout, he watches its effect on his audience, pausing once to tell us—the ultimate audience—that their bright eyes were fixed on him, their lips apart. Shortly after he finishes, however, the ladies begin to laugh and chatter, piquing his artistic ego and determining him to test their emotions with history rather than with fiction. With twilight setting the proper atmosphere, he summons up the past: he envisions a procession of accused and guilty persons proceeding toward Gallows Hill; he tells us how he "strove to realize and faintly communicate" to the young ladies "the deep, unutterable loathing and horror, the indignation, the affrighted wonder, that wrinkled on every brow, and filled the universal heart." Building toward his climax, the narrator says that he "plunged" into his "imagination for a blacker horror, and a deeper woe, and pictured the scaffold—"; but here his companions interrupt him and seize his arm; their nerves are trembling; and, "sweeter victory still, I had reached the seldom trodden places of their hearts, and found the wellspring of their tears."

Gratified with the reaction he has evoked from his audience, the narrator concludes that "the past had done all it could." The party leaves the hill, regretting that its barren summit has "no relic of old, nor lettered stone of later days, to assist the imagination in appealing to the heart." Earlier in the tale Hawthorne prefigures this barrenness by writing that "we are not a people of legend or tradition"; we are, rather, a people of the present, with "no heartfelt interest in the olden time." But in telling an effective story about telling an ineffective story he has moved from the conventional extravagance of Gothic fiction to a kind of summoned-up-on-the-spot Gothic history and thereby demonstrated a new way of making the past work upon the present.

Hawthorne's mature work enacts, even as it depends on, his sense both of past and of community. In "The Custom-House" sketch, the Custom House itself embodies memory gone blank; an enervated present nods over a forgotten past, which (as symbolized by the scarlet letter) has failed to clear customs and find its way into the present. In "The Custom-House," Hawthorne reopens commerce with this past. He bandies imaginary remarks with his inflexible ancestors. By "discovering" the letter he puts the vitality and suppressed emotion of the past into the service of his art. The final product, *The Scarlet Letter*, takes its fictional life from a profound sense of community, dramatic evidence of Hawthorne's triumph in possessing the Puritan past for the purposes of his imagination.

In its widest implications Hawthorne's sense of community involves mankind. His isolated individuals stand apart from humanity, obsessed with their guilt, their pride, their need for revenge or perfection—obsessed, finally, with self. Such characters involve themselves in futile efforts to find nourishment amid the barren wastes of abstraction, while the tales in which they figure proclaim the importance of community, whose bond is of the heart. Even the artist, as we have seen, can draw apart from humanity and adopt the self-defeating role of manipulator.

American fiction has inherited Hawthorne's fascination with the relation of the individual and society as well as his commitment to learning what we were as a way of knowing what we are and might be. Among writers who explore the meaning of the human condition in a similar way, Henry James, William Faulkner, and Robert Penn Warren stand out as preeminent (as I pointed out in the 1965 edition of this study and as Hyatt H. Waggoner has come to see in a more recent essay).[1] Profitable comparisons of Hawthorne and James have appeared steadily for many years. In 1918, for example, T. S. Eliot invited us to consider *Roderick Hudson* in relation to *The Marble Faun* and *The Sense of the Past* in relation to *The House of the Seven Gables* as a way of defining the "Hawthorne aspect" of James's imagination. Eliot thus focused on the role of the artist and the role of the past as significant topics for both writers. In 1952 Marius Bewley investigated the place of Hawthorne and James in the tradition of the American novel and pointed out similarities between *The Blithedale Romance* and *The Bostonians* and between *The Marble Faun* and *The Wings of the Dove*. And in 1979 Robert Emmet Long traced the effect of Hawthorne's fictional practice on the early and middle years of James's career in the most thorough discussion of the subject we have had.[2]

In James's work, one finds a deep and implied sense of community, which sustains the various judgments he makes on his Americans who confront European experience. Christopher Newman in *The American* may go to Europe because of moral repugnance toward the society which has made him rich; but he is, as he comes to understand, essentially a part of that society. In the novel, James gives us not Newman's society but rather a sense of his community—sprawling, inchoate, yet vibrant. Lambert Strether in *The Ambassadors* perceives what he has missed in life only in terms of what Woollett, Massachusetts, has made him. Although Mrs. Newsome and Woollett are not *in* the novel, no one would doubt their importance *for* the novel.

In *Portrait of a Lady*, Isabel Archer's refusal of the best offers of marriage that two continents and two cultures can make is possible only on the grounds of her being an American. Americans estranged from a sense of community abound in *Portrait of a Lady*, and they prove to be pitiful or villainous; Ned Rosier is as futile as he is precious; the mask of the cosmopolite hides Madame Merle's helplessness; and Gilbert Osmond is a consummate egotist, whose self-devotion is worthy of a Hawthorne villain. These characters, unlike Casper Goodwood who brings increasing force and virility into the novel, are cut off from the provincial and no doubt vulgar resources of their community. At best, they could but echo Mrs. Touchett when she objects that her point of view is not American: "that's shockingly narrow," she exclaims; "thank God, my view is personal."

James also shares Hawthorne's interest in the relation of the artist to society. The problems of his artists are not precisely those of Hawthorne's. But a theme in James's work second in importance only to that of American innocence confronting European experience concerns the artist, his work, and his audience. It is a theme to which American writers have been perennially attracted.

James's American characters, like those of Hawthorne, are equipped with Puritan consciences, which have become portable, more refined, but not attenuated with the passage of time. When Madame de Mauves (which is the title marriage has given to the American Euphemia Cleve) says to Longmore that she has "only a clinging, inexpugnable conscience" to sustain her, she speaks for any James character who has not surrendered his or her birthright. Throughout a lengthy career, James gave us European society, carefully portrayed; he also gave us an American sense of community, deeply implied.

Faulkner's use of a Southern past suggests a number of comparisons with Hawthorne's use of a New England past. In Faulkner's work, history yields myth, which, in turn, explores the meaning of history. Yoknapatawpha County, like Hawthorne's neutral ground, becomes a fiction for creating fiction. In that county there is "strife amongst kindred" (to use Holgrave's words about the Pyncheon family in *The House of the Seven Gables*), pride fed by futile hope and by embellishment of the past, ancient wrong which continues to haunt the present. There is also a strong sense of community which allows Faulkner to range freely in time, to chronicle the depredations of the Snopes clan in one era and to depict the high ambition of Thomas Sutpen in another. In Faulkner's fiction, too, there is the powerful convergence of historical and personal guilt found most dramatically in *Go Down, Moses*. As noble as his intentions are, Isaac McCaslin's attempt to repudiate his tainted heritage is doomed by the inexorable swirl of history, forever impure, endlessly repetitive, yet paradoxically entangled with possibilities of love Isaac has missed. One cannot escape the consequences of history in Faulkner's world anymore than in Hawthorne's.

Perhaps no one would contend that *The Wild Palms* gives us Faulkner at his best. Yet in the way Harry Wilbourne chooses life rather than death at the end of that novel one sees the legacy that came through Homer, Dante, Hawthorne, and other writers reenacted with authority. First Wilbourne realizes that *"if memory exists outside of the flesh it wont be memory,"* that man needs the flesh (*"the old meat"*) to ratify his experience, no matter how painful. And out of that realization comes his final affirmation: *"Yes,"* he concludes, *"between grief and nothing I will take grief."* Thus the bumbling Wilbourne echoes the gallant Achilles.

The fiction of Robert Penn Warren bears closer affinities with that of Hawthorne than does the work of any other writer. Happily, this is a compliment to both of them. Warren's observation that "My Kinsman, Major Molineux," "The Gentle Boy," and *The Scarlet Letter* are examples "of Hawthorne's inclination to treat violent materials in the long perspective of the past" surely reminds us of his own practice in such works as *Night Rider, World Enough and Time*, and *Brother to Dragons*.[3] In Warren's fiction the man of idea stands revealed again in his essential inhumanity. No matter that Adam Stanton (with his "surgical smile") is the friend of Jack Burden's youth in *All the King's Men*; confronted with the fact that all human beings have fallen, he explodes into violence. Characteristically, Warren's latter-day Adams—unable to tolerate a world of lost innocence—lash out with a violence that is as helpless as it is destructive. In the manner of Jeremiah Beaumont in *World Enough and Time*, Percy Munn in *Night Rider* gets caught up in a just cause that turns to threat, arson, and murder in pursuit of its goal. Repeatedly in Warren's work the means defile the end; when the end becomes abstract and obsessive, the means become inhuman. Warren shows, too, that a man can know himself only by accepting the past which has made him what he is. The burden of the past involves guilt, which is both difficult and necessary to bear. One who repudiates that past (often portrayed as the father) is consequently a person without identity; for only in and through history can identity be achieved. And only by means of history can the present acknowledge its responsibility to the future.[4]

One need not protest Hawthorne's importance too much. It is profound and demonstrable in many ways. Warren credits Hawthorne with being the first American writer "in whose work we can sense the inner relation of life to fiction" and sees him (along with Poe) pioneering "the kind of hallucinatory fiction which is characteristic of modernity."[5] Both observations suggest additional relevance for Hawthorne's art in our time. Radical changes in fictional technique, of course, have taken place since Hawthorne wrote, in the light of which the meditative pace of his sketches and longer romances may seem at times ponderous and old-fashioned. But the economy and brilliance of *The Scarlet Letter* and of his most searching tales have come undisturbed through alterations in fashion and taste to command the respect given only to triumphs in form. And in writing fiction about the problems of writing fiction (as in "Alice Doane's Appeal," "Main-street," and other tales) Hawthorne anticipated a mode that has been virtually institutionalized by contemporary wirters such as John Barth and John Updike. We recognize that Hawthorne came early and did much. That significant later writers have found it important and even necessary to do similar things is the fullest tribute to the enduring quality of his achievement.

Notes and References

Chapter One

1. Whipple's provocative survey of Hawthorne's work appeared, unsigned, in the May, 1860, issue of the *Atlantic Monthly*. It is reprinted in *The Recognition of Nathaniel Hawthorne: Selected Criticism Since 1828*, ed. B. Bernard Cohen (Ann Arbor, Mich., 1969), pp. 78–90. For Hawthorne's response to Whipple's essay, see James T. Fields, *Yesterdays with Authors* (Boston, 1871), p. 89.

2. Although his later work in the romance continued to be meditative and analytical, Hawthorne expressed admiration for fiction very different from his own. From England in the 1850s he wrote to Fields asking if he had ever read the work of Anthony Trollope, whose novels "precisely suit my taste; solid and substantial, written on the strength and through the inspiration of ale, and just as real as if some giant had hewn a great lump out of the earth and put it under a glass case. . . ."

3. The developing contrast between Septimius and Robert Hagburn is drawn more sharply in the earlier version of this story, "Septimius Felton," than in the revision, "Septimius Norton," principally because the "Norton" draft (which added much narrative detail) broke off approximately two thirds of the way through what Hawthorne had sketched out as the full plot. Both drafts are included in *The Elixir of Life Manuscripts: Septimius Felton, Septimius Norton, The Dolliver Romance*, ed. Edward H. Davidson, Claude M. Simpson, and L. Neal Smith, Centenary Edition, vol. 13 (Columbus, Ohio, 1977).

4. Horatio Bridge recalls that Hawthorne added the *w* to the spelling of his name several years after he left college. Hawthorne told Bridge that "in tracing the genealogy of his family, he had found that some of his ancestors used the *w*, and he had merely resumed it."

5. Arlin Turner pieces together the publishing history of "The Story-Teller" in *Nathaniel Hawthorne: A Biography* (New York, 1980), pp. 72–79.

6. *The House of the Seven Gables* was completed in January, 1851; Hawthorne had actually been at work on it from August to January.

7. Hawthorne planned to write a sketch of Thoreau (who died in 1862) as a preface for "The Dolliver Romance," incorporating the legend of a man who believed he was deathless which he had heard from Thoreau

in the 1850s. The preface would discharge "the duty of a live literary man to perpetuate the memory of a dead one." At Hawthorne's funeral the incomplete manuscript of "Dolliver" lay on his coffin.

8. James R. Mellow, *Nathaniel Hawthorne in His Times* (Boston, 1980), p. 371.

9. Turner, pp. 217, 221.

10. For the texts of Hawthorne's unfinished romances and a full account of their composition, see *The American Claimant Manuscripts: The Ancestral Footstep, Etherege, Grimshawe*, ed. Edward H. Davidson, Claude M. Simpson, and L. Neal Smith, Centenary Edition, vol. 12 (Columbus, Ohio, 1977) and *The Elixir of Life Manuscripts* cited in note 3, above.

Chapter Two

1. Leo B. Levy, "The Notebook Source and the 18th Century Context of Hawthorne's Theory of Romance," *Nathaniel Hawthorne Journal* 3 (1973):121.

2. R. W. B. Lewis studies the effects of the American feeling of being emancipated from history in *The American Adam: Innocence, Tragedy, and Tradition in the Nineteenth Century* (Chicago: University of Chicago Press, 1955). See chapter 1, "The Case Against the Past," pp. 13–27.

3. *North American Review* 6 (1818):237–38.

4. *Edinburgh Review* 50 (1829):127.

5. Northrop Frye distinguishes such a relationship among these genres in *Anatomy of Criticism* (Princeton, N.J.: Princeton University Press, 1957), pp. 304–5.

6. See, for example, Richard Chase, *The American Novel and Its Tradition* (New York: Anchor Books, 1957), especially chapter 1.

7. Although it is not presented as a literal dream, "The Haunted Mind" has the important dreamlike qualities identified by Rita K. Gollin in *Nathaniel Hawthorne and the Truth of Dreams* (Baton Rouge, 1979). In Hawthorne's fiction, Gollin writes, a dream "may take shape as a spectral procession, a preternatural hallucination, or simply a mystifying episode imperfectly recalled when awake. But always, dreaming in the fiction invites and requires penetration beyond material surfaces: the dreamer moves unsteadily toward an enlarged understanding of himself and the natural universe, sometimes confronting his own buried secrets of guilt and desire" (pp. 94–95).

8. James Beattie, *Dissertations Moral and Critical*, 2 vols. (Dublin, 1783), 1:113.

Chapter Three

1. Neal Frank Doubleday discusses Hawthorne's use of the Gothic tradition in *Hawthorne's Early Tales, A Critical Study* (Durham, N.C., 1972), pp. 52–62.

2. In *A Wonder-Book for Girls and Boys* (1852) and in *Tanglewood Tales for Girls and Boys* (1853), Hawthorne again used versions of the fairy-tale opening in his retelling of the Greek myths. Thus: "Once upon a time" ("The Golden Touch"); "Long, long ago, when this old world was in its tender infancy" ("The Paradise of Children"); "One evening, in times long ago" ("The Miraculous Pitcher"); "Once in the old, old times (for all the strange things which I tell you about happened long before anybody can remember)" ("The Chimaera"); "A great while ago, when the world was full of wonder" ("The Pygmies").

3. Hawthorne seems to have been unable to make use of the Indian as a subject in his fiction. In the section of "Sketches from Memory" entitled "Our Evening Party Among the Mountains," he writes: "It has often been a matter of regret to me, that I was shut out from the most peculiar field of American fiction, by an inability to see any romance, or poetry, or grandeur, or beauty in the Indian character, at least, till such traits were pointed out by others. I do abhor an Indian story."

4. Ursula Brumm, "A Regicide Judge as 'Champion' of American Independence," *Amerikastudien* 21 (1976):178–79. Michael Davitt Bell examines the role of regicide figures in fiction in *Hawthorne and the Historical Romance of New England* (Princeton, N.J., 1971), pp. 27–33.

5. See Seymour L. Gross, "Hawthorne's Revision of 'The Gentle Boy,'" *American Literature* 26 (1954):196–208, for an analysis of how Hawthorne balanced the culpability of Puritans and Quakers in his revision of this tale for *Twice-Told Tales* in 1837.

Chapter Four

1. W. B. Carnochan, "'The Minister's Black Veil': Symbol, Meaning, and the Context of Hawthorne's Art," *Nineteenth-Century Fiction* 24 (1969):185.

2. James B. Reece sees Mr. Hooper bound by the solemn vow he has made to God in return for the power of bringing sinners (everyone) to salvation ("Mr. Hooper's Vow," *ESQ* 21 [1975]:94, 98).

3. In "Hawthorne as Poet" (*Sewanee Review* 49 [1951]:179–205, 426–58), Q. D. Leavis demonstrated the manner in which Hawthorne blocks off sympathies from both Merry Mounters and Puritans and thereby established the basic terms for future analysis of this tale.

4. Frederick C. Crews observes that the entire plot of "The May-

pole" moves "toward reconciliation." The contending parties, he writes, "are less different from one another than they seem. If the Puritans, in trying to exclude sensual pleasure, nevertheless readmit in the form of sadism, the Merry Mounters are just as unsuccessful in trying to exclude conscience" (*The Sins of the Fathers: Hawthorne's Psychological Themes* [New York, 1966], p. 23).

5. David Levin, "Shadows of Doubt: Specter Evidence in Hawthorne's 'Young Goodman Brown,'" *American Literature* 34 (1962):351.

6. Levin, p. 352.

7. Michael J. Colacurcio, "Visible Sanctity and Spectral Evidence: The Moral World of Hawthorne's 'Young Goodman Brown,'" *Essex Institute Historical Collections* 110 (1974):274.

8. Ibid., p. 296.

9. James W. Clark, Jr., argues convincingly that once Goodman Brown allows the devil to revise his view of the past he has compromised himself beyond repair. See "Hawthorne's Use of Evidence in 'Young Goodman Brown,'" *Essex Institute Historical Collections* 111 (1975):15.

10. Kent Bales sees Beatrice's "literary namesake" as Beatrice Cenci and does not mention Dante's figure of Beatrice in "Sexual Exploitation in Rappaccini's Garden," *ESQ* 24 (1978):135. My sense is that the allusions to Dante in this tale should not be minimized. Bales offers a good review of recent psychological readings of "Rappaccini's Daughter" and argues the case for Beatrice's fall from nature persuasively.

11. Roy R. Male identifies Ethan Brand's quest as essentially that of Satan in *Hawthorne's Tragic Vision* (Austin, Tex., 1957), pp. 86–87.

12. Nina Baym, *The Shape of Hawthorne's Career* (Ithaca, N.Y., 1976), p. 117.

13. For an incisive discussion of the function of saturnalian ritual in this tale, see Peter Shaw, "Fathers, Sons, and the Ambiguities of Revolution in 'My Kinsman, Major Molineux,'" *New England Quarterly* 49 (1976):559–76, especially pp. 567–70.

Chapter Five

1. Henry James, *Hawthorne* (Ithaca, N.Y.: Cornell University Press, 1967), pp. 90–92. James's study of Hawthorne was originally published in the English Men of Letters Series in 1879. Although Hawthorne apparently knew Lockhart's *Valerius, A Roman Story* (1821) and *Matthew Wald* (1824), there is no record of his having read *Adam Blair* (1822).

2. Charles Feidelson, Jr., *Symbolism and American Literature* (Chicago, 1953), pp. 9–13.

3. Taken out of context, these words (from the beginning of chapter

9) would undoubtedly be seen as a reference to Dimmesdale; that they refer to Chillingworth emphasizes his refusal to acknowledge either Hester or himself and thus points up a subtle analogy between the physician and the minister.

4. For a fuller discussion of the possibility that Dimmesdale may convert himself by means of his own sermon, see my "Dimmesdale's Ultimate Sermon," *Arizona Quarterly* 27 (1971):230–40.

5. Crews examines this final section of *The Scarlet Letter* carefully in *Sins of the Fathers*, pp. 148–53.

6. Baym, *Hawthorne's Career*, p. 132.

7. In his *American Notebooks*, Hawthorne made the following brief entry in 1844: "The life of a woman, who, by the old colony law, was condemned always to wear the letter A, sewed on her garment, in token of her having committed adultery." In 1636 the New Plymouth colony enacted a law which stated that persons convicted of adultery should be whipped and made to wear "two Capitall letters viz. AD. cut out in cloth and sowed on theire upermost Garments on theire arme or backe." Had Hester worn the letters *AD* on her gown, Arthur Dimmesdale would probably have swooned in an ecstasy of guilt.

8. T. S. Eliot, "Henry James: The Hawthorne Aspect" (1918), in *Recognition*, ed. Cohen, p. 161.

Chapter Six

1. Male, *Tragic Vision*, p. 133.

2. Ibid., p. 137; Kenneth Dauber, *Rediscovering Hawthorne* (Princeton, N.J., 1977), pp. 147–48; Turner, *Hawthorne*, p. 226.

3. Richard Harter Fogle, *Hawthorne's Fiction: The Light and the Dark*, rev. ed. (Norman, Okla., 1964), p. 155.

4. Hyatt H. Waggoner, *Hawthorne: A Critical Study* (Cambridge, Mass., 1955), pp. 171–72; John Gatta, Jr., "Progress and Providence in *The House of the Seven Gables*," *American Literature* 50 (1978):40, 48.

5. James, *Hawthorne*, p. 97.

6. F. O. Matthiessen, *American Renaissance: Art and Expression in the Age of Emerson and Whitman* (New York: Oxford University Press, 1941), p. 333.

7. Melville's remark can be found in *The Letters of Herman Melville*, ed. Merrell R. Davis and William H. Gilman (New Haven: Yale University Press, 1960), p. 124; for T. S. Eliot, see Cohen, *Recognition*, p. 162; James, *Hawthorne*, p. 103.

Chapter Seven

1. Coverdale also has roots in Hawthorne's life: see Arlin Turner, "Autobiographical Elements in Hawthorne's *The Blithedale Romance*," *University of Texas Studies in English* 15 (1935):39–62.

2. Robert C. Elliot succinctly observes that the "most tantalizing puzzle" in *Blithedale* is "the relation between Hawthorne and the man he created to tell his story." See "*The Blithedale Romance*," in *Hawthorne Centenary Essays*, ed. Roy Harvey Pearce (Columbus, Ohio, 1964), pp. 110–13.

3. Male, *Tragic Vision*, p. 144.

4. Hawthorne, like a number of his contemporaries, frequently uses "either" where today we would use "any."

5. Frank Davidson, "Toward a Revaluation of *The Blithedale Romance*," *New England Quarterly* 25 (1952):374–83.

6. Waggoner, *Hawthorne*, p. 175.

7. James H. Justus, "Hawthorne's Coverdale: Character and Art in *The Blithedale Romance*," *American Literature* 47 (1975):23.

8. Edgar A. Dryden sees Coverdale's final confession not as a valid statement of love but as an instance of "bad faith" in *Nathaniel Hawthorne: The Poetics of Enchantment* (Ithaca, N.Y., 1977), pp. 101–4.

Chapter Eight

1. For a more inclusive discussion of Hawthorne's sense of home and its importance to his writing, see my "Hawthorne's Public Decade and the Values of Home," *American Literature* 46 (1974):141–52.

2. Roy Harvey Pearce considers Hawthorne's use of the sketch in "Hawthorne and the Twilight of Romance," *Yale Review* 37 (1947–48):487–506, especially pp. 500–504. In *The Marble Faun*, says Pearce, the sketch "becomes the structural core of the romance."

3. Henry James, "A Chain of Cities" (1873), in *Italian Hours* (London: William Heinemann, 1909), p. 238. A visitor to Perugia, wrote James, "must uncap to the irrecoverable, the inimitable style of the statue of Pope Julius III. before the cathedral, remembering that Hawthorne fabled his Miriam, in an air of romance from which we are well-nigh as far today as from the building of Etruscan gates, to have given rendezvous to Kenyon at its base."

4. In *Nathaniel Hawthorne: An Approach to an Analysis of Artistic Creation* (Cleveland, 1970), Jean Normand argues that Hawthorne betrayed "his own esthetic" by not placing the crime of Donatello and Miriam "at the beginning or even before the beginning" of his romance

(p. 330). Normand's contention adds to our sense that Hawthorne was working with different conceptional strategies in *The Marble Faun.*

5. Baym, *Hawthorne's Career*, p. 246.

Chapter Nine

1. Hyatt H. Waggoner, "The Presence of Hawthorne," in *The Presence of Hawthorne* (Baton Rouge, La., 1979), pp. 143–62.

2. T. S. Eliot, in *Recognition*, ed. Cohen, pp. 157–63; Marius Bewley, *The Complex Fate: Hawthorne, Henry James, and Some Other American Writers* (London, 1956), pt. 1, Chaps. 1–3; Robert Emmet Long, *The Great Succession: Henry James and the Legacy of Hawthorne* (Pittsburgh, 1979).

3. Robert Penn Warren, "Hawthorne Revisited: Some Remarks on Hellfiredness," *The Sewanee Review* 81 (1973):95.

4. James H. Justus offers a cogent analysis of the relation of Hawthorne's work and that of Warren in *The Achievement of Robert Penn Warren* (Baton Rouge: Louisiana State University Press, 1981), part 1.

5. Warren, "Hawthorne Revisited," pp. 75, 81.

Selected Bibliography

PRIMARY SOURCES

1. Books

Fanshawe: A Tale. Boston: Marsh and Capen, 1828.

Peter Parley's Universal History. Boston: American Stationers Co., 1837.

Twice-Told Tales. Boston: American Stationers Co., 1837. Expanded ed., Boston: James Munroe and Co., 1842. Cited as *TTT* in section 2 below.

Grandfather's Chair. Boston: E. P. Peabody; New York: Wiley and Putnam, 1841.

Biographical Stories for Children. Boston: Tappan and Dennet, 1842.

Mosses from an Old Manse. New York: Wiley and Putnam, 1846. Rev. ed., Boston: Ticknor and Fields, 1854.

The Scarlet Letter: A Romance. Boston: Ticknor, Reed, and Fields, 1850.

The House of the Seven Gables. Boston: Ticknor, Reed, and Fields, 1851.

True Stories from History and Biography. Boston: Ticknor, Reed, and Fields, 1851.

The Snow-Image, and Other Twice-Told Tales. Boston: Ticknor, Reed, and Fields, 1852.

A Wonder-Book for Girls and Boys. Boston: Ticknor, Reed, and Fields, 1852.

The Blithedale Romance. Boston: Ticknor, Reed, and Fields, 1852.

Life of Franklin Pierce. Boston: Ticknor, Reed, and Fields, 1852.

Tanglewood Tales for Girls and Boys. Boston: Ticknor, Reed, and Fields, 1853.

The Marble Faun; or, The Romance of Monte Beni. Boston: Ticknor and Fields, 1860.

Our Old Home. Boston: Ticknor and Fields, 1863.

2. Tales and Sketches

For those who are interested in the pattern of Hawthorne's publishing, the following list gives for individual tales and sketches the date and place of original publication and also the book in which Hawthorne collected each tale and sketch. Items marked "not collected" are included in volume 11 of the Centenary Edition of Hawthorne's work unless otherwise noted. Volume 11 also contains an explanation of items attributed to Hawthorne. (To find the date of any tale or sketch, consult the index to this study.)

1830

> "The Hollow of the Three Hills." *Salem Gazette*, November 12, 1830, p. 1. *TTT*, 1837.
>
> "The Battle-Omen." *Salem Gazette*, November 2, 1830, p. 1. Not collected. Attributed.
>
> "An Old Woman's Tale." *Salem Gazette*, December 21, 1830, pp. 1–2. Not collected. Attributed.

1831

> "Sights from a Steeple." *Token*, 1831, pp. 41–51. *TTT*, 1837.
>
> "The Haunted Quack." *Token*, 1831, pp. 117–37. Not collected. Attributed.

1832

> "The Gentle Boy." *Token*, 1832, pp. 193–240. *TTT*, 1837.
>
> "My Kinsman, Major Molineux." *Token*, 1832, pp. 89–116. *Snow-Image*.
>
> "Roger Malvin's Burial." *Token*, 1832, pp. 161–88. *Mosses*, 1846.
>
> "The Wives of the Dead." *Token*, 1832, pp. 74–82. *Snow-Image*.

1833

> "The Canterbury Pilgrims." *Token*, 1833, pp. 153–66. *Snow-Image*.
>
> "The Seven Vagabonds." *Token*, 1833, pp. 49–77. Expanded *TTT*, 1842.

1834

> "Mr. Higginbotham's Catastrophe." *New-England Magazine* 7 (December 1834):450–59. *TTT*, 1837.
>
> "Passages from a Relinquished Work." *New-England Magazine* 7 (November 1834):352–58. Revised *Mosses*, 1854.

1835

> "The Ambitious Guest." *New-England Magazine* 8 (June 1835): 424–31. Expanded *TTT*, 1842.
>
> "The Devil in Manuscript." *New-England Magazine* 9 (November 1835):340–45. *Snow-Image*.
>
> "Graves and Goblins."*New-England Magazine* 8 (June 1835):438–44. Not collected. Attributed.
>
> "The Gray Champion." *New-England Magazine* 8 (January 1835): 20–26. *TTT*, 1837.
>
> "My Visit to Niagara." *New-England Magazine* 8 (February 1835): 91–96. Not collected.

"Old News." *New-England Magazine* 8 (February 1835):81–88; (March 1835):170–78; (May 1835):365–70. *Snow-Image.*

"A Rill from the Town-Pump." *New-England Magazine* 8 (June 1835):473–78. *TTT*, 1837.

"Sketches from Memory." *New-England Magazine* 9 (November 1835):321–26; (December 1835):398–409. Revised *Mosses*, 1854.

"The Vision of the Fountain." *New-England Magazine* 9 (August 1835):99–104. *TTT*, 1837.

"Wakefield." *New-England Magazine* 8 (June 1835):341–47. *TTT*, 1837.

"The White Old Maid." *New-England Magazine* (under the title "The Old Maid in the Winding-Sheet") 9 (July 1835):8–16. Expanded *TTT*, 1842.

"Young Goodman Brown." *New-England Magazine* 8 (April 1835): 249–60. *Mosses*, 1846.

"Alice Doane's Appeal." *Token*, 1835, pp. 84–101. Not collected.

"The Haunted Mind." *Token*, 1835, pp. 76–82. Expanded *TTT*, 1842.

"The Village Uncle." *Token*, 1835 (under the title "The Mermaid"), pp. 106–21. Expanded *TTT*, 1842.

"Little Annie's Ramble." *Youth's Keepsake*, 1835, pp. 146–59. *TTT*, 1837.

1836

"Old Ticonderoga." *American Monthly Magazine* 1 (February 1836):138–42. *Snow-Image.*

"A Visit to the Clerk of the Weather." *American Monthly Magazine* 1 (May 1836):483–87. Not collected. Attributed.

"The May-pole of Merry Mount." *Token*, 1836, pp. 283–97. *TTT*, 1837.

"The Minister's Black Veil." *Token*, 1836, pp. 302–20. *TTT*, 1837.

"The Wedding-Knell." *Token*, 1836, pp. 113–24. *TTT*, 1837.

1837

"Fragments from the Journal of a Solitary Man." *American Monthly Magazine* 4 (July 1837):45–56. Not collected. Attributed.

"The Toll-Gatherer's Day." *Democratic Review* 1 (October 1837): 31–35. Expanded *TTT*, 1842.

"A Bell's Biography." *Knickerbocker* 9 (March 1837):219–23. *Snow-Image.*

"Dr. Heidegger's Experiment." *Knickerbocker* (under the title "The Fountain of Youth") 9 (January 1837):27–33. *TTT*, 1837.

"Edward Fane's Rosebud." *Knickerbocker* 10 (September 1837): 195–99. Expanded *TTT*, 1842.

"David Swan." *Token*, 1837, pp. 147–55. *TTT*, 1837.

"Fancy's Show Box." *Token*, 1837, pp. 177–84. *TTT*, 1837.

"The Great Carbuncle." *Token*, 1837, pp. 156–75. *TTT*, 1837.

"The Man of Adamant." *Token*, 1837, pp. 119–28. *Snow-Image.*

"Monsieur du Miroir." *Token*, 1837, pp. 49–64. *Mosses*, 1846.

"Mrs. Bullfrog." *Token*, 1837, pp. 66–75. *Mosses*, 1846.

"The Prophetic Pictures." *Token*, 1837, pp. 289–307. *TTT*, 1837.

"Sunday at Home." *Token*, 1837, pp. 88–96. *TTT*, 1837.

1838

"The Threefold Destiny." *American Monthly Magazine* 9 (March 1838):228–35. Expanded *TTT*, 1842.

"Chippings with a Chisel." *Democratic Review* 3 (September 1838): 18–26. Expanded *TTT*, 1842.

"Edward Randolph's Portrait." *Democratic Review* 2 (July 1838): 360–69. One of the four "Legends of the Province-House." Expanded *TTT*, 1842.

"Foot-prints on the Sea-shore." *Democratic Review* 1 (January 1838):190–97. Expanded *TTT*, 1842.

"Howe's Masquerade." *Democratic Review* 2 (May 1838):129–40. One of the four "Legends of the Province-House." Expanded *TTT*, 1842.

"Lady Eleanor's Mantle." *Democratic Review* 3 (December 1838): 321–32. One of the four "Legends of the Province-House." Expanded *TTT*, 1842.

"Snow-flakes." *Democratic Review* 1 (February 1838):355–59. Expanded *TTT*, 1842.

"Endicott and the Red Cross." *Token*, 1838, pp. 69–78. Expanded *TTT*, 1842.

"Night Sketches: Beneath an Umbrella." *Token*, 1838, pp. 81–89. Expanded *TTT*, 1842.

"Peter Goldthwaite's Treasure." *Token*, 1838, pp. 37–65. Expanded *TTT*, 1842.

"The Shaker Bridal." *Token*, 1838, pp. 117–25. Expanded *TTT*, 1842.

"Sylph Etherege." *Token*, 1838, pp. 22–32. *Snow-Image.*

"Time's Portraiture." *Salem Gazette* (broadside), January 2, 1838, p. 1. Not collected.

1839

"Old Esther Dudley." *Democratic Review* 5 (January 1839):51–59. One of the four "Legends of the Province-House." Expanded *TTT*, 1842.

"The Sister Years." *Salem Gazette* (broadside), January 4, 1839, p. 1. Expanded *TTT*, 1842.

"The Lily's Quest." *Southern Rose* 7 (January 1839):161–64. Expanded *TTT*, 1842.

1840

"John Inglefield's Thanksgiving." *Democratic Review* 7 (March 1840):209–12. *Snow-Image.*

1842

"A Virtuoso's Collection." *Boston Miscellany* 1 (May 1842):193–200. *Mosses,* 1846.

1843

"Little Daffydowndilly." *Boy's and Girl's Magazine* 2 (August 1843): 264–69. *Snow-Image.*

"Buds and Bird-Voices." *Democratic Review* 13 (June 1843): 604–8. *Mosses,* 1846.

"The Celestial Rail-road." *Democratic Review* 12 (May 1843):515–23. *Mosses,* 1846.

"Egotism; or, the Bosom-Serpent." *Democratic Review* 12 (March 1843):255–61. *Mosses,* 1846.

"Fire-Worship." *Democratic Review* 13 (December 1843):627–30. *Mosses,* 1846.

"The New Adam and Eve." *Democratic Review* 12 (February 1843): 146–65. *Mosses,* 1846.

"The Procession of Life." *Democratic Review* 12 (April 1843):360–66. *Mosses,* 1846.

"The Birth-mark." *The Pioneer* 1 (March 1843):113–19. *Mosses,* 1846.

"The Hall of Fantasy." *The Pioneer* 1 (February 1843):49–55. *Mosses,* 1846.

"The Antique Ring." *Sargent's New Monthly Magazine* 1 (February 1843):80–86. Not collected.

"The Old Apple-Dealer." *Sargent's New Monthly Magazine* 1 (January 1843):21–24. *Mosses,* 1846.

1844

"A Good Man's Miracle." *Child's Friend* 1 (February 1844):151–56. Not collected.

"The Artist of the Beautiful." *Democratic Review* 14 (June 1844): 605–17. *Mosses,* 1846.

"A Book of Autographs." *Democratic Review* 15 (November 1844):454–61. Not collected.

"The Christmas Banquet." *Democratic Review* 14 (January 1844): 78–87. *Mosses,* 1846.

"The Intelligence Office." *Democratic Review* 14 (March 1844):
269–75. *Mosses*, 1846.

"Rappaccini's Daughter." *Democratic Review* 15 (December 1844):
545–60. *Mosses*, 1846.

"A Select Party." *Democratic Review* 15 (July 1844):33–40.
Mosses, 1846.

"Drowne's Wooden Image." *Godey's Magazine and Lady's Book* 29
(July 1844):13–17. *Mosses*, 1846.

"Earth's Holocaust." *Graham's Magazine* 25 (May 1844):193–200.
Mosses, 1846.

1845

"P's Correspondence." *Democratic Review* 16 (April 1845):337–45.
Mosses, 1846.

1846

"The Old Manse." First appeared in *Mosses*, 1846.

1849

"Main-street." *Aesthetic Papers*. Boston: E. P. Peabody, 1849,
pp. 145–74. *Snow-Image*.

1850

"Ethan Brand." *Boston Weekly Museum* 2 (January 5, 1850):234–
35. Also appeared in the *Dollar Magazine* 7 (May 1851):193–
201. *Snow-Image*.

"The Snow-Image." *International Miscellany* 1 (November 1850):
537–43. *Snow-Image*.

"The Great Stone Face." *National Era* 4 (January 1850):16. *Snow-
Image*.

1852

"Feathertop." *International Monthly Magazine* 5 (February, March
1852):182–86; 333–37. Revised *Mosses*, 1854.

1862

"Chiefly about War-Matters." *Atlantic Monthly* 10 (July 1862):43–
61. Not collected. Scheduled to appear in the volume of miscel-
laneous writings in the Centenary Edition. Presently available in
the Riverside Edition, vol. 12.

3. Editions of Hawthorne's Work

The Centenary Edition of the Works of Nathaniel Hawthorne. William
Charvat, Roy Harvey Pearce, and Claude M. Simpson, general editors. Columbus: Ohio State University Press, 1964–. The definitive
edition. Fourteen volumes, including all the tales and romances, have
been published. Six volumes, including Hawthorne's letters, remain
to be published. Prior to the publication of the Centenary Edition,

The Complete Works of Nathaniel Hawthorne, 12 vols. (Boston: Houghton Mifflin, 1883, the "Riverside Edition"), was standard.

4. Other Material by Hawthorne

Love Letters of Nathaniel Hawthorne, 1839–1863. 2 vols. Chicago: Society of the Dofobs, 1907. Reprinted in 1 vol., Washington, D.C.: NCR/Microcard, 1972.

Letters of Nathaniel Hawthorne to William D. Ticknor, 1851–1864. 2 vols. Newark: Carteret Book Club, 1910. Reprinted in 1 vol., Washington, D.C.: NCR/Microcard, 1972.

Hawthorne's Lost Notebook, 1835–1841. Edited by Barbara Mouffe. Foreword by Charles Ryskamp. Introduction by Hyatt H. Waggoner. University Park: Pennsylvania State University Press, 1978. Had been thought to exist only in a copy made by Sophia Hawthorne. Valuable addition to American notebook material.

Nathaniel Hawthorne: Poems. Edited by Richard E. Peck. Charlottesville: Bibliographical Society of the University of Virginia, 1967. Twentynine youthful and unpromising poems.

Hawthorne as Editor: Selections from His Writings in The American Magazine of Useful and Entertaining Knowledge. Edited by Arlin Turner. Baton Rouge: Louisiana State University Press, 1941. Convenient place to sample some of Hawthorne's hack work.

"A Sophia Hawthorne Journal, 1843–1844." Edited by John J. McDonald. *Nathaniel Hawthorne Journal* 4 (1974):1–30. Fascinating record of Sophia's thoughts about her husband.

SECONDARY SOURCES

1. Bibliographical Studies

Blair, Walter. "Nathaniel Hawthorne." In *Eight American Authors: A Review of Research and Criticism,* edited by James Woodress. Rev. ed. New York: W. W. Norton, 1971, pp. 85–128. Excellent coverage and evaluations.

Byers, John R., Jr., and Owen, James J. *A Concordance to the Five Novels of Nathaniel Hawthorne.* 2 vols. New York: Garland Publishing, 1979. Obviously helpful for research on words, images, recurrent ideas.

Clark, C. E. Frazer, Jr. *Nathaniel Hawthorne: A Descriptive Bibliography.* Pittsburgh: University of Pittsburgh Press, 1978. Thorough listing of editions of Hawthorne's work. Nicely illustrated.

Jones, Buford. *A Checklist of Hawthorne Criticism, 1951–1966.* Hartford, Conn.: Transcendental Books, 1967. Excellent coverage, carefully organized for reference.

Warren, Austin. ed. *Nathaniel Hawthorne: Representative Selections.* New York: American Book Company, 1934. Well annotated bibliography of early material.

2. Critical and Biographical Studies

Abel, Darrel. "Hawthorne's Dimmesdale: Fugitive from Wrath." *Nineteenth-Century Fiction* 11 (1956):81–105. Traces Puritan notions of degeneration and moral regeneration in character of Dimmesdale.

———. "Black Glove and Pink Ribbon: Hawthorne's Metonymic Symbols." *New England Quarterly* 42 (1969):163–80. Focuses on *The Scarlet Letter* and "Young Goodman Brown." Argues that the true meaning of history lies in the consciousness of the characters.

Adams, Richard P. "Hawthorne's *Provincial Tales.*" *New England Quarterly* 30 (1957):39–57. Analysis of this abandoned collection of tales (including "Young Goodman Brown" and "My Kinsman, Major Molineux") and of its dynamic structure.

Adkins, Nelson F. "The Early Projected Works of Nathaniel Hawthorne." *Papers of the Bibliographical Society of America* 39 (1945):119–55. Shows principles of unity in Hawthorne's abandoned collections of tales. Thorough treatment of subject, still very helpful.

Arvin, Newton. *Hawthorne.* Boston: Little, Brown, 1929. Judicious treatment of Hawthorne's fiction in its relation to his life. Study marks shift to psychological consideration of Hawthorne as an artist.

Askew, Melvin W. "Hawthorne, the Fall, and the Psychology of Maturity." *American Literature* 34 (1962):335–43. Hawthorne's characters "fall" not into theologically conceived hell but into human condition. Good definition of recurrent pattern in Hawthorne's work.

Astrov, Vladimir. "Hawthorne and Dostoevski as Explorers of the Human Conscience." *New England Quarterly* 15 (1942):296–319. Dostoevski could have known Hawthorne's work. Traces patterns of guilt in *The Scarlet Letter, The Marble Faun,* and *Crime and Punishment* to suggest further lines of inquiry.

Bales, Kent. "Hawthorne's Prefaces and Romantic Perspectivism." *ESQ: A Journal of the American Renaissance* 23 (1977):69–88. Analogues of Hawthorne's perspectivist techniques are to be found in the work of German and English romantic writers. Strong on "The Old Manse," the introduction to "Rappaccini's Daughter," and "The Custom-House."

———. "Sexual Exploitation and the Fall from Natural Virtue in Rappaccini's Garden." *ESQ: A Journal of the American Renaissance* 24

(1978):133–44. Beset by the selfishness of others, Beatrice enacts the romantic myth of the fall from Nature, accepting a final sacrificial role as part of her fallen fate. Well argued.

Baughman, Ernest W. "Public Confession and *The Scarlet Letter.*" *New England Quarterly* 40 (1967):532–50. Ending of *The Scarlet Letter* historically and theologically justified. Sound scholarship supports ideas.

Bayer, John G. "Narrative Techniques and the Oral Tradition in *The Scarlet Letter.*" *American Literature* 52 (1980):250–63. Need to win over an audience he was unsure of led Hawthorne to use techniques of an oral tradition in both "The Custom-House" and *The Scarlet Letter.*

Baym, Nina. *The Shape of Hawthorne's Career.* Ithaca, N.Y.: Cornell University Press, 1976. Major study of Hawthorne's work as it developed voices, narrative stances, and ideas over more than two decades. Insists on the importance of *when* a work was written. Perceptive on tales and on romances.

Bell, Michael Davitt. *Hawthorne and the Historical Romance of New England.* Princeton, N.J.: Princeton University Press, 1971. Whereas other historical romances portrayed Puritans as either liberators or oppressors, Hawthorne saw first-generation Puritans as liberators, later Puritans as oppressors. Provides interesting context but tends to overlook Hawthorne's complex characterizations.

Bell, Millicent. *Hawthorne's View of the Artist.* New York: State University of New York, 1962. Hawthorne cannot find a valid place for the artist in society. Careful consideration of relevant work. Attention to romantic and antiromantic elements in Hawthorne's work.

Bewley, Marius. *The Complex Fate: Hawthorne, Henry James and Some Other American Writers.* London: Chatto and Windus, 1952. Considerations of Hawthorne's romances and some of James's novels—*Blithedale* and *The Bostonians,* for example. Suggests more than it accomplishes.

Bier, Jesse. "Hawthorne on the Romance: His Prefaces Related and Examined." *Modern Philology* 53 (1955):17–24. One of the first analyses of Hawthorne's attitude toward fiction as exemplified in the prefaces to his major romances.

Bridge, Horatio. *Personal Recollections of Nathaniel Hawthorne.* New York: Harper, 1893. Valuable. Includes important letters from Hawthorne to Bridge.

Brodhead, Richard H. *Hawthorne, Melville, and the Novel.* Chicago: University of Chicago Press, 1976. Analyzes the differing strategies Hawthorne and Melville developed for writing romances. Strong on the period that includes *The Scarlet Letter, Seven Gables*, and *Blithedale*.

Brownell, W. C. "Hawthorne." In *American Prose Masters*. New York: Scribner's, 1909, pp. 63–130. Excellent example of adverse criticism of Hawthorne's work. Admits greatness of *The Scarlet Letter*, but objects to ineffective allegory, bad symbolism, and fatalism in other works.

Brumm, Ursula. "A Regicide Judge as 'Champion' of American Independence." *Americkastudien* 21 (1976):177–86. Identifies the regicide judge William Goffe as the Gray Champion. Effective use of history and folklore to explain the movement of Hawthorne's story.

Bush, Sargent, Jr. "Bosom Serpents before Hawthorne: The Origins of a Symbol." *American Literature* 43 (1971):181–99. Traces instances of bosom serpents from *The Fairie Queene* to medical treatises and newspaper accounts to show what Hawthorne had available for his tale.

Cameron, Kenneth Walter. *Hawthorne Among His Contemporaries: A Harvest of Estimates, Insights, and Anecdotes from the Victorian Literary World*. Hartford, Conn.: Transcendental Books, 1968. A conglomeration of reviews, notices, information, and trivia. Worth rummaging through. Helpful index.

Charney, Maurice. "Hawthorne and the Gothic Style." *New England Quarterly* 34 (1961):36–49. Hawthorne's response to Gothic art in England and Italy. Hawthorne equates Gothic and romantic and thinks of the romance as a Gothic form. Well done.

Clark, James W., Jr. "Hawthorne's Use of Evidence in 'Young Goodman Brown.'" *Essex Institute Historical Collections* 111 (1975):12–34. Excellent study of witchcraft sources, Puritan assumptions, and Hawthorne's creative response to history. Highly recommended.

Cohen, B. Bernard, ed. *The Recognition of Nathaniel Hawthorne: Selected Criticism Since 1828*. Ann Arbor: University of Michigan Press, 1969. Balanced and comprehensive selection of Hawthorne criticism, including some early reviews and important later assessments.

Colacurcio, Michael J. "Footsteps of Ann Hutchinson: The Context of *The Scarlet Letter*." *ELH: Journal of English Literary History* 39 (1973):459–94. Hawthorne's "romantic" themes are extensions of an unrecognized romantic individualism to be found in Ann Hutchinson's "heresy." Hawthorne seems to have intended parallels between Arthur Dimmesdale and John Cotton.

———. "Visible Sanctity and Specter Evidence: The Moral World of Hawthorne's 'Young Goodman Brown.'" *Essex Institute Historical Collections* 110 (1974):259–99. Detailed analysis of tale as an

expression of its historical and moral climate. Suggests the profound
and prophetic import of the story. A superior piece of scholarship.

Conway, Moncure D. *Life of Nathaniel Hawthorne*. New York: A. Lovell,
1890. Perceptive on Hawthorne's ideas and art. Has good bibliography of early material on Hawthorne.

Cox, James M. "*The Scarlet Letter*: Through the Old Manse and the
Custom House." *Virginia Quarterly Review* 51 (1975):431–47.
Traces the interrelationship of Hawthorne's life and art from "The
Old Manse" to "The Custom-House" and *The Scarlet Letter*. Points
out the guilt inherent in Hawthorne's commitment to literary art.
Excellent, wide-ranging essay.

Crews, Frederick C. *The Sins of the Fathers: Hawthorne's Psychological
Themes*. New York: Oxford University Press, 1966. Important psychological (Freudian) interpretation of Hawthorne's work. At times
demonstrates new ways of arriving at familiar perceptions, but offers some excellent readings of major texts.

Crowley, J. Donald. "The Artist as Mediator: The Rationale of Hawthorne's Large-Scale Revisions in His Collected Tales and Sketches."
In *Hawthorne and Melville in the Berkshires*, edited by Howard P.
Vincent. Kent, Ohio: Kent State University Press, 1968, pp. 79–88,
156–57. Authoritative essay on revisions in Hawthorne's tales and
sketches. Shows Hawthorne himself responsible for changes.

———. ed. *Hawthorne: The Critical Heritage*. New York: Barnes and
Noble, 1970. Contains contemporary reviews of Hawthorne's work
and other useful assessments.

———. "The Unity of Hawthorne's *Twice-Told Tales*." *Studies in American Fiction* 1 (1973):35–61. Finds unifying patterns of tone, theme,
and narrative stance in *TTT*. Perceptive, with a dash of ingenuity.

Crowley, John W. "Hawthorne's New England Epochs." *ESQ: A Journal
of the American Renaissance* 25 (1979):59–70. Studies the complementary views of history seen in *Seven Gables* and *Grandfather's
Chair*. Illuminating analysis.

Daly, Robert J. "History and Chivalric Myth in 'Roger Malvin's Burial.'"
Essex Institute Historical Collections 109 (1973):99–115. Considers
historical event behind this tale and how Hawthorne transformed it.
Good on Hawthorne and the writing of history.

Dauber, Kenneth. *Rediscovering Hawthorne*. Princeton, N.J.: Princeton
University Press, 1977. Provides some incisive readings of tales and
romances. Disagrees with much previous criticism. But the Hawthorne we rediscover is in large part the Hawthorne we already
know.

Davidson, Edward H. *Hawthorne's Last Phase*. New Haven: Yale University Press, 1949. Informative study of Hawthorne's difficulties in composing his four late fragmentary romances.

Davidson, Frank. "Toward a Revaluation of *The Blithedale Romance*." *New England Quarterly* 25 (1952):374–83. Concise survey of former views. Studies significance of veil imagery in the romance.

Doubleday, Neal F. "Hawthorne's Inferno." *College English* 1 (1940): 658–70. On Hawthorne's knowledge of Dante. Sees similar treatments of pride.

———. *Hawthorne's Early Tales: A Critical Study*. Durham, N.C.: Duke University Press, 1972. Surveys the conventions and influences that bore on Hawthorne's tales from 1825 to 1838. Responsible, clear, worthwhile.

Dryden, Edgar A. *Nathaniel Hawthorne: The Poetics of Enchantment*. Ithaca, N.Y.: Cornell University Press, 1977. Seeks to define the relation of self to art in Hawthorne's work, noting recurrent patterns and structures that inform his fiction and characterization.

Eakin, Paul John. "Margaret Fuller, Hawthorne, James, and Sexual Politics." *South Atlantic Quarterly* 75 (1976):323–38. Perceptive essay. Focuses on Margaret Fuller, Zenobia in *Blithedale*, and Olive Chancellor in James's *Bostonians*, with implications reaching to our times.

Eisinger, Chester E. "Hawthorne as Champion of the Middle Way." *New England Quarterly* 27 (1954):27–52. Shows Hawthorne shying away from extremes toward a balanced life in which home and love played central part. Thorough and intelligent.

Fairbanks, Henry G. *The Lasting Loneliness of Nathaniel Hawthorne: A Study of the Sources of Alienation in Modern Man*. Albany, N.Y.: Magi Books, 1965. Examines Hawthorne's persistent quest for a unity of vision that would include God, Nature, and Man. Specialized argument.

Feidelson, Charles, Jr. *Symbolism and American Literature*. Chicago: University of Chicago Press, 1953. Excellent section on Hawthorne and symbolism. Basic for subject.

Fick, Leonard J. *The Light Beyond: A Study of Hawthorne's Theology*. Westminster, Md.: Newman Press, 1955. Explores Hawthorne's concern with guilt, remorse, and penance in the light of Christian theological concepts.

Fields, James T. "Hawthorne." In *Yesterdays with Authors*. Boston: J. R. Osgood, 1871, pp. 41–124. Valuable reminiscences of Hawthorne's publisher.

Fisher, Marvin. "The Pattern of Conservatism in Johnson's *Rasselas* and Hawthorne's *Tales*." *Journal of the History of Ideas* 19 (1958): 173–96. Both writers concerned with "preservation of traditional human values." Notes Hawthorne's remarks on Johnson in *Our Old Home*. Discussion includes "Young Goodman Brown," "Minister's Black Veil," "Birth-mark."

Flint, Allen. "Hawthorne and the Slavery Crisis." *New England Quarterly* 41 (1968):393–408. Surveys Hawthorne's comments on black Americans and on slavery. Careful treatment of a topic frequently ignored.

Fogle, Richard Harter. *Hawthorne's Fiction: The Light and the Dark*. Rev. ed. Norman: University of Oklahoma Press, 1964. One of the basic critical studies of Hawthorne. Excellent analysis of the romances and several of the major tales.

———. *Hawthorne's Imagery: The "Proper Light and Shadow" in the Major Romances*. Norman: University of Oklahoma Press, 1969. Supplements the analyses in *Hawthorne's Fiction*. Focuses helpfully on prefaces and romances.

Fossum, Robert H. "The Summons of the Past: Hawthorne's 'Alice Doane's Appeal.' " *Nineteenth-Century Fiction* 23 (1968):294–303. Tale exemplifies Hawthorne's problems as a writer of historical romance.

Garlitz, Barbara. "Pearl: 1850–1955." *PMLA* 72 (1957):689–99. Summarizes views on Pearl. Sees her as "a microcosm of Hester's moral chaos."

Gatta, John, Jr. "Progress and Providence in *The House of the Seven Gables*." *American Literature* 50 (1978):37–48. Finds three ideas of progress in *Seven Gables*, the visionary being the most important and most problematic because it represents the design of Providence.

Gollin, Rita K. *Nathaniel Hawthorne and the Truth of Dreams*. Baton Rouge: Louisiana State University Press, 1979. Studies Hawthorne's attitudes toward dreams and daydreams and the function of dreaming in his fiction. Excellent on Hawthorne's feeling that dreams can uncover basic truths as well as fears.

Gross, Robert Eugene. "Hawthorne's First Novel: The Future of a Style." *PMLA* 78 (1963):60–68. Strong analysis of Hawthorne's language, imagery, and use of the horrific as they prefigure characteristic features of his later work.

Gross, Seymour L. "Hawthorne's Revision of 'The Gentle Boy.' " *American Literature* 26 (1954):196–208. Revisions are in the interest of balancing responsibility between Puritans and Quakers.

———. "Hawthorne and the Shakers." *American Literature* 29 (1958): 457–63. Importance of Thomas Brown's *Account of the People Called Shakers . . .* (1812) in setting Hawthorne's attitude.

Hall, Lawrence Sargeant. *Hawthorne: Critic of Society*. New Haven: Yale

University Press, 1944. Details Hawthorne's interest in political and social affairs. Convincing treatment.

Hawthorne, Julian. *Nathaniel Hawthorne and His Wife.* 2 vols. Boston: J. R. Osgood, 1884. Still valuable for the material it presents in bulk. Has been very useful for later biographers.

Hedges, William L. "Hawthorne's *Blithedale*: The Function of the Narrator." *Nineteenth-Century Fiction* 14 (1960):303–16. Objects to Frederick C. Crews's reading of *Blithedale* (first published in *American Literature* in 1957, later in *The Sins of the Fathers* [1966]). Coverdale goes to Blithedale out of need for friendship and love; rediscovers evil in paradise.

Himelick, Raymond. "Hawthorne, Spenser, and Christian Humanism." *Emerson Society Quarterly* 21 (1975):21–28. Hawthorne responded to a balanced and profound vision in Spenser, complex, ambivalent in its own way.

Hoeltje, H. H. *Inward Sky: The Mind and Heart of Nathaniel Hawthorne.* Durham, N.C.: Duke University Press, 1962. Thorough coverage of Hawthorne's work in relation to his life. Critically naive at times (with "Major Molineux," for example). Avowed paraphrasing of Hawthorne's language "wherever possible" produces curious and inflated rhetoric.

Hoffman, Daniel C. *Form and Fable in American Fiction.* New York: Oxford University Press, 1961. Section on Hawthorne includes perceptive discussion of *The Scarlet Letter, Seven Gables, Blithedale,* and "My Kinsman, Major Molineux."

Hull, Raymona E. *Nathaniel Hawthorne: The English Experience, 1853–1864.* Pittsburgh: University of Pittsburgh Press, 1980. Thorough account of Hawthorne and his family in England, then back in Concord. One hundred and fifty biographical sketches at end of book give much information on people Hawthorne knew.

Jacobson, Richard J. *Hawthorne's Conception of the Creative Process.* Cambridge: Harvard University Press, 1965. Appraises metaphors of imaginative creation in Hawthorne's work in light of classical and romantic theories. Important.

James, Henry. *Hawthorne.* London: Macmillan, 1879. Hawthorne and his milieu from James's perspective. Perceptive, with the added importance that it tells us much about James.

Johnson, Claudia D. *The Productive Tension of Hawthorne's Art.* University, Ala.: University of Alabama Press, 1981. Hawthorne's sense that art centered on self was offset by a religious tradition that taught sacrifice of self for others—hence, the "productive tension" in his work. Good thesis.

Jones, Buford. "Hawthorne and Spenser: From Allusion to Allegory." *Nathaniel Hawthorne Journal* 5 (1975):71–90. Hawthorne reworked Spenserian themes, images, and characters throughout his career. Mammon, for example, can be seen in Judge Pyncheon, Talus in Hollingsworth.

Justus, James H. "Hawthorne's Coverdale: Character and Art in *The Blithedale Romance*." *American Literature* 47 (1975):21–36. Major achievement in *Blithedale* is the creation of a vacillating Coverdale (as narrator) whose quality of failure measures Hawthorne's success. Coverdale has affinities with James's Winterbourne and John Marcher.

Kesselring, M. L. *Hawthorne's Reading, 1828–1850*. New York: New York Public Library, 1949. An informative listing.

Laser, Marvin. " 'Head,' 'Heart,' and 'Will' in Hawthorne's Psychology." *Nineteenth-Century Fiction* 10 (1955):130–40. Suggests that Hawthorne's ideas were influenced by the psychology of Thomas C. Upham. Convincing.

Lathrop, George P. *A Study of Hawthorne*. Boston: J. R. Osgood, 1876. The first biography of Hawthorne, by his son-in-law. Used as virtually the only source of biographical information by Henry James for his *Hawthorne*.

Lawrence, D. H. "Nathaniel Hawthorne and *The Scarlet Letter*." In *Studies in Classic American Literature*. New York: T. Seltzer, 1923, pp. 121–47. Hawthorne has presented in disguised form the demonism underlying American experience. Hester Prynne typifies the destructive American female who delights in seducing the pure American male. Wild and provocative. Volume also contains essay on *Blithedale*.

Lease, Benjamin. "Hawthorne and the Archeology of the Cinema." *Nathaniel Hawthorne Journal* 6 (1977):133–71. Shows popularity of such things as the daguerreotype, the diorama, and mesmerism—all used by Hawthorne in his fiction.

Leavis, Q. D. "Hawthorne as Poet." *Sewanee Review* 59 (1951):179–205, 426–58. Hawthorne's fiction shows concern about the workings of his society. Very good comments on "May-pole of Merry Mount."

Levin, David. "Shadows of Doubt: Specter Evidence in Hawthorne's 'Young Goodman Brown.' " *American Literature* 34 (1962):344–52. Brings Puritan idea of "specter" or counterfeit evidence to bear on tale. Argument very well handled.

Levy, Leo B. "The Notebook Source and the 18th Century Context of

Hawthorne's Theory of Romance." *Nathaniel Hawthorne Journal* 3 (1973):120–29. Notebook source for "neutral ground" passage in "The Custom-House" does not contain the terms "Actual," "Imaginary," or "neutral ground." Simplified account of Scottish Common Sense "context."

Loggins, Vernon. *The Hawthornes: The Story of Seven Generations of An American Family*. New York: Columbia University Press, 1951. General treatment of Hawthorne family from colonial times to the twentieth century.

Lohmann, Christoph K. "The Agony of the English Romance." *Nathaniel Hawthorne Journal* 2 (1972):219–29. Good study of Hawthorne's inability to complete a romance juxtaposing England and America, past and present.

Long, Robert Emmet. *The Great Succession: Henry James and the Legacy of Hawthorne*. Pittsburgh: University of Pittsburgh Press, 1979. Most comprehensive coverage of a much discussed topic. Does not, however, deal with Hawthorne and the later work of James.

McCall, Dan E. "The Design of Hawthorne's 'Custom House.'" *Nineteenth-Century Fiction* 21 (1967):349–58. Excellent analysis of sketch as related to *The Scarlet Letter* by means of Hawthorne's artistic transformation of guilt from his ancestors to himself.

McDonald, John J. " 'The Old Manse' and Its Mosses: The Inception and Development of *Mosses from an Old Manse*." *Texas Studies in Literature and Language* 16 (1974):77–108. Focuses perceptively on function of "Old Manse" in *Mosses* and addresses larger question of Hawthorne's work in this period. A superior article.

McPherson, Hugo. *Hawthorne as Myth-Maker: A Study in Imagination*. Toronto: University of Toronto Press, 1969. Informative study of Hawthorne's versions of the Greek myths in *A Wonder-Book* and *Tanglewood Tales* and of Hawthorne's mythmaking imagination as a New England romancer. Reflects influence of Northrop Frye.

McWilliams, John P. Jr. " 'Thorough-Going Democrat' and 'Modern Tory': Hawthorne and the Puritan Revolution of 1776." *Studies in Romanticism* 15 (1976):549–71. Juxtaposes Hawthorne's complex presentation of the Revolutionary experience with popular simplified versions. Excellent on "Major Molineux" and "Legends of the Province House."

———. "Fictions of Merry Mount." *American Quarterly* 29 (1977):3–30. Presents accounts of the Merry Mount controversy by contemporaries and by nineteenth- and twentieth-century historians, novelists, and poets as a context for Hawthorne's shaping of the story. Very helpful.

Male, Roy R. *Hawthorne's Tragic Vision*. Austin: University of Texas Press, 1957. Contains perceptive analysis of the romances and of dominant themes in Hawthorne's work. A basic critical study.

Marks, Alfred H. "German Romantic Irony in Hawthorne's Tales." *Symposium* 7 (1953):274–305. Formulates Hawthorne's debt to such writers as Schlegel and Tieck.

———. "Who Killed Judge Pyncheon? The Role of the Imagination in *The House of the Seven Gables*." *PMLA* 71 (1956):355–69. Death of materialistic Judge Pyncheon signals victory for the forces of the imagination. Terms of essay viable for Hawthorne's work as a whole.

Martin, Terence. "Dimmesdale's Ultimate Sermon." *Arizona Quarterly* 27 (1971):230–40. Suggests possibility that Dimmesdale converts himself by means of his Election Sermon. Interesting idea.

———. "Hawthorne's Public Decade and the Values of Home." *American Literature* 46 (1974):141–52. Identifies three senses of home (New England, England, Rome) and their meaning for Hawthorne's imagination.

Mellow, James R. *Nathaniel Hawthorne in His Times*. Boston: Houghton Mifflin Co., 1980. Impressive narrative biography placing Hawthorne in a rich public and personal context. Manner of using documents gives a readable romantic tone to the presentation.

Newberry, Frederick. "Tradition and Disinheritance in *The Scarlet Letter*." *ESQ: A Journal of the American Renaissance* 23 (1977):1–26. Sets *The Scarlet Letter* in a full historical context from which it derives incisive and ironic value as a work of art. A significant essay that illuminates many details in the romance.

Newman, Lea Bertani Vozar. *A Reader's Guide to the Short Stories of Nathaniel Hawthorne*. Boston: G. K. Hall & Co., 1979. A very helpful assemblage of material on fifty-four tales. Responsible to previous criticism and scholarship, conveniently arranged. A superior research tool for all students of Hawthorne's work.

Nissenbaum, Stephen. "The Firing of Nathaniel Hawthorne." *Essex Institute Historical Collections* 114 (1978):57–86. A detailed study of the events and personal politics that led to Hawthorne's dismissal from the Salem Custom House. Concludes that *The Scarlet Letter* rather than "Custom-House" is Hawthorne's true autobiographical statement.

Normand, Jean. *Nathaniel Hawthorne: An Approach to an Analysis of Artistic Creation*. Translated by Derek Coltman. Foreword by Henri Peyre. Cleveland, Ohio: Press of Case Western Reserve University, 1970. Lengthy study of Hawthorne's life, the creative processes of his work, and his individual stylistic habits.

O'Conner, William Van. "Hawthorne and Faulkner: Some Common Ground," *Virginia Quarterly Review* 33 (1957):105–23. Both authors exploit their legendary and their family pasts and are preoccupied with gloomy wrong.

Pearce, Roy Harvey. "Hawthorne and the Sense of the Past, or, the Immortality of Major Molineux." *ELH* 21 (1954):327–49. Analysis of "Major Molineux" reveals a "Molineux theme" in Hawthorne's work, "the imputation simultaneously of guilt and righteousness through history." Places story in total context of Hawthorne's fiction.

————, ed. *Hawthorne Centenary Essays.* Columbus: Ohio State University Press, 1964. A collection of eighteen essays on various aspects of Hawthorne's art; includes essays by Charles Feidelson, Jr., R. W. B. Lewis, and Edwin H. Cady. Contains some fine work.

————. "Day-Dream and Fact: The Import of *The Blithedale Romance.*" In *Individual and Community: Variations on a Theme in American Fiction*, edited by Kenneth H. Baldwin and David K. Kirby. Durham, N.C.: Duke University Press, 1975. Relates Miles Coverdale and Eustace Bright, regressive behavior of Blithedalers and children in *A Wonder-Book*, and Hawthorne's "dream" of Blithedale and the "fact" of his residence at Brook Farm. Important.

Person, Leland S., Jr. "Aesthetic Headaches and European Women in *The Marble Faun* and *The American.*" *Studies in American Fiction* 4 (1976):65–77. Problems posed by European culture emanate from the woman. Very good on Miriam in *The Marble Faun* (and on Newman and Claire in *The American*).

Reece, James B. "Mr. Hooper's Vow." *Emerson Society Quarterly* 21 (1975):93–102. Hooper deserves "a happier fate" because his solemn vow is made so that he may have the power to bring others to salvation. Strong on the historical situation of a Puritan minister.

Rees, John O., Jr. "Hawthorne's Concept of Allegory: A Reconsideration." *Philological Quarterly* 54 (1975):494–510. Carefully defined essay which characterizes Hawthorne's allegorical method as discontinuous and prophetic, a testing of absolute modes in the interest of an increased perception of the moral world.

Ruland, Richard. "Beyond Harsh Inquiry: The Hawthorne of Henry James." *ESQ: A Journal of the American Renaissance* 25 (1979): 95–117. Assesses *Hawthorne* as a reflection of James's artistic mind. Detailed and slow-paced.

St. Armand, Barton Levi. "Hawthorne's 'Haunted Mind': A Subterranean Drama of the Self." *Criticism* 13 (1971):1–25. Sees the "haunted mind" as a manifestation of the hypnagogic state, which invites inner terrors even as it seeks assurance in conventional images of the outer world.

Sandeen, Ernest. "*The Scarlet Letter* as a Love Story." *PMLA* 77 (1962): 425–35. Reads *The Scarlet Letter* as a "tragedy of the grand passion rather than as a tale of sinful passion." Perceptive and vital analysis.

Schubert, Leland. *Hawthorne the Artist: Fine-Art Devices in Fiction.* Chapel Hill: University of North Carolina Press, 1944. Works by analogy from sculpture, painting, and music to discover artistic techniques and formal patterns in Hawthorne's work.

Schwartz, Joseph. "Three Aspects of Hawthorne's Puritanism." *New England Quarterly* 36 (1963):192–208. Defines Hawthorne's attitude toward Puritan theology, toward Puritanism as a way of life, and toward the Puritan contribution to political liberty. Clear and valuable.

Shaw, Peter. "Fathers, Sons, and the Ambiguities of Revolution in 'My Kinsman, Major Molineux.'" *New England Quarterly* 49 (1976): 559–76. Rich interpretation which takes account of Hawthorne's use of disparate materials. Strong on the function of saturnalian ritual in the tale.

————. "Hawthorne's Ritual Typology of the American Revolution." *Prospects: An Annual of American Cultural Studies* 3 (1977:)483–98. Sees "May-pole," "Endicott," "Gray Champion," "Major Molineux," and "Howe's Masquerade" as making "a ritual history of pro-torevolutionary events in New England." Convincing treatment.

Shulman, Robert. "Hawthorne's Quiet Conflict." *Philological Quarterly* 47 (1968):216–36. Examines the "conflict" between Hawthorne's commitment to art and his allegiance to a Puritan-Protestant ethic and the consequent effect on his fiction.

Simpson, Lewis P. "John Adams and Hawthorne: The Fiction of the Real American Revolution." *Studies in the Literary Imagination* 9 (1976):1–18. Focuses on "Major Molineux" as the "archetypal story of the American imagination" in the mode of John Adams's search for origins rather than of Jefferson's faith in reason.

Stanton, Robert. "Hawthorne, Bunyan, and the American Romances." *PMLA* 71 (1956):155–65. Explores parallels of moral vision and its narrative treatment in these writers.

Stein, William Bysshe. *Hawthorne's Faust: A Study in Mythmaking.* Gainesville: University of Florida Press, 1953. Advances thesis based on Faustian archetype to show an "unbroken continuity" in Hawthorne's artistic career. At times ingenious, more often provocative.

Stewart, Randall. "Hawthorne and *The Faerie Queene*." *Philological Quar-*

terly 12 (1933):196–206. Important early article indicating parallels and relationships.

———. *Nathaniel Hawthorne: A Biography*. New Haven: Yale University Press, 1948. An excellent study. Succinct, thorough, perceptive blending of Hawthorne's life and work.

Stoehr, Taylor. *Hawthorne's Mad Scientists: Pseudoscience and Social Science in Nineteenth-Century Life and Letters*. [Hamden, Conn.]: Archon Books, 1978. Takes *Blithedale* as its center and investigates pseudoscience, "trivia," and the processes of Hawthorne's fiction. Much of interest.

Stubbs, John. *The Pursuit of Form: A Study of Hawthorne and the Romance*. Urbana: University of Illinois Press, 1970. Studies the manner in which Hawthorne's romances give pattern and order to otherwise incoherent experience.

Trollope, Anthony. "The Genius of Nathaniel Hawthorne." *North American Review* 129 (1879):203–22. Trollope's response to Hawthorne's avowed admiration for his work. Interesting because it is Trollope. Praises weirdness, mystery, and drollery of Hawthorne's fiction.

Turner, Arlin. *Nathaniel Hawthorne: A Biography*. New York: Oxford University Press, 1980. The definitive biography. Thorough and well documented. Focuses on significant patterns in Hawthorne's work and thus gives an excellent understanding of a writer's life and career.

Von Abele, Rudolph. *The Death of the Artist: A Study of Hawthorne's Disintegration*. The Hague: Nijhoff, 1955. Gives some good readings but is militantly intent on establishing its thesis. Oversimplifies problems of Hawthorne as an artist.

Wagenknecht, Edward C. *Nathaniel Hawthorne: Man and Writer*. New York: Oxford University Press, 1961. A "psychograph" rather than a conventional biography. Contains much information and many perceptive ideas.

Waggoner, Hyatt H. *Hawthorne: A Critical Study*. Cambridge: Harvard University Press, 1955. A basic critical study. Strong on Hawthorne's tales. Close attention to the imagery and patterns of the romances.

———. "The New Hawthorne Notebook." *Novel: A Forum on Fiction* 11 (1978):218–26. A good description of the contents of Hawthorne's *Lost Notebook*. Earlier version of this description appeared as "A Hawthorne Discovery: The Lost Notebook, 1835–1841." *New England Quarterly* 49 (1976):618–26.

———. *The Presence of Hawthorne*. Baton Rouge: Louisiana State University Press, 1979. A collection of eight essays (seven published previously) by a major critic of Hawthorne.

Warner, Lee, H. "With Pierce, and Hawthorne, in Mexico." *Essex Institute Historical Collections* 111 (1975):213–20. Examines Hawthorne's revisions of Franklin Pierce's Mexican War diary for the campaign biography. For an account of changes Pierce made in Hawthorne's manuscript, see Claude M. Simpson, Jr., "Correction or Corruption: Nathaniel Hawthorne and Two Friendly Improvers," *Huntington Library Quarterly* 36 (1973):367–86.

Warren, Robert Penn. "Hawthorne Revisited: Some Remarks on Hellfiredness." *Sewanee Review* 81 (1973):75–111. Surveys Hawthorne's career, then discusses "Gentle Boy," "Major Molineux," and *The Scarlet Letter* as representative of his achievement.

Weber, Alfred. *Die Entwicklung der Rahmenerzählungen Nathaniel Hawthornes: "The Story Teller" und andere frühe Werke 1825–1838.* Berlin: Erich Schmidt, 1972. Close study of the development of the framed narrative in Hawthorne's career. For a laudatory review (in English), see Christoph Lohmann in *Nathaniel Hawthorne Journal* 2 (1972):267–70.

Wentersdorf, Karl P. "The Elements of Witchcraft in *The Scarlet Letter.*" *Folklore* 83 (1972):132–53. References to the "Black Man" and to Mistress Hibbins have a historical as well as a dramatic dimension. Helpful scholarship.

Whipple, Edwin P. "Hawthorne," in *Character and Characteristic Men.* Boston: Houghton, Mifflin, 1866. Originally appeared in *Atlantic,* May, 1860. Perceptive analysis of Hawthorne's work by a critic Hawthorne respected greatly. Hawthorne called essay "a really keen and profound article."

Index

Adam Blair (Lockhart), 105–108
"Alice Doane's Appeal" (1835), 12, 183–84, 187
All the King's Men (Warren), 187
"Allegories of the Heart," 67
Ambassadors, The (James), 185
"Ambitious Guest, The" (1835), 65
American, The (James), 185
American Magazine of Useful and Entertaining Knowledge, 13–14
"Ancestral Footstep, The," 70
"Artist of the Beautiful, The" (1844), 5, 60–62, 67–68, 135, 152
Atlantic Monthly, 25, 26, 36

Bacon, Delia, 24–25
Bacon, Francis, 24
Bales, Kent, 192n10
Barth, John, 188
Baym, Nina, 96, 119, 174
Beattie, James, 39–40
Belknap, Jeremy, 32
"Benito Cereno" (Melville), 98
Benjamin, Park, 13
Bewley, Marius, 185
"Birth-mark, The" (1843), 20, 54–56, 67, 74, 93–94, 95, 163
Blackstone, Reverend William, 78
Blithedale Romance, The (1852), 21, 22, 29, 32, 54, 59, 65–66, 93–94, 147–62, 175, 185
Boston Custom House, 17
Bostonians, The (James), 185
Bowdoin College, 7, 9, 11, 14, 15

Bridge, Horatio, 1, 8, 9, 12, 14, 18, 21, 22, 189n4
Brook Farm 17–18, 29
Brother to Dragons (Warren), 187
Brown, Charles Brockden, 53
Brumm, Ursula, 51
Bunyan, John, 3, 19, 20, 53, 67

"Canterbury Pilgrims, The" (1833), 56–57
Carnochan, W. B., 74
"Celestial Rail-road, The" (1843), 19
Channing, Ellery, 64
"Chiefly About War Matters" (1862), 26–27
"Christmas Banquet, The" (1844), 19, 67
Cilley, Jonathan, 9
Civil War, 27, 28, 35
Clark, James W., Jr., 192n9
Claxton, Reverend Lawrence, 78
Colacurcio, Michael J., 84
Cooper, James Fenimore, 32, 34
"Custom-House, The" (1850), 8, 30, 33, 69–70, 108, 168, 184

Dante, 20, 53, 63, 81, 87–88, 181–82, 186
Dauber, Kenneth, 141
"David Swan" (1837), 45–46
Davidson, Frank, 158
de Staël, Madame, 20
"Dr. Heidegger's Experiment" (1837), 147
"Dolliver Romance, The," 28, 70, 189n7

Duyckinck, Evert Augustus, 10, 133, 145

"Earth's Holocaust" (1844), 19, 45, 62, 163
Edinburgh Review, 31
"Edward Randolph's Portrait" (1838), 62
"Egotism; or, the Bosom Serpent" (1843), 47, 62, 67
Eliot, T. S., 126, 146, 184–85
Emerson, Ralph Waldo, 18, 22–23, 25, 26, 27, 45, 64
"Endicott and the Red Cross" (1837), 49–51, 62
"Ethan Brand" (1850), 43, 54, 62, 63, 92–98, 167–68

fairy tale opening, 45
"Fancy's Show Box" (1837), 45–46, 74, 168
Fanshawe: A Tale (1828), 4–5, 9, 12, 17, 20, 68
Faulkner, William, 145, 184, 186
Faun of Praxiteles, 170–71
"Feathertop" (1852), 47
Feidelson, Charles, Jr., 107
Felt, Joseph, 20
Fields, James T., 1, 12, 21–22, 68, 132, 165, 189n1
"Fire-Worship" (1843), 65
Fogle, Richard Harter, 142
"Footprints on the Sea-shore" (1838), 147

Gatta, John, Jr., 143
"Gentle Boy, The" (1832), 11, 13, 57–58, 66, 163, 187
Go Down, Moses (Faulkner), 186
Godwin, William, 3
Goffe, William, 51
Gollin, Rita K., 190n7
Goodrich, Samuel G., 12–13

"Goody Two-Shoes," 81
"Gray Champion, The" (1835), 11, 49, 51, 62
"Great Carbuncle, The" (1837), 45, 48, 65, 68
"Great Stone Face, The" (1850), 65, 68

"Hall of Fantasy, The" (1843), 19, 48, 53, 181
"Haunted Mind, The" (1835), 38–41, 48, 80, 190n7
Hawthorne, Elizabeth, 4, 9, 10, 13
Hawthorne, Elizabeth Manning (Hawthorne's mother), 3, 9, 10–11, 17
Hawthorne, Julian, 10, 18
Hawthorne, Louisa, 3–4, 10, 18
Hawthorne, Sophia Peabody (Hawthorne's wife), 1, 10–11, 12, 15–17, 18, 21, 64, 65, 66, 178
Hawthorne, Una, 3, 10, 18, 26, 165
Hilliard, George, 19
"Hollow of the Three Hills, The" (1830), 44–45, 163
Hogg, James, 3
Homer, 53, 181–82, 186
House of the Seven Gables, The (1851), 21, 22, 24, 29, 35, 54, 59, 62, 65, 93–94, 128–46, 147, 168, 184, 186
Howells, William Dean, 26, 36

Indian stories, 191n3
Irving, Washington, 32, 33–34

James, Henry, 36–38, 41, 47, 105–108, 144, 145, 146, 169, 184–86
Jefferson, Thomas, 136
"John Inglefield's Thanksgiving" (1840), 65
Johnson, Samuel, 160
Judd, Sylvester, 34

Justus, James H., 161, 195n4

"Lady Eleanore's Mantle" (1838), 68
"Legends of the Province House," 33, 48–49
Levin, David, 81, 83
Levy, Leo B., 30
Lewis, R. W. B., 31
Life of Franklin Pierce (1852), 21
"Lily's Quest, The" (1839), 43, 45, 47
Lincoln, Abraham, 26–27
Lockhart, John Gibson, 105–106
Long, Robert Emmet, 185
Longfellow, Henry Wadsworth, 9, 14, 145

Madame Bovary (Flaubert), 36
"Madame de Mauves" (James), 186
"Main-street" (1849), 51, 187
Male, Roy H., 140, 151
"Man of Adamant, The" (1837), 47, 56, 75
Manning, Robert, 3, 7
Manning, Samuel, 9
Manning, William, 4
Marble Faun, The (1860), 20, 22, 25–26, 29, 32, 34, 65–66, 122, 141, *163–80*, 184, 185
Mather, Cotton, 20
Mather, Increase, 20
Matthiessen, F. O., 144
"May-pole of Merry Mount, The" (1836), 43, 68, 77–*80*, 98
Mellow, James R., 23
Melville, Herman, 10, 20, 23–24, 43, 51, 52, 67, 81, 98, 138, 145–46
Metropolitan, London, 1
Milton, John, 20, 53, 63
"Minister's Black Veil, The" (1836), 47, 68, 72–77, 82

Mitchell, Isaac, 32
Moby-Dick (Melville), 23, 24
Mosses from an Old Manse (1846), 1, 19–20, 21, 23, 43, 81
"Mrs. Bullfrog" (1837), 43
"My Kinsman, Major Molineux" (1832), 13, 43, *98–104*, 187

Nature (Emerson), 18
"New Adam and Eve, The" (1843), 53, 163
New-England Magazine, 13
Night Rider (Warren), 187
"Night Sketches: Beneath an Umbrella" (1838), 47, 69, 147
North American Review, 14, 31

Oberon, 11
Odyssey, The (Homer), 181–82
"Old Manse, The" (1846), 20, 22, 64, 69, 70
"Old-Time Legends: Together with Sketches, Experimental and Ideal," 70
Our Old Home (1863), 25, 28, 163–64

Patch, Sam, 48
Paul Pry, 17, 58–59, 147–48
Peabody, Elizabeth, 10
"Peter Goldthwaite's Treasure" (1838), 1, 4, 5–6
Peter Parley's Universal History (1837), 13
Pierce, Franklin, 9, 11, 24, 25, 28
Pin Society, 4
Poe, Edgar Allan, 20, 32, 43, 74, 187
Pope Julius III, 168, 169–70, 194n3
Portrait of a Lady, The (James), 185
Pot-8-o Club, 9

"Procession of Life, The" (1843), 19

processionals, 19, 51

"Prophetic Pictures, The" (1837), 59–60

"Provincial Tales," 12–13

pseudonyms, 11–12

"Rappaccini's Daughter" (1844), 20, 32, 43, 54, 87–92, 93–94, 95, 192n10

Rasselas (Johnson), 160

Ripley, George, 17

Roderick Hudson (James), 184

"Roger Malvin's Burial" (1832), 13, 65

Royce, A. A., Reverend, 11

Royce, Ashley A., 11

Salem Custom House, 19, 21, 30

Scarlet Letter, The (1850), 1, 2, 12, 15, 21, 22, 27, 30, 31, 36, 43, 50, 54, 68–71, 74, 93, *105–27*, 147, 164, 167, 169, 171, 175, 184, 187, 193n7

Scott, Walter, 3, 20, 32, 53

"Select Party, A" (1844), 19, 51–52

Sense of the Past, The (James), 184

"Septimius" manuscripts, 4, 6–7, 28, 70, 189n3

"Seven Tales of My Native Land," 9, 12, 183

Sewell, Samuel, 20

"Shaker Bridal, The" (1838), 1, 56, 117

Shakers, 9–10

Shakespeare, William, 3, 20, 24, 53

"Sights from a Steeple" (1831), 58–59, 69, 147

Simms, William Gilmore, 35–36

"Sister Years, The" (1839), 147

sketch, function of, 69–70, 168, 194n2

"Snow-flakes" (1838), 147

"Snow-Image, The" (1850), 5–6, 67, *152–53*

Snow-Image and Other Twice-Told Tales, The (1851), 14, 15, 21, 58, 98

South Sea Exploring Expedition, 17

Spectator, 4

Spenser, Edmund, 3, 20, 51

Stewart, Dugald, 39

Stewart, Randall, 4

"Story-Teller, The," 13

sub-titles, use of, 46–47

"Sunday at Home" (1837), 147

Swift, Jonathan, 20

Tanglewood Tales for Girls and Boys (1853), 21, 191n2

Thomson, James, 3

Thoreau, Henry David, 23, 70, 151, 168, 189n7

"Threefold Destiny, The" (1838), 46–47, 48, 62, 67

Ticknor, William D., 4, 25

Tieck, Ludwig, 20

Token, 12, 13, 14, 78, 98

"Toll-Gatherer's Day, The" (1837), 147

Transformation, 179

Trollope, Anthony, 189n2

True Stories from History and Biography (1851), 21

Turner, Arlin, 24, 141

Twice-Told Tales (1837), 2, 11, 14, 19–20, 21, 43

twilight, use of, 48–49

Unpardonable Sin, 93–94, 95, 97

Updike, John, 188

"Village Uncle, The" (1835), 47

"Virtuoso's Collection, A" (1842), 19
"Vision of the Fountain, The" (1837), 65, 147

Waggoner, Hyatt H., 143, 160, 184
"Wakefield" (1835), 65, 87
War and Peace (Tolstoy), 144–45
Warren, Robert Penn, 145, 184, 186–87
Webster, Noah, 31
"Wedding-Knell, The" (1836), 56, 117, 147
Whipple, E. P., 1, 145, 189n1
Whitman, Walt, 27
Wild Palms, The (Faulkner), 186

Williams, Roger, 78
Wings of the Dove, The (James), 185
Winthrop, John, 20, 114, 115
"Wives of the Dead, The" (1832), 13
Wonder-Book for Girls and Boys, A (1852), 21, 191n2
Woodworth, Samuel, 32–33
World Enough and Time (Warren), 187
workshop method, 46, 98

"Young Goodman Brown" (1835), 20, 21, 43, 48, 62, *81–86*, 117, 192n9